Around the Reading Workshop in 180 Days

Around the Reading Workshop in 180 Days

A Month-by-Month Guide to Effective Instruction

FRANK SERAFINI
with Suzette Serafini-Youngs

HEINEMANN • PORTSMOUTH, NH

Heinemann
A division of Reed Elsevier Inc.
361 Hanover Street
Portsmouth, NH 03801–3912
www.heinemann.com

Offices and agents throughout the world

Library of Congress Cataloging-in-Publication Data
Serafini, Frank.
    Around the reading workshop in 180 days : a month-by-month guide to effective instruction / Frank Serafini with Suzette Serafini-Youngs.
        p. cm.
    Includes bibliographical references.
    ISBN 0-325-00830-2 (alk. paper)
    1. Reading (Elementary). 2. Reading comprehension. 3. Reading (Middle school).
I. Serafini-Youngs, Suzette.   II. Title.
LB1573.S4525 2006
372.4—dc22   2005029058

Editor: Lois Bridges
Production: Elizabeth Valway
Cover design: Jenny Jensen Greenleaf
Cover art: Brennan Blazer Bird
Composition: Publishers' Design and Production Services, Inc.
Manufacturing: Steve Bernier

Printed in the United States of America on acid-free paper
10   09   08   ML   4   5

This book is dedicated to Sharon Zastrow (Z) and Kevin Youngs (the K-Man), the loves of our lives. We thank you for your sense of humor, your zest for life, and for always being there when we needed you most. You help us remain grounded and make each new day an adventure worth experiencing. We love ya both!

Contents

Acknowledgments

Frank would like to acknowledge:

The many teachers I have worked with throughout North America who have helped me articulate my thoughts and reconsider my teaching through their eyes; I celebrate your dedication to the many children whose lives you have changed forever.

My colleagues at the University of Nevada, Las Vegas, for their continued help and support.

Lois Bridges and the wonderful staff at Heinemann; you make my writing shine.

Tracy Heine, whose belief in me as a speaker has kept me very busy over the past three years; I thank you for all the opportunities you have made possible.

My graduate assistant, Sophie; thanks for your invaluable help with the many references I needed and used throughout the book.

Suzette would like to acknowledge:

Ali Gamble, who was the best teaching partner I ever had; your love for children is an inspiration. Thanks for making my last year of teaching the best. Your voice and ideas ring throughout the Windows.

The staff at Bailey Charter School; thanks for giving me a home and a place to practice my craft.

Marc DeVoti and Butch Madrid, my two principals in Pagosa Springs, and all the wonderful parents who let me fly with my ideas. You gave me space to learn and grow.

Special thanks to Morgan and Chandler, for being the best two little girls a mom could ask for. Thanks for keeping busy while I was writing.

In closing, Frank and Suzette would like to acknowledge our mom, Dolores Serafini, whose love, help, and support made this book, and our lives, possible.

Introduction—The Journey Begins

I'm glad I did it, partly because it was well worth it, but
chiefly because I shall never have to do it again.
—MARK TWAIN

I was reminded of these words from Mark Twain after pitching another book proposal to Lois Bridges, my editor at Heinemann, about the reading workshop. After writing *The Reading Workshop: Creating Space for Readers*, I believed the quote in the epigraph to be prophetic: I would never write another book about the reading workshop; I was glad I had written the first one, but I had said all that I wanted to say about reading workshops, and I would eventually be moving on to write about new ideas and theories.

Well, here I am again, thinking and writing in greater depth than ever about my preferred visions for the reading workshop, about the lessons I have conducted during my years of teaching elementary school, and about the various communities of readers I have tried to create and support in every class I have taught, fourth grade through college. Through my experiences with conducting workshops around North America, I have decided that I have more to say about reading workshops and am ready to write about my new ideas and approaches to helping intermediate-grade students develop into sophisticated readers.

In my first book, *The Reading Workshop: Creating Space for Readers*, I explained how my preferred vision of a reading workshop looked and operated, but I did not explain in detail the things I had to do to get the expectations and procedures I described into place. I did not describe in detail how the procedures, comprehension lessons, learning experiences, and discussions that took place in September were different from the ones that took place in March. The reading workshop evolves over time. All of the necessary components do not get introduced in the first week of school and then remain the same for the next forty or so weeks.

The basic premise of this book, *Around the Reading Workshop in 180 Days: A Month-by-Month Guide to Effective Instruction*, is to help teachers understand how to implement a workshop approach to reading instruction in the intermediate and middle grades, beginning with the first day of school and continuing until the day we say good-bye to students sometime around May or June. Throughout this book, I will describe the details of my teaching practices and workshop procedures that I enacted in my classrooms as the school year progressed. I will also share various lesson plans, resources, assessment forms, and instructional strategies that I have found to be successful in the reading workshop.

However, what is really at the heart of a workshop approach to reading instruction is helping readers change the way they think and talk about what they read, not accumulating various resources or instructional strategies. The reading workshop is not primarily about procedures, although consistent procedures help teachers and students make sense of and organize their school day. Reading consists of both cognitive operations and social practices, and our pedagogical strategies should reflect this dual theoretical orientation.

Make no mistake, in *Around the Reading Workshop in 180 Days,* I describe how I organized my reading workshop, how I helped children choose appropriate texts, how I encouraged invested discussions, how I helped students comprehend what they read, and other equally important instructional strategies. But, what I am really trying to convey is how I tried to change the nature of the interactions among teachers, students, and texts.

Martin Nystrand (1997) suggests the quality of student learning is closely linked to the quality of classroom talk. I fully agree. If we are going to improve the quality of literacy learning and reading instruction in elementary and middle school classrooms, we must elevate the quality of the talk that occurs there. We must bring to our teaching a level of integrity and intellectual rigor that seems to be absent in the current educational and political climate, with its focus on increasing standardized test scores.

Aidan Chambers (1996) has suggested that literature discussions become spaces for "shared contemplation." He contends students need to be able to offer ideas in a spirit of communal investigation, a space where "half-baked" ideas can be offered and considered without fear of retribution. I agree. If my students have to wait until their ideas are fully baked, there will be little or no worthwhile conversations about what we have read and thought.

Reading comprehension is the process of generating, articulating, negotiating, and revising interpretations and understandings within a community of readers. These four processes of comprehension provide a theoretical basis for many of the instructional strategies conducted in my reading workshop. The reading workshop should become a space for students to feel comfortable sharing ideas, where students can generate and negotiate interpretations without fear of punishment, and where they have opportunities and support for revising their interpretations and understandings. In other words, a space where readers are supported and challenged to make sense of what they read and experience.

In my third book, *Lessons in Comprehension: Explicit Instruction in the Reading Workshop,* I described in detail how my reading comprehension lessons went, not how other teachers' lessons should proceed. There is a fine line between *describing* what I did and *prescribing* what teachers should do, and I walk this line with every chapter I write. As I described the lessons, resources, and procedures I used in my reading workshop in that book, I provided readers with a window into my thinking and the decisions I made during various comprehension lessons. The goal of that book was not to have teachers try to sound like me or to sequentially deliver the comprehension lessons I described. I just wanted teachers to get a sense of what I did and what was possible for them.

At a workshop I conducted recently, a concerned classroom teacher asked me why I included only 64 lessons in my book when there were 180 days in her school year. An alarm went off! After taking a deep breath and recognizing the sincerity in her question, I tried to explain that *she* was responsible for the lessons that took place in her classroom, not *me*. I suggested that she consider my book as a guide for her teaching, not a scripted curriculum to obediently follow. I explained that she would have to draw upon all of her resources, instructional strategies, and knowledge of readers and reading to construct and conduct lessons that would be successful for her students. I finished by suggesting it was her responsibility to make informed decisions about the types of lessons she should offer, not mine. She went away a bit dismayed, but then, so did I.

There are numerous components that I believe to be essential in establishing an effective reading workshop, such as reading aloud and discussing literature, explicit comprehension lessons, literature study groups, classroom-based literacy assessment, and a well-stocked classroom library. However, how these components are organized and enacted can vary from classroom to classroom. My goal in writing professional development materials is to support teachers in their teaching, not to take over their curriculum. I hope the descriptions of my classroom and teaching that I provide throughout this book help you see a preferred vision for your own teaching, not simply a better window into mine.

How the Book Is Organized

In *Around the Reading Workshop in 180 Days*, I begin with a theoretical discussion that provides the foundation for the practices described throughout the rest of the chapters in the book. I have titled this section "Summer Vacation." In this chapter, I explain some of the theories and insights that support the organization, procedures, and comprehension lessons I use in my reading workshop. I use this section to discuss various literary theories and reading research that support effective reading instruction.

"Summer Vacation" provides readers with the reasons I do what I do in my reading workshop and should help teachers articulate why a reading workshop is an effective approach to reading instruction to concerned stakeholders like parents and administrators. I never begin a university class or one of my many seminars on the reading workshop without discussing the theoretical foundations of my teaching. It is important to understand *why* certain practices are enacted, not just *how* they are enacted. Until teachers' theories and understandings of reading and reading processes expand, any changes made in their teaching practices will be mostly cosmetic.

Of course, you could always skip this chapter and jump ahead to Chapter 2 and start reading, but I highly recommend reading Chapter 1 first. But, as T. S. Elliot said in his *Book of Practical Cats* when referring to the Rum Tum Tugger, "for you will do as you do do, and there is no doing anything about it" (1939, 13).

After the first chapter, I have organized the rest of the book by chapters that coincide with each month, September through May, of a traditional school year in the United States. The months I have chosen to begin and end with are arbitrary, and teachers at year-round schools or schools down under should have little difficulty transposing these chapters to fit their school schedules.

In addition to an extensive list of recommended professional resources and children's literature, each chapter will include the following components:

- ❖ an introduction
- ❖ detailed descriptions of the various lessons and learning experiences I provided each month
- ❖ recommended lessons from my book *Lessons in Comprehension: Explicit Instruction in the Reading Workshop*
- ❖ a featured lesson in comprehension for each month
- ❖ various assessments I used to come to know my students as readers
- ❖ connections to the writing workshop
- ❖ a list of things I hoped to see, hear, and have established by month's end
- ❖ suggestions for further reflection
- ❖ a classroom vignette, titled "Window on the Workshop," focusing on a particular unit of study, written by my coauthor, Suzette Serafini-Youngs

At this point I should probably introduce my coauthor, Suzette Serafini-Youngs. Suzette is an experienced intermediate-grade teacher who has incorporated a reading workshop into her teaching for more than ten years. She's also a doctoral student in literacy education and a visiting instructor at the University of Nevada, Reno, where she teaches courses in literacy methods and children's literature. Fortunately for me, she is also my sister. I have had the pleasure of spending time in Suzette's elementary classroom over the past ten years. I respect the intellectual space she established in her classroom and the rapport she developed with her students. I believe that her vignettes will provide the reader with a window into the workings of a reading workshop, giving voice to the various experiences and lessons from Suzette's own unique point of view. Each month she focuses on a particular unit of study, providing descriptions of how she planned, organized, and enacted these units in her elementary classrooms. I hope that her vignettes help teachers visualize how a reading workshop looks, feels and sounds throughout a school year.

Some Concluding Thoughts for the Introduction

So many of the things that make reading instruction truly effective cannot be simply incorporated into lesson plans, no matter the detail. There are nuances to quality instruction that remain unseen to the casual observer or educational novice. What often goes unnoticed is the language of instruction, the relationships developed between students and teachers, the reflective qualities of the teaching process, the ways students respond to the instruction provided, and the environment in which effective learning experiences take place.

The fact that I am an avid reader of children's literature, spend countless hours reading and analyzing picture books and novels, and have an extensive collection of children's literature to share with my students, may have as much to do with my effectiveness as a reading teacher as does the quality of the lessons I design. The fact that I am a reflective person, spending time writing about my teaching in my writer's notebook, supports my ability to teach effectively. The fact that I subscribe to numerous professional journals and read most of the professional development literature on literacy education available supports my ability to design and implement a reading workshop. The fact that I enjoy being around children, have a somewhat warped sense of humor, and like to listen to my students' ideas has as much to do with the quality of my teaching as the lessons I create and enact. I hope that my passion for teaching, reading, literature, and children shows through in my writing.

I have created a literacy education website at serafini.nevada.edu that allows me to provide booklists and other up-to-date information for teachers and reading educators. I refer throughout the book to various resources that are available on the website for you to consider. I hope that you will wander around the site and find the ideas and resources helpful.

This book builds upon the foundation I created in my earlier writings yet adds to that foundation in new and exciting ways. I believe that *Around the Reading Workshop in 180 Days: A Month-by-Month Guide to Effective Instruction* represents the most complete platform statement about reading instruction that I may ever make. But, as the epigraph suggests, never say never.

Teaching is a courageous act. Therefore, so must be the act of writing about teaching. I have spent countless hours with teachers talking about teaching. I am reminded of how daunting the task of facing twenty-five or more children each morning can be, and I have developed an enormous respect for what teachers do each and every day. In this book, I want to describe what I did in my classroom without suggesting that other teachers do the exact same thing. To do so will require some restraint and finesse as I walk the fine line between *describing* what I did and *prescribing* what other teachers should do. It is with this in mind that I begin my journey around the reading workshop in 180 days.

CHAPTER 1

Summer Vacation—Preparing for the Reading Workshop

> I suggest that the only books that influence us are those for which we are ready, and which have gone a little further down our particular path than we have gone ourselves.
> —E. M. FORSTER

Summer vacation has a long tradition in American education. Originally created to provide time for children to work on their parents' farms in our once-agrarian society, summer vacation has evolved into a three-month hiatus for teachers and students from the pressures of the classroom. Today, many teachers use summer vacation to rejuvenate from the arduous days of the previous school year, while others work extra jobs to supplement their grossly inadequate teacher salaries. Whatever the circumstances, summer is a time to travel, relax with friends and family, and recharge one's batteries.

In addition, I have always viewed summer vacation as a time to catch up on my reading. During the summer months, I get a chance to attend to the stack of professional journals that may have gone unread throughout the school year and some of the new professional development materials from my favorite educational publishers, like Heinemann.

I try to balance my professional reading with classic and contemporary children's and young adult literature, novels, magazines,

SUMMER VACATION CHAPTER OUTLINE

In Service of Meaning
Changing the Questions
Readers Who . . .
Five Critical Dispositions
Literary Theory 101
❖ A Modernist Perspective
❖ A Transactional Perspective
❖ A Sociocultural Perspective
Making a Theoretical Shift
Rethinking Comprehension
Creating Space for Thinking-Talking
Selecting Resources for the Reading Workshop
The Role of Language and Word Study in the Reading Workshop
Essential Components of the Reading Workshop
❖ Creating a Literate Environment
❖ Reading Aloud as the Foundation of the Reading Workshop
❖ Invested Discussions
❖ Transactional Units of Study
❖ Lessons in Comprehension
❖ Literacy Assessment

travel brochures, photography books, and whatever else piques my interest. I treasure the days of summer and feel fortunate to be a forty-something-year-old who has been able to have an extended summer vacation and spring break every year of my life. I read to expand my knowledge base, assuage my curiosity, and keep current with theoretical and pedagogical advancements in the educational field. It is a time to discover and enjoy those books that have gone a little further down my particular path than I have gone myself.

Before summer vacation comes to an end, I begin to plan for the upcoming school year. I consider some of the new selections of children's and young adult literature that I have read over the summer for my literature study groups. I create and add to the resource files I maintain for the various units of study and literary experiences I provide each school year. If there is time, I reread some professional literature that has had a tremendous impact on my thinking for the past fifteen years. Some of the books that I have revisited many times during the summer months are *Life in a Crowded Place* (1992), by Ralph Peterson, *In the Middle* (1998), by Nancie Atwell, *The Reader, the Text, the Poem* (1978), by Louise Rosenblatt, *The Culture of Reading and the Teaching of English* (1994), by Kathleen McCormick, and *The Pleasures of Children's Literature* (1996), by Perry Nodelman. Rereading these books helps me remember the theoretical foundations upon which I build my reading workshop, and they provide an impetus for refocusing my thinking about the complexities of teaching reading and writing.

In this chapter, I share some of the theoretical assertions and pedagogical approaches that provide a foundation for my reading workshop. I believe it is vital to discuss the research and theories that support our practice in order to grow as teachers. As teachers, we need to be able to make more informed pedagogical decisions and defend our instructional approaches to concerned stakeholders like principals, parents, legislators, and school board members. We need to be able to explain why we do what we do if we are going to be treated as professionals and have any chance of making informed pedagogical decisions in our reading workshops.

In Service of Meaning

Throughout the past few years I have been offering a statement in my workshops that has become a pedagogical slogan for my thinking about reading instruction. That pedagogical slogan is *in service of meaning*. What I mean by this phrase is that everything we do in the reading workshop must be done *in service of making meaning when we read*. Whether we are discussing literature, investigating the relationship between written symbols and oral language, helping readers choose an appropriate book to read independently, or working on understanding the nature of the alphabet, I am constantly assessing how the practices and procedures I am enacting in my reading workshop serve the primary goal of supporting readers' construction of meaning in transactions with texts.

The slogan *in service of meaning* also has implications for the types of learning experiences that we provide in our classrooms. These experiences, sometimes referred to as learning activities, range from authentic literary experiences that closely relate to the types of experiences we have outside of school to inauthentic instructional activities, like phonics worksheets, building dioramas or story mobiles, and using flash cards to practice reading words in isolation, that occur only in school settings. Don Holdaway once referred to these inauthentic activities as "dummy runs"; I sometimes call them literacy scrimmages. I use this metaphor because when athletes play a scrimmage against other players, their efforts are significantly different from their efforts during an actual game. The same goes for students during the act of reading. As teachers, we can't expect students' motivation, cognitive operations, and social practices to be the same in an inauthentic literacy scrimmage as they are when the students are reading an authentic text for an authentic purpose.

Because of the differences between an authentic literacy experience and a dummy run, we have to evaluate our instructional practices to understand whether they are acting in service of meaning. This shift from activities to authentic literary experiences also means changing our expectations for readers, the questions we ask about teaching, and the definitions we construct for reading and reading comprehension.

Changing the Questions

It seems the question "What is the best way to teach reading?" has been asked by at least one student in every university class, or one teacher at a workshop I have conducted, since I began working in literacy education. I understand teachers' and students' concerns about teaching reading and their sincerity in asking this question. Sometimes I think that students believe education professors know the answer to this question but are waiting until the course is almost over before sharing the hidden secrets about teaching reading. Maybe they think that once they pay enough tuition, professors are allowed share the secrets of reading education, but not until then.

The problem with trying to answer the question about what is the *best* way to teach reading is the assumption that reading is a singular, universal concept or process, and that teacher educators are simply required to demonstrate the quickest path to get students to the goal of reading proficiency. However, reading is a multifaceted concept; there are many definitions of what it means to read and to be a proficient reader. Does reading proficiently mean being able to read with oral accuracy? Does it mean being able to identify the main idea of a selection? Does it mean bringing a variety of theoretical perspectives in order to construct meanings in transaction with a text? There are commercial programs and instructional approaches that address each of these definitions to varying degrees. However, the decisions we make about the instructional approaches we employ should be aligned with our own definition of proficient reading and successful readers.

I believe there is no single, true path to achieving proficiency in reading. The federal government's goal of all children being able to read by third grade is a nice political slogan, but hardly a pedagogical reality. Depending upon how reading is defined and assessed, some children will fit the definition of a proficient reader and some won't. Most importantly, this slogan begs the question "What is meant by third-grade reading?" In most settings, reading at the third-grade level means achieving average or above-average levels on a norm-referenced test. It is a statistical impossibility for all children to achieve above-average results on a norm-referenced test, except maybe in Garrison Keillor's Lake Wobegon, where, as you know, everyone is above average and good-looking.

The criteria for deciding what is the best way to teach reading are directly associated with one's definition of what it means to be a proficient reader, how one defines comprehension, and how reading ability and comprehension are assessed and evaluated. Based on one's definitions of reading and reading comprehension, many programs could be shown to be somewhat effective. Unfortunately, this is the case with many of the commercial programs being touted as scientifically research based by the federal government. All reading programs help some children learn to read, to some degree, at some time, depending on how reading is defined and assessed. We have to remember, the most important variable shown in numerous research studies on effective reading instruction remains the quality of the teacher in the classroom, not the purchased resources. The better the teacher, the better the teaching.

Many teachers have become quite skeptical of claims made by companies selling scripted reading programs touted as scientifically based. Wandering around the International Reading Association's annual conference exhibit hall the past several years, I was hard-pressed to find a booth that did not have "scientifically based" stamped on the products. It is very frustrating for teachers to ask the question, "What is the best way to teach reading?" and have researchers, politicians, commercial publishers, and teacher educators give a variety of answers or simply dodge the question. Sometimes, teachers want to know the answer to the question "What works in reading education?" Before we can begin to answer this question, we have to clarify it by asking, "Works for what?"

The paradigm wars in reading theory and education may seem confusing at times; however, the challenge is not finding what works, but understanding what it works for, what effect it has on readers, and what definition of reading it is supporting. So what is a reading teacher to do? I believe that if you can't answer a question satisfactorily, you should change the question! This strategy has proved quite beneficial in many workshops and university courses over my professional career. So, let me suggest a more appropriate question: "What types of readers do we want to create and support?" This question goes beyond determining which program works best to uncovering what each program does for readers and teachers. The reading workshop may be considered the best way to teach reading once we describe the types of readers we want coming out of our classrooms and schools.

Readers Who . . .

I believe that it is important to create and articulate a preferred vision of a sophisticated, proficient reader so that we will know if our instructional practices are having a positive effect on developing readers toward this vision. That is, as reading teachers, we need to be able to describe in detail the characteristics of proficient, sophisticated readers in order to evaluate the literary experiences we provide. Our preferred vision of a proficient, sophisticated reader must remain flexible and open to revision. We don't want to limit our readers to one way of reading. However, we will not be able to tell whether our instructional approaches are having any positive impact if we don't know where we are headed.

At this point, I should explain that I have chosen the terms *proficient, sophisticated reader* rather than *good* and *bad reader* because of the connotations of such terms. I get very upset when teachers refer to their students as the low group or the slow readers. This is an example of the disabling language of deficits. These teachers tell me at length what their students *can't* do. They frequently offer a long list of deficits for many of their students. However, the list of what a student *can't* do is a poor place to start creating a reading curriculum. We need to begin with what readers *can* do and then provide instructional experiences that support their needs and interests, not ones that expose their deficits.

I am not naïve enough to believe that all students come to my classroom with the same experiences and abilities. However, I believe that most of my readers' problems stem from lack of experience rather than lack of ability. I recommend thinking about our students as having differing degrees of experience, something we as teachers can provide more of, rather than differing amounts of ability. We can't inject more gray matter into students' heads, but we can provide richer literary experiences for them.

I will share in later chapters how I develop a preferred vision of proficient readers *with* my students, but for now, let me outline some of the characteristics of a reader that, if things go well in my classroom, my students will begin to demonstrate.

I want to develop and support readers who . . .

1. *Find a place for reading in their lives.* By this, I mean I want children to engage in reading as well as play soccer, watch television, play guitar, go to sleepovers, clean their rooms, and play outdoors. I don't want reading to be seen as something that *replaces* the things children already enjoy doing. I just want them to find a place to *include* reading in their already busy schedules. If it comes down to soccer or reading, many children will opt out of reading. I love to do many things besides read; however, I have carved out time in my schedule to make reading a part of my everyday life. I want to help children appreciate what reading can do for them so they will choose to read throughout their lives.

2. *Enjoy reading and its challenges.* Reading is not a skill that, once developed, can simply be dragged from text to text without encountering challenges. In other words, even sophisticated, proficient readers encounter texts they struggle to understand. Some young readers assume that once you learn to read, you simply understand everything regardless of content, genre, or textual features. This is certainly not the case, and not the image of a proficient, sophisticated reader I want to develop with my readers. Reading can be enjoyable and easy to do at times while at other times challenging for the most proficient of readers. I know successful readers tend to enjoy the act of reading and engage with texts more frequently. However, these readers are also more willing to work through a text rather than give up in the face of challenges. Proficient readers understand that reading is about the construction of meaning and are willing to work toward this goal.

3. *Utilize a variety of reading strategies to make sense of texts.* Reading is a complex act, involving the flexible orchestration of many strategies and practices during the reading process. Readers draw upon cues provided in the written text, the context

of the reading event, their purposes for reading, and their prior experiences to make sense of what they read. Proficient readers rely upon a variety of strategies, not just the ability to sound words out, when constructing meaning with texts.

4. *Are willing and able to generate, articulate, and negotiate interpretations.* Readers need to know that they are responsible for making sense of what they read and are responsible for sharing their ideas with other readers. During teacher-initiated read-alouds, students are expected to listen carefully, enjoy the story, and once completed, share their ideas about the text. Once ideas are shared, readers must allow their interpretations to remain open to negotiation and revision. Within this process of negotiation and revision lies the power of a community of readers.

5. *Become emotionally invested in what they read.* In order for readers to become emotionally invested in what they read, they need to be given the opportunity to choose many of the texts they read, have the stories they read relate to their lives and experiences, and be able to empathize with the challenges the characters in the selected stories face. We cannot expect readers to become emotionally invested in what they read if we continually take away the responsibility for choosing appropriate texts and limit their access to quality reading materials. Teachers and school librarians must provide access to quality reading materials and time to browse and explore what has been provided. As Nancie Atwell (1998) suggests, *time to read, choice in what one reads, and response to one's efforts* are the foundations of the reading workshop.

6. *Read a wide variety of texts.* As they say, variety is the spice of life. Nowhere is this more important than in exposing readers to new genres, authors, illustrators, and topics in literature. Readers should be exposed to science fiction, mystery, fantasy, historical fiction, poetry, and many other types of literature. As Ralph Peterson, a wonderful professor I took classes from at Arizona State University, once told me, "There are no children who hate reading, just children who haven't found the right book!" I believe this is true, but I also know the challenges inherent in this statement. Monies provided for classroom and school libraries have become marginal, at best. Because of federal mandates, school districts are forced to spend their dismal resources on tests and commercial programs. When classroom libraries sit empty, children are not provided access to quality reading materials or the opportunity to enter the world of reading and literature.

7. *Understand that images and texts may possess meanings beyond what is represented.* When E. B. White wrote about Charlotte and Wilbur in *Charlotte's Web*, he was not describing some alien world where pigs and spiders are able to talk. He was using literary personification to reveal the tensions and wonders of human existence. That is, Wilbur and Charlotte were created to illuminate *our* lives and experiences, not provide factual information about farm life. It is important for young readers to make this symbolic connection, so when they are asked to discuss symbolism in Shakespeare's plays in high school, they understand that literature relates to the world outside the text.

8. *Understand that texts are social artifacts.* All texts are written and created by people vested in particular versions of reality. Until readers understand this fact, they will be reticent to question the version of reality presented by the author or publisher. In certain texts, for example, editorials and advertisements, the perspective of the au-

thor may be readily apparent. However, *all* texts have a particular perspective and represent a particular version of the world and reality. Starting in the primary grades, children need to be introduced to the authors and illustrators who construct the various versions of reality that are presented in the books they read. Through discussions and support from more capable, critical readers, novice readers will learn that it is not only allowable to see the world differently and question the versions of reality presented in the books they read but necessary to do so to support a democratic way of life. In order to question the reality presented in texts, one must understand that texts are socially constructed and interpretations are open to negotiation and revision.

I know these eight characteristics may seem a bit unrealistic for every reader in every class but as I suggested at the outset of this section, the construction of this list was part of the process of creating a preferred vision for the readers in our classrooms. These characteristics are what I want to see emerging in my students during our time spent together. I will also begin to use these characteristics as an evaluation instrument to understand readers' progress toward these goals.

For many years, I have shared a list like this with the parents of my students to help them understand the goals of our reading workshop. To construct a list of proficient reader characteristics with my students, rather than simply hand them a completed taxonomy of characteristics they need to develop, we read and discuss various picture books that contain images of readers and reading. I have written an article in *The Reading Teacher* (April 2004a) that explains this process in further detail. The characteristics of proficient readers form a basis for the expectations I hold for readers in my classroom, and they will guide the instructional approaches I employ in my reading workshop. This process is further discussed in Chapter 2.

Five Critical Dispositions

In addition to the more global reader characteristics I have just presented, there are five critical dispositions that readers need to develop if they are to become proficient, sophisticated readers. These five critical dispositions need to be adopted or understood by readers before reading comprehension instruction can be effective. These critical dispositions provide a framework for our lessons in comprehension to hang on, and they set readers up for success by focusing their attention on reading as a meaning-making process. By providing experiences and setting expectations about what is important during the act of reading, we are able to develop these critical dispositions in our novice readers.

Disposition 1: Proficient and sophisticated readers understand that reading is a process of making meaning with texts.

If readers do not understand that making sense of what they read is the goal of transacting with a text, they are simply wasting their time. Some students think fluency, oral proficiency, or accurate decoding is the ultimate goal. However, these are intermediary goals that are important when working toward constructing meaning in transaction with a text. There are strong correlations between oral fluency and comprehension; however, fluency must be valued in service of making meaning, not as a primary goal in and of itself. Oral fluency and automatic decoding may be strong predictors of reading comprehension, but fluency and decoding alone do not guarantee that comprehension has occurred.

In addition, as readers progress into more complicated texts, their decoding abilities become *less and less* an indicator of comprehension. Let me explain. If a reader accurately decodes a simple picture book, for example, *Mrs. Wishy-Washy*, by Joy Cowley, one could say with a great deal of confidence she probably understood what she read. For one reason, the book is rather literal in its presentation, without multiple layers of meaning. Secondly, the book includes enough illustrations to support the construction of meaning by the reader. And most importantly, the book was not written to be used for in-depth literary or critical discussions.

However, when a student reads literature, poetry, and more complex, postmodern picture books, for example, *The Tunnel, Zoo*, or *Voices in the Park*, by Anthony Browne, his oral fluency may not be enough to indicate that he was able to understand the references, metaphors, or allusions presented in these texts. When students are reading these more complex picture books, comprehension requires the ability to connect the text and images to the world, understand the grammars of visual design, bring relevant prior experiences to the text, and connect seemingly disparate elements in the text in order to make sense of what they are reading. It also requires the ability to suspend closure and entertain ambiguity, but I discuss these later in the book.

One of the most important aspects of this disposition is the fact that readers who read for meaning make more appropriate choices for their independent reading. Readers who make sense of what they read do not spend much time with texts they cannot understand.

Ensuring that readers understand that reading is the process of constructing meaning in transaction with texts is the cornerstone of the reading workshop. Developing a variety of reading comprehension strategies for readers to use to make sense of what they read is the primary instructional objective of the lessons I create. Like my pedagogical slogan *in service of meaning* suggests, the lessons I develop, the expectations I set, and the critical dispositions I help readers adopt are all intended to ensure that students are comprehending what they're reading.

Disposition 2: Proficient and sophisticated readers assume responsibility for understanding what they are reading.

Readers need to understand that they are the ones responsible for making sense of what they read or hear, not the teacher or other students. During a read-aloud, students need to understand that it is their responsibility to pay attention to the story being read. If readers don't understand that it is their responsibility for making sense of texts, how will they know when to apply the reading comprehension strategies we are teaching? It's not like we ring a bell in the classroom when it is time to read on and go back or a press a buzzer when it is time to break a word down into chunks. That would be rather silly.

Readers who read for meaning assume responsibility for making sense of their selections. They self-correct and look for cues when meaning breaks down. They understand that reading is a meaning-making process and know that it is their responsibility to construct meaning. They also know that if they need help, their teacher is available. What I think is important is that readers have strategies for making meaning that go beyond sounding it out, staring at the page, or immediately asking someone for help. In order to get readers to know what strategies to use, we need to make them aware that it is their responsibility to make sense of what they are reading and not to rely immediately on help from more capable readers.

Disposition 3: Proficient and sophisticated readers develop an awareness of reading as a thinking process.

As readers get older, they become aware of their thinking processes. This is often referred to as *metacognitive awareness* or *metacognition*. Metacognition is defined as "thinking about one's thinking." It is a developing awareness of what goes on in one's mind as one is thinking or reading a text. According to many educational psychologists, this awareness begins to develop in children around age six or seven. Metacognitive awareness, that is, the ability to focus on one's cognitive processes when reading, is an important factor in comprehension strategy instruction. If we are going to try to explain to novice readers how to visualize when reading, they have to become aware of their thinking and be able to recognize and discuss what happens in their minds when they are reading. For young readers, I describe metacognition by asking them, "Is your brain listening to your mouth?" This makes more sense than asking a nine-year-old if he is becoming more metacognitively aware.

As teachers, we need to develop a language for talking about our thinking that makes sense to our students. I had one student who referred to reading as "watching a mind movie." When he got bored, he fast-forwarded the movie, and when he was confused, he rewound it. This explanation worked for him. We need to help readers develop their understandings about what they are doing when they read.

Disposition 4: Proficient and sophisticated readers are willing and able to recognize and acknowledge confusion.

Before readers are able to apply a reading comprehension strategy, they have to know when and why to do so. Let me give you an example. You are sitting on a beach in Fiji and you are reading a novel. You come to the end of the page and realize that you have no idea what you just read, having been distracted by the beautiful scenery surrounding you. You recognize this lack of attention and comprehension long before you decide what to do about it. As a matter of fact, if you didn't recognize that your mind had been wandering, you would simply keep on reading. Once you become aware that you haven't been paying attention to what you have been reading, as the reader responsible for making sense of the text, you have a decision to make. Do you go back and reread the page because you feel that you missed something important, or do you simply turn to the next page because it's a cheap romance novel and you are sure you will be able to catch up? The decision is based on your purposes for reading, what you are reading, and the context in which you are reading.

Readers who don't recognize that meaning has broken down rarely apply any comprehension strategies. This is one reason that proficient and sophisticated readers make self-corrections during reading. Self-correcting is a good indicator that readers are reading for meaning. If readers are self-correcting, they are usually attending to meaning and recognizing when confusion has set in.

In addition to recognizing confusion, readers also need to feel comfortable enough in our community of readers to acknowledge and share their confusion. That is, during a read-aloud or independent reading, I need to know when my students are confused so we can do something about it. Whether it is an issue of vocabulary, text structure, references made in the text, or another factor, if my students are not able to recognize confusion, acknowledge this confusion, and share their challenges, I will have a much harder time helping them become strategic readers.

Disposition 5: Proficient and sophisticated readers apply a variety of reading comprehension strategies when meaning breaks down.

Once the first four critical dispositions are in place, teaching reading comprehension strategies will make more sense to our students. In my opinion, all too often teachers try to demonstrate reading comprehension strategies before readers are ready to understand how these strategies can help them in the reading process. In order to know when to apply particular comprehension strategies when meaning breaks down, readers have to understand that reading is a meaning-making process, understand that they are the ones responsible for making sense of what they read, become aware of their thinking during the reading process, and begin to recognize and acknowledge confusion if and when it sets in. Then, and only then, will reading comprehension strategy instruction have a foundation to build on or become effective.

Let me give you an example to bring these critical dispositions into focus. Recently, I was in an intermediate-grade classroom where the teacher told me she had been teaching reading comprehension strategies, in particular the strategy of predicting. I wandered around and asked some of her students what they were doing during their reading time. What I hoped to hear from her students was that they were reading a particular genre, studying a particular author, or delving into some interesting topic or theme during an interdisciplinary unit of study. One young man in the class told me that they were working on prediction. When I asked him what they were predicting, he replied, "Everything, man!"

As you can see, there was no place for him to contextualize the comprehension strategy lessons that were being taught. In that classroom, children were practicing predicting, not comprehending. The strategy lessons had become an end in themselves. It wasn't that students were learning to predict in order to anticipate what was happening in a mystery novel; predicting had become a context-free, universal strategy with no purpose. Being explicit in our instruction is not sufficient. We must also contextualize the comprehension strategies we teach so readers know when and why to use them. This may seem like an extreme example to illustrate a point, but I am concerned that this type of instruction is happening in more classrooms than we care to admit.

Comprehension strategy instruction is not simply about learning to predict; it's about knowing when to predict, why to predict, and how to use prediction to help make sense of what is being read. We want to help readers orchestrate comprehension tools flexibly and strategically in a variety of contexts, with a variety of texts, for a variety of purposes. It is the conscious application of comprehension strategies that makes for more proficient and sophisticated readers.

In summary, long before reading comprehension strategy instruction begins, readers need to know that reading is a meaning-making process, that they are responsible for making sense of what they read, that they need to become aware of their thinking during the reading process, that they are safe to recognize and acknowledge confusion in our community of readers, and that there are particular reading comprehension strategies they can use when texts don't make sense. If we try to put the strategy before the disposition, readers will not understand when or why to apply a particular comprehension strategy. We should focus on the various texts and units of study we're providing, and fold the comprehension strategies into this context.

Literary Theory 101

I would like to take you on a brief foray into the world of literary criticism. I do so because the theoretical perspectives with which we align affect the discussions we conduct with children's literature, what we consider proficient reading, the expectations we set for our students, and the role children's literature plays in our classrooms. Whether we acknowledge these theoretical perspectives or not, they affect how we teach and how we assess reading comprehension.

I will not to dumb down any of the concepts that I am addressing in this section; however, trying to make rather complex ideas accessible for classroom teachers who have not encountered any of these theoretical discussions in their educational coursework or professional development opportunities may be challenging. It is not my intention to cover the complete intellectual terrain of every literary theory available today in this text. For those of you with deeper interests in this area, I have provided an extensive reference section at the end of the book for further reading and investigation into various literary and reading theories.

The ways in which children's literature is used in elementary and middle school classrooms is directly related to a teacher's definition of reading and her beliefs about meaning, how knowledge is constructed, the role of the reader in the act of reading, and how context, both immediate and cultural, plays a role in the construction of meaning. Teachers need to not only understand and reflect on their instructional practices but also to understand and reflect on the literary theories that inform and support those practices. Whether teachers can explicitly articulate their theoretical perspectives or not, these perspectives play a significant role in the resources teachers choose, the instructional practices they employ, and the literate environment they create in their classrooms. I firmly believe that without a substantial change in teachers' theoretical perspectives, there will be little or no change in the role that children's literature plays in the reading curriculum, how reading is taught, and how comprehension is assessed.

There are three primary theoretical perspectives that inform reading comprehension and literary criticism. Although they are referred to by a variety of names and organized into different categories by various reading and literary theorists, I have organized them into the following three categories: (1) modernist, also referred to as the new criticism, focusing primarily on the text in and of itself, (2) transactional, often referred to as reader response theory, focusing on the transaction between a reader and the text, and (3) sociocultural, sometimes referred to as critical theory, focusing on the cultural, political, and historical relationships and contexts among readers and texts. Each theoretical perspective supports a particular set of reading practices, or pedagogies. These reading practices vary according to the amount of time allocated to reading instruction and self-selected reading, the way that reading is defined, the assumptions about where knowledge is located and whether it is discovered or constructed, and the emphasis placed on the roles of the text, the reader, and the context in the reading process.

A Modernist Perspective

A modernist perspective is based on the beliefs that (1) meaning is located in the text and can be "uncovered" through close textual analysis, (2) comprehension is a result of cognitive processes and has little to do with the social context of the reading event, (3) there is one "pure essence" of a text that only competent readers can gain access to, and (4) various readings of a text can be evaluated for their correctness based on predetermined meanings constructed by literary scholars. Only the most competent of readers, usually university professors and literary scholars, can ever truly understand the pure essence of a text, and all subsequent readings by individual readers can be measured against this one true meaning.

From a modernist perspective, meaning is conceptualized as an entity that resides *in* the text and can be objectively measured and assessed. The reader's response to the text, conceptualized as the affective fallacy, is not to be considered, nor are the author's intentions, conceptualized as the intentional fallacy. A modernist perspective focuses on the text in and of itself, where meaning is discovered, not constructed.

From this perspective, being literate is associated with a set of universal skills applied to a specific set of texts in order to comprehend the meaning that resides within the text itself. You can see how the notion of main idea emerges from this theoretical perspective. You can also see how reading instruction informed by a modernist orientation has often become a game of "guess what is in the teacher's head." From a modernist perspective, it is probably more advantageous to read the Cliffs Notes than the actual piece of literature in many high school and college classrooms.

There are certain works of literature, usually written by white males who are now dead, that are considered worthy of reading, and other works, generally associated with common or pop culture, that are not worthy of attention. Theorists who align with a modernist perspective view literature as a vehicle for transmitting important values from generation to generation. Canons of literature, constructed by scholars and school administrators, prescribe what is to be read. Teachers are simply required to make sure that readers get the correct messages from these authorized texts. Little educational space is left for an individual's response or the questioning of which texts should be read.

A Transactional Perspective

In a transactional perspective, meaning is constructed by the reader in transaction *with* literature, not discovered in the text. From a transactional perspective, the reader plays a more prominent role in the act of reading, bringing prior knowledge and experiences to selectively attend to specific aspects of a text in order to make sense of what he is reading. In other words, readers bring meaning to the text, in order to construct meaning *with* the text.

There are aspects of both schema theory and reader response theory in the transactional perspective. Adopting a constructivist theory of meaning, theorists who align with a transactional model reject the notion that meaning resides in the text and instead focus their attention on the transaction between a reader and a text, the interpretive communities involved with discussing a piece of literature, the gaps that readers fill in during the reading event, and the various stances that a reader assumes while reading.

According to Louise Rosenblatt (1978), the focus is on a particular reader, transacting with a particular text, in a particular context. Reading is often conceptualized as the construction of meaning in the internal, cognitive space of the individual reader in transaction with a particular text. One primary difference between the transactional and the sociocultural perspective is the individual reader is given more agency to construct meanings with a text in the transactional perspective, while in the sociocultural perspective, meanings are viewed as more socially or culturally determined.

From a transactional perspective, children's literature is seen as a vehicle for learning about the world, sharing one's personal experiences and interpretations, and creating a sense of personal identity. Readers, as members of various interpretive communities, generate, articulate, negotiate, and revise their interpretations in the company of other readers. It is the lived-through or aesthetic experience of reading literature, and the ways that literature develops one's identities and understandings of the world, that become the primary focus in this perspective.

A Sociocultural Perspective

Finally, a sociocultural perspective focuses on the ways that texts are constructed in social, political, and historical contexts and how these various contexts position readers and texts and endorse particular interpretations. From this perspective, reading is seen as a social practice of constructing meaning that cannot be separated from the cultural, historical, and political contexts in which it occurs. Allan Luke (1995) states that reading and comprehension are tied up in the politics and power relations of everyday life in literate cultures.

From this perspective, texts are not considered neutral receptacles of information; rather, they are viewed as cultural artifacts, created for specific purposes by people with political, cultural, and historical experiences. Texts are regarded as social constructions that promote particular interests and versions of reality, and therefore texts are seen as sites for the construction of plural and possibly conflicted meanings. There is a variety of meanings available during the act of reading, and the concept of main idea is simply viewed as one possible meaning available to readers, usually considered an officially sanctioned interpretation of a particular text.

Jerry Harste and colleagues (2000) suggest children's literature be regarded as a space for constructing critical conversations, where both teachers and students negotiate meanings, discuss the systems of power inherent in the meanings available, and share experiences of how these stories relate to their lives and communities. That is, reading practices associated with a sociocultural perspective provide alternative ways of organizing classroom experiences around texts to address cultural, political, and historical forces and their impact on the lives of the students in the classroom. Pedagogical decisions are made at the classroom level, taking into consideration larger societal contexts and forces. The classroom is no longer seen as an independent neutral space, isolated from political agendas and cultural contexts; rather, it is seen as a part of society, influenced by the political, cultural, and historical forces contained therein.

In today's schools, the modernist perspective remains the dominant force in reading instruction. Reader response theories have begun to make an impact on high school literature and English classes, but the search for a single main idea still goes on in many classrooms. One of the last pedestals of the modernist theory that challenges a shift to a transactional or sociocultural perspective is contemporary assessment instruments and practices. If there is more than one correct interpretation or meaning for a text, how do teachers assess reading comprehension? How do we ensure that all readers have comprehended what they've read? Though space does not allow for a complete discussion, I present numerous assessment devices throughout each chapter that help teachers assess the quality of readers' interpretations without resorting to assessing main ideas or using chapter quizzes that focus on the literal recall of textual elements.

Making a Theoretical Shift

Making a shift from a modernist perspective to a transactional or sociocultural perspective requires teachers to reject the notion of a single, objective main idea that resides somewhere in the text. Teachers have to promote discussions that provide opportunities for readers to construct a plurality of meanings from a single text, bringing their prior experiences, knowledge of the world, and cultural understandings to bear on the text.

In this shift, the reader has to be reconceptualized as a constructor of meanings, not the discoverer of a reclusive main idea. The shift from a modernist to a transactional perspective places the reader and the text, not simply the text alone, at the center of the meaning-making process. It is in the transaction between reader, context, and text that meaning is constructed. Reconceptualizing the reader as a cultural entity, one who brings to the act of reading not only individual agency but socially determined interpretations, one begins to make the shift from a transactional to a sociocultural perspective. From a sociocultural perspective, both readers and texts are always grounded in a social context, with all the cultural, political, and historical baggage this entails. One cannot read from a neutral position, nor can one find a book written from a neutral stance. Acknowledging the sociocultural relationships of power that are inherent in public institutions, gender roles, socioeconomic class structures, and across racial boundaries supports this shift.

A shift from a modernist perspective to a sociocultural one means that readers are no longer simply acquiring reading skills transmitted through direct instruction. Instead, readers are appropriating reading practices through guided participation in literacy activities with more capable others. I see this as a shift from learning universal reading strategies that can be applied at will to acquiring reading *practices* that are contextually grounded and learned through apprenticeship with other readers. Learning to read is shaped by one's interactions and relationships with more knowledgeable readers, not simply advanced by the accumulation of context-free reading comprehension strategies.

Leaving a modernist orientation behind, the teacher no longer sees herself as the arbiter of meaning or the sole interpretive authority in the classroom. The teacher becomes simply one voice, albeit a voice with a great deal more experience as a reader than most students, in the interpretive community. The role of the teacher is to support readers' ability to generate, articulate, negotiate, and revise meanings within a community of readers.

Rethinking Comprehension

Comprehension is defined differently within each of the theoretical perspectives previously discussed. From a modernist perspective, comprehension means the ability to discover a single meaning or main idea that resides within the text and has been predetermined by more capable readers. From this perspective, the text takes center stage over the reader and the reading context. From a transactional perspective, comprehension means constructing meaning, based on one's linguistic knowledge and prior experiences, with texts. Readers bring meaning to the text to construct meaning in transaction with it. From a sociocultural perspective, readers are no longer considered autonomous entities capable of constructing any meanings they prefer. So comprehension means constructing meaning that is constrained by cultural, political, and historical factors with texts, which are social artifacts of a particular time and place.

Before continuing, I want to offer a definition—which I have been revising throughout my time in education—of reading comprehension. It is important that our ideas and beliefs remain open to revision; however, there are times when we must articulate what we think in order to start a dialogue about a particular topic. Therefore, at this time I consider reading comprehension to be *the ability to use a variety of perspectives, including an author's intentions, specific textual references, personal experiences, and sociocultural influences, to generate viable interpretations or meanings in transaction with a variety of texts.* To elaborate, I consider reading comprehension as:

❖ *A process, not a commodity.* It is more important to consider comprehending as a verb rather than comprehension as a noun. When we read, we are in a continual process of making meaning with a text. The process of comprehending ends only momentarily. We may read a book over and over again and construct entirely different meanings because of a change in purpose, contexts, or prior experiences. Therefore, it is vitally important that we consider comprehending texts as a process, not as some residual commodity we can calculate after the act of reading is completed.

❖ *The ability to generate viable interpretations. Viable* is defined as "practicable, able to successfully exist." Interpretations that are viable are open to negotiation, cannot be rejected outright, and are able to sustain interrogation. Interpretations that are viable cannot be directly rejected by referring to the text and are deemed plausible by the community of readers in which these interpretations are offered.

❖ *The ability to draw upon multiple perspectives to interpret a text.* Readers who comprehend what they read construct meaning from a variety of perspectives, are able to draw upon a variety of theoretical lenses, for example, a feminist or critical perspective, and consider what each lens does for them as readers. It is the ability to read across theoretical lenses that makes a reader proficient.

❖ *The ability to understand official meanings.* In order to be successful in schools today, readers need to be able to handle passages on a standardized test as well as interpret literature for class discussions. Although I am theoretically opposed to the notion of a main idea, and believe that one does not, in fact, exist within a text, I realize that readers will be asked to identify the main idea on the standardized tests they take each year. In the context of a standardized test, the question readers need to consider is, "What main ideas, officially predetermined by the creators of the test, do you think the scorers are looking for?" In other words, "What do you think test makers would say is the main idea?" This may be in contradiction to my theoretical beliefs, but it is part of our reality as teachers in American public schools.

❖ *The ability to provide evidentiary warrants for the interpretations constructed.* Readers must learn to make a case for the interpretations they offer in an interpretive community. Although the evidence presented may come from textual and nontextual sources, the reader must still be able to articulate why he has constructed the meanings he has offered. Readers should be able to explain how they arrived at the interpretations they share in discussions and be able to offer evidence and support for these interpretations.

❖ *The ability to understand the various systems that affect meanings and interpretations.* Meaning is not simply out there, waiting to be discovered; rather, it is constructed by particular readers, reading particular texts, in particular immediate and cultural contexts. We need to help readers go beyond simply responding to texts. We need to help readers understand why they respond the way they do and what political, historical, and sociocultural factors influence them to respond the way they do. After immediate responses to a text are generated, we must help readers interrogate these responses and understand what has affected their interpretive decisions.

❖ *The ability to generate, articulate, negotiate, and revise meanings in a community of readers.* This is the most important aspect of reading comprehension, not simply because it helps students do well in school, but because it is the foundation of a democratic society. Our interpretive communities must remain intellectually rigorous contexts, where readers offer, defend, and revise what they think. This means that we have to raise the level of intellectual rigor in our literature discussions and not allow readers to simply state that they like a book without expanding their response strategies and abilities. Many discussions begin with readers sharing favorite parts; they just shouldn't end there.

The abilities that I have just described are part of my preferred vision for the readers in my reading workshop. Before finishing this opening chapter, I need to expand on the concepts of generating, articulating, negotiating, and revising meanings. In order to do so, I will begin by discussing the concept of thinking-talking.

Creating Space for Thinking-Talking

In defining how I conceptualize the reading and sharing of literature in the reading workshop, I have come to think of the atmosphere around the acts of reading aloud, discussing literature, and independent reading as creating a space for thinking-talking. By thinking-talking, I mean the sense of shared contemplation suggested by Aidan Chambers (1996), in which readers and teachers are invited to share their half-baked ideas in order to work through their thoughts about a particular text.

The act of thinking-talking involves the following four practices, or processes, that occur within a community of readers:

1. generating meanings
2. articulating meanings
3. negotiating meanings
4. revising meanings

These four processes of thinking-talking are grounded in the social context of the classroom and are supported by an open, honest, and accepting environment that should be established as a community of readers comes together during the school year under the careful guidance of a literary docent. Thinking-talking cannot be supported if students make fun of each other's ideas or are unwilling to listen to other students when they share their interpretations. By expanding the ways in which we generate, articulate, negotiate, and revise our ideas about literature, we are creating the foundation, in essence a theoretical space, for thinking-talking to occur.

❖ *Generating meanings* means that readers are constructors of meaning and are expected to actively participate and engage with the various texts we read and share. Readers cannot just allow a text to waft over them; instead, they need to pay attention, think about what is read, and consider what the text means to them. Comprehension is a constructive process that occurs over time. Readers actively consider ideas and language presented in the text and assimilate these with their prior experiences, beliefs, and understandings. They need to assume the responsibility for making sense of what they read and be prepared to share their interpretations with other readers.

❖ *Articulating meanings* means the ability and willingness to share ideas within a community of readers. It is a process of making one's thinking public for it to be considered by other students through oral, written, and artistic representations. This sharing of ideas and interpretations involves feeling comfortable enough to say what one really thinks. It is not easy to establish this level of trust and respect in a community of readers, but literature discussions have little chance of being effective without it. As teachers, we have to provide multiple opportunities and points of entry for readers to articulate their understandings. Using small groups for discussions, paired reading buddies, and individual teacher-student conferences, in addition to whole-group discussions, we are able to provide more opportunities for readers to have their individual voices heard.

❖ *Negotiating meanings* involves readers remaining available to new ideas, entertaining ambiguity, thinking through half-baked ideas, and using their imaginations to consider alternative possibilities. Shared contemplation, or what I have called thinking-talking, relies on a reader's ability to negotiate meaning. Readers offer interpretations in their discussions and come away with new ideas to consider. This signals a shift from *conversation*, where readers tend to talk around a text, to *dialogue*, where readers interrogate a text and the alternative meanings offered by other readers.

❖ *Revising meanings* is accomplished on an individual level as well as on a community level. Individuals may revise the meanings they originally constructed before a discussion, and whole groups may reconsider what they thought about a book after articulating and negotiating various interpretations. Describing how this looks in practice is one of the primary goals of this text.

Robert Scholes (1985) described the difference between centripetal forces and centrifugal forces that may influence a literary discussion. Centripetal forces drive interpretations to the center, forcing readers to come to consensus and reach agreement on what a piece of literature means. These centripetal forces can be imposed by a teacher or can develop on their own because of students' prior experiences with literature in school settings. They close down discussion and limit possibilities. Contrarily, centrifugal forces expand ideas, opening up spaces for interrogation of ideas and shared contemplation, allowing for new possibilities and alternative interpretations. In a community of readers, the goal is not consensus but rather the intellectual challenges posed by contradictory interpretations. As classroom teachers, we need to be mindful of the presence of both types of forces and how they may affect our literature discussions.

Selecting Resources for the Reading Workshop

I have shared my ideas about readers, teachers, and the processes necessary for quality literature discussions. Now I think it is important to discuss what texts should be the focus of these discussions. Selecting literature and other texts for one's classroom and reading instruction experiences is not a disinterested process, nor can it be defended by referring to some neutral criteria of quality. Teachers select what they will read aloud and provide in their classroom libraries from a limited selection of what has been published, is made available in bookstores and school libraries, and fits with their view of childhood and literary theories.

Teachers choose what is appropriate to read to children based on what Perry Nodelman (1996) has called their "constructions of childhood." Teachers, and other adults, have a version of reality that includes a version of childhood, that is, what it means to be a child, what children should be exposed to, and what they should be allowed or required to experience. Some teachers believe that childhood should be a time of innocence, so they select only Disneylike stories with happy endings. Other teachers believe that children need to be exposed to the challenges they will face in the world, the harsh realities of living in modern times. These teachers tend to select realistic fiction with characters who deal with situations and issues that make some people uncomfortable.

There is a fine line between what is considered *censorship* and what is considered *selecting* literature. The tendency in many public schools to stay away from controversial issues and attempt to "sanitize" the reading curriculum often leads to a disconnect between the readers in our classrooms and the literature we provide or require children to read. Too often, our selections privilege children from mainstream backgrounds and marginalize children from diverse cultures and lower socioeconomic groups. We need to be vigilant to concepts of diversity and inclusiveness in our selections of literature and ensure that the texts we provide reflect our students' cultures, experiences, and values as well as those of middle-class America.

As classroom teachers, we need to be aware of the versions of reality portrayed in the various literature selections we provide for our students and provide support for students to question the realities portrayed therein. Texts invite readers to read in particular ways, but readers have the option of accepting this invitation or constructing an alternative interpretation, asking a different set of questions in transaction with a particular text. We need to ensure that readers have the option of asking questions of a text that it may not invite them to ask.

Since teachers select most of the books that are read aloud or included in the classroom library, when students disagree with something in a text or question the version of reality presented in the text, they are, in effect, questioning the teacher and her choice of reading material. If they "talk back" to the text, do we view this as talking back to the teacher? That is, are we creating a space where students can feel comfortable disagreeing with our selections and interpretations?

In order to create this type of space for discussion and disagreement, teachers need to be more open and transparent with their processes of selecting texts for the classroom library and for reading aloud. We must be willing to analyze our selections and the reasons we have for choosing particular texts. Shared contemplation begins by sharing the reasons we read particular texts and not others. It is supported by creating a community of readers who are willing to share their honest reactions to a text. We need to unpack our criteria, and the criteria of committees who give out prominent children's literature awards like the Newbery, Caldecott, and Orbus Pictus awards, to make clear why we choose to read what we do.

In continuing with this line of thought, not only do we need to be aware of the selections of literature we provide, but we also need to be aware of the various roles that children's literature assumes in the elementary reading curriculum. For example, literature may be conceived as an *add-on* to the reading curriculum, where students are allowed to read real books only when their seatwork is done or their basal lessons are completed. On the other hand, literature may be conceived as a *space for thought*, where the reading of literature opens up opportunities for discussion, reflection, and interrogation of multiple perspectives. Both of these roles are contingent upon the theoretical perspectives and definitions of reading comprehension constructed and adopted by the classroom teacher.

In the past few years, I have come to consider literature as a space for thinking-talking. I have adapted some of the ideas in the following list from an article in *Language Arts*, a journal of the National Council of Teachers of English, written by Carolyn Burke and Jody Copenhaver (2004).

Literature as a Space for Thinking-Talking

❖ Literature provides a way to make sense of our world and to understand the structures and patterns of our society.

❖ Literature serves as a device for preserving our understandings, knowledge, culture, and social beliefs.

❖ Literature provides a platform, or intellectual space, for people to consider alternative realities (i.e., the way things could be) and have discussions about those possibilities.

❖ Literature provides opportunities to question the way things are in our world, for example, social institutions, public schools, or race relations.

- Literature illuminates the life we lead and the people we are in the process of becoming.
- Literature creates a safe place to question the world and to realize possibilities. We can say things about characters that we can't always say about actual people.
- Literature allows readers to reflect upon their life's experiences and revisit them time and again. Reflection brings intellectual flexibility.
- Literature provides momentary escapes from our current situations.
- Literature enables us to see the universality of human experience.
- Literature is a product of convention that is rooted in, if not determined by, the dominant belief systems and ideologies of the times in which it is created.
- Literature can be experienced aesthetically, as a lived-through experience, or efferently, concerned about what the reader takes away from the reading experience.
- Literature is based on elements of story or narrative conventions. It is concerned with plot, characters' motives, setting, and themes.
- Literature can educate the heart as well as the mind.
- Literature can do things for readers that other types of texts cannot. It can provide readers with new ways of thinking about the world and themselves and revising their versions of reality. Its role cannot be underestimated.

As children learn *how* to read, they also learn what reading *is*. That is, what counts as proficient reading is defined through the expectations and practices enacted in our classrooms. Students are constructed as readers of particular types by the reading practices made available to them in schools and by the discourse regimes that locate and situate practices and readers. Readers construct readings, not as originators of meaning, but as human subjects positioned through social, political, and historical practices that remain the location of a constant struggle over power.

Every reading workshop is a site for the construction of meanings. Every interpretive community has some allegiance to a particular literary tradition or perspective, and it draws upon these traditions to decide what it means to be a proficient reader. Readers learn to speak in certain ways and offer certain interpretations based on the theoretical orientations of the teacher and the interpretive community. Each instructional practice and theoretical perspective functions to close off possible readings and meanings from some perspectives and privilege others. It is the interrogation of these perspectives and the meanings generated by individual readers that needs to become a central component of the reading workshop.

The Role of Language and Word Study in the Reading Workshop

So far, I have focused my attention on the reading, discussing, and analysis of literature, the role of the teacher, and the role of literature across the elementary curriculum. However, another essential component of the reading workshop is the role of language or word study. In language study, we draw students' attention to the qualities and characteristics of the English language, for example, parts of speech like nouns and verbs, word structures and families, and alphabetic principles. Although I believe that language study has been overemphasized in many reading programs, I firmly believe that it is an essential component in a reading workshop framework.

Frank Smith (1988a) said navigation of text is a conscious decision-making process based on readers' growing awareness of the concepts and conventions of printed text. I consider navigation the processes of decoding and beyond. It involves decoding and knowledge of words and language but also includes knowledge of text structures, genre characteristics, design elements, directionality, and punctuation. The lessons we provide focusing on word and language study must go beyond simple lessons in word-attack skills. These lessons in linguistics must help readers understand the contexts for using these skills and how decoding and navigating texts can be used *in service of meaning*.

Essential Components of the Reading Workshop

The reading workshop is nothing more than an organizational framework for reading instruction. That's it! It is not a program to be delivered, nor is it a series of scripted lessons. It is a structure within which to locate reading instruction that provides an array of learning experiences for developing proficient, sophisticated readers. The reading workshop provides space for interactions among students and teachers, large blocks of time for students to engage in the act of reading, and demonstrations of proficient reading by more capable readers. That is, the reading workshop is a place for engaged reading.

Fostering engaged reading means more than just providing time for students to read, although this is an important aspect of it. Too often, I have seen sustained silent reading (SSR) or drop everything and read (DEAR) programs become anything but sustained, silent, or engaging. During engaged reading, readers are asked to assume the responsibility for making appropriate choices concerning what they read. In addition, they are given ample time to read in and out of school, provided with appropriate feedback to their interpretations, and provided with an opportunity to generate, articulate, negotiate, and revise meanings in a community of readers. If these components are not a part of the block of time set aside for the reading workshop, mandating silent reading for twenty minutes somewhere else during the school day won't give readers the time, access, opportunity, and support necessary to become proficient, sophisticated readers.

Specifically, the essential components of the reading workshop that are described in the chapters to follow are:

❖ creating a literate environment

❖ reading aloud as the foundation of the reading workshop

❖ invested discussions

❖ transactional units of study

❖ lessons in comprehension

❖ literacy assessment

I briefly introduce each component here and explain how it emerged and what role it played in my reading workshop throughout the rest of the book.

Creating a Literate Environment

Readers don't learn to read in a vacuum, nor do they learn to read in classrooms that don't provide access to quality reading materials. In *The Reading Workshop: Creating Space for Readers*, I shared my vision of a literate environment, drawing parallels between the elaborate children's section of many commercial bookstores and the literate environments I wanted to see in intermediate classrooms. I discussed how classroom environments must provide access to high-quality reading materials, time for engaged reading, and opportunities to share and discuss what has been read. These ideas have not changed. What I hope to do in the chapters to follow is share more of the specifics of how this literate environment comes together over time and what particular aspects are vital for success.

Reading Aloud as the Foundation of the Reading Workshop

Unlike Las Vegas, everything that happens during the read-aloud does not stay in the read-aloud. What occurs during reading aloud and discussing literature affects how individuals transact with texts independently and the expectations and procedures for paired reading and small-group literature studies. How literature is discussed during the read-aloud provides the most concrete demonstration of the ways we want students to read and think on their own and in small groups. If things don't happen during whole-group discussions, why would we expect them to happen when we send students off on their own to read?

As I described in *Reading Aloud and Beyond: Fostering the Intellectual Life in Older Readers*, the read-aloud sets the stage for other components of the reading workshop. Reading aloud and discussing literature is by far the most influential component of the reading workshop. Unfortunately, it is often the least valued and utilized by intermediate- and middle-grade teachers. Reading aloud is enjoyable and relaxing, but it is also a time to demonstrate fluent oral reading, a way of exposing children to new genres, authors, illustrators, themes, and titles, a way of setting expectations for responding to texts, and a primary opportunity to develop an effective community of readers.

Invested Discussions

Read-aloud time does not mean just reading aloud a book. It also includes time for discussing ideas, sharing interpretations, and negotiating meaning. Over the past ten years, I have created numerous invested discussion strategies that I have used to help students move beyond "I like the book." Invested discussions employ quality literature and support the notion of shared contemplation. These various invested discussion strategies provide an opportunity for readers to offer half-baked ideas and see how they rise.

Most of the invested discussion strategies that I have utilized contain some aspect of visual representation. I use classroom charts to maintain a record of what we have discussed each day in order to return to our ideas in subsequent discussions. These charts also support readers in stepping back from the details of a text to analyze the structures of the text as a whole or contemplate the big picture. The goal of these invested discussion strategies is not to get good at them in isolation; rather, they should be seen as vehicles for generating, articulating, doing, and revising interpretations in a community of readers.

Transactional Units of Study

I organize my reading and writing curricula around the concept of transactional units of study. In general, units of study in the reading workshop focus on particular genres, the works of an author or an illustrator, topics from the content areas, themes in literature, social issues, or elements of literature. These units last from two to six weeks, depending upon their importance in the language arts curriculum, the needs and interests of my students, and the resources available.

Like my college syllabi, the transactional units of study I conduct never remain exactly the same from semester to semester or year to year. The students in my classes change, and so should my teaching and resources. I am constantly reflecting on how each unit of study worked the previous semester and adding new resources as they become available, in particular newly published selections of children's literature. Some units of study have worked for several years; others have been abandoned immediately.

Each transactional unit of study contains a cornerstone text that focuses our attention on the topic or theme and provides an extended learning experience from which to construct the rest of the unit. For example, in a unit on the theme escaping reality, I have used the picture book *Where the Wild Things Are* for many years as a cornerstone text. We read this book for several days, discussing the illustrations, written text, and textual structure, and use these experiences as the foundation for discussing the other texts in the unit of study.

Transactional units of study are different from traditional thematic units in one significant way: they are not created over the summer by a group of teachers to be delivered in the fall. Transactional units of study are developed alongside the readers in the classroom, responding to their needs and interests, in addition to being planned over the summer or school year. It is this blend of preplanned lessons and response-centered teaching that is the core of the transactional unit of study. These units are created with students, not in front of them.

Lessons in Comprehension

In my third book, *Lessons in Comprehension: Explicit Instruction in the Reading Workshop,* I delineated many of my favorite and most successful lessons for teaching readers to comprehend. Some of these lessons reappear in this book, but many new ones have been added as well. I didn't give away all my secrets in that book, you can be assured.

The reading workshop provides the structure for our lessons in comprehension to proceed. Learning to become a proficient and sophisticated reader is enhanced through access to quality reading materials, demonstrations of literate behavior, and lessons in reading and comprehension. Teachers using the workshop approach to reading instruction teach explicitly every day, using a variety of approaches and strategies. Explicit comprehension lessons are an essential component of an effective reading workshop.

Literacy Assessment

Unlike standardized tests, literacy assessment should not exist as a separate entity but rather should be embedded in the day-to-day interactions and experiences of the reading workshop. Because of this, I include various assessments within each chapter to demonstrate the instruments and observational procedures I use to come to know my students as readers. Assessment should be used to inform one's practice, not merely to offer up scores for comparing readers. Each type of classroom-based assessment provides a different window into a child's literate abilities, needs, and interests. As we come to know the children in our classrooms as readers, we become better positioned to develop effective lessons and learning experiences.

Professional Development or Training?

In the past few years, there has been a shift in teacher education and district inservices away from *professional development*, which focuses on expanding teachers' knowledge base, theories of reading, and pedagogical abilities, and toward *training*, which focuses on the correct application of someone else's ideas and practices, usually contained in a commercial reading program.

During several trainings I have attended, provided by federally mandated reading programs, teachers were rarely, if ever, asked or allowed to question what they were doing. The instructional practices contained in these programs are scripted out for teachers in their teachers' manual. I do not believe that this form of training builds capacity for effective reading instruction; rather, these trainings force teachers to blindly follow a recipe without any input into what or how they are teaching. They are simply asked to give up their professional judgment and follow a program written by some professor or educator who may or may not have been in a classroom in the past decade.

In a workshop approach to reading instruction, teachers are supported to make instructional decisions based on their knowledge of the reading process, their understanding of the students in their classroom, and the resources available to them. When teachers are given room to make decisions, reflect on their teaching practices, evaluate the effectiveness of their instructional choices, share and discuss their teaching with other teachers, read professional literature, and make changes to their practices based on these reflections, we are truly building capacity for effective reading instruction. Training provides little opportunity for this level of reflection and professional development to occur.

On the other hand, I don't want teachers to simply teach whatever they want; I want them to be able to explain in detail how they will address the standards for achievement set forth in district and state standards documents using their chosen pedagogical approaches. We, as classroom teachers, must learn to make a better case for what we are doing in the reading workshop; otherwise, we will be continually forced to deliver scripted lessons.

The Literary Docent

I have been using the term *literary docent* for several years now as a metaphor for my vision of a quality teacher of reading and literature. As I observed and participated in numerous museum tours during my travels across the country, I paid close attention to what the docents did during guided tours. I listened to what they said and, more importantly, what they didn't say. I researched the types of professional development sessions that docents were required to attend, their job descriptions, and how they interacted with museum patrons. These experiences led me to begin making connections to the various roles constructed by reading workshop teachers.

Museum docents conduct museum tours, leading patrons through the museum's collections of art or exhibits and helping them attend to important aspects of the museum that may otherwise go unnoticed. They enable visitors to see and understand aspects of the art or artifacts they encounter that they wouldn't see and understand on their own. In the same way, I would define the literary docent as someone who helps readers navigate the world of literature, helping them see and understand what they wouldn't see and understand on their own. The literary docent calls readers' attention to aspects of literature that may go unnoticed.

Museum docents do not interpret art for their patrons; they give them the tools to interpret art for themselves. That is, they help us understand what we are seeing as we wander around the museum while keeping the joy of the museum experience alive. In my opinion, this is also the key to quality teaching. My role as a teacher of literature, or literary docent, is to help children develop the theoretical tools to interpret literature for themselves, and to help them come to more sophisticated interpretations by applying various lenses, without destroying the joy of reading. It is this fine line between critical interpretation and enjoyment that I walk as I introduce readers to the world of literature.

In addition to positioning teachers as literary docents, the reading workshop also requires teachers to be literacy promoters. In this role, teachers not only facilitate students' development as literate human beings but also, like vaudeville barkers, promote and advertise the advantages and joys of being literate. If you think back on the teachers who have had an impact in your life, most likely there was a particular teacher who interested you in a particular subject and had a tremendous impact on your thinking and beliefs. It is my guess that this teacher loved what he or she was teaching. The teacher was able to show you new things and pique your interest in the subject at hand. His or her love of English, science, art, or whatever made you love it as well. It is this love of learning we try to inspire in the students we meet every year.

When students arrive in my classroom and see the hundreds of books I set out for them and talk with me about my favorite books or the books I am currently reading, I hope they see me as a joyfully literate human being. Being lifelong readers and learners ourselves is one of the best ways we can invite students into the world of reading and literature.

Structure Versus Control

Before leaving the characteristics of the reading workshop teacher, I want to briefly discuss the differences between a *controlled* and a *structured* classroom environment. Many teachers share with me their concerns about classroom management and their fears of trying a reading workshop approach because it won't be structured enough. What they are really concerned about is giving up control. The challenge is sharing responsibilities with students so that both parties gain control over the procedures, learning experiences, and choices made in the reading workshop, not determining which group will dominate the other. I want to make a case for structured reading workshops, not controlled reading workshops.

In a controlled classroom environment, the teacher makes almost all of the decisions while students wait to find out what they are doing next. When students are sitting quietly in rows, waiting for directions, the classroom is controlled, not structured. All students are doing the same thing at the same time. The teacher serves as arbiter of meaning and evaluator of all learning. Students submit work in order to find out how they have done. The classroom interactions follow the traditional initiate-respond-evaluate pattern, in which a teacher initiates a discussion by asking questions, students respond, and the teacher evaluates the responses. In a controlled classroom environment, the teacher controls the learning from *outside* the experiences of her students. The teacher watches over it, rather than participates in it.

In a structured classroom environment, the schedule is posted so that students, as well as the teacher, are aware of what is coming next. The teacher takes time to establish consistent, predictable structures and procedures that provide a framework for students to work and make choices within. These procedures become ritualized as students make them their own. Students share the responsibilities of the reading workshop, completing their daily jobs and making appropriate decisions about what reading and learning experiences to engage in. The teacher works from the inside in a structured classroom environment, participating in discussions and helping students interact with each other as well as the teacher.

A structured classroom environment opens up possibilities for students, requires consistency and predictability, and provides students a framework to work within. It requires forethought but allows for teachable moments to occur and student input and ideas to flourish. A controlled classroom environment is a regimented place where students are required to simply follow the rules, not help create them. Reading workshops certainly need structure to operate effectively, but they do not need to be controlled.

Some Final Thoughts and Concerns

At the heart of the reading workshop lies a commitment to changing the way we think and talk about texts. It demands a momentous philosophical shift from an objectivist or modernist perspective, where meaning is thought to reside within a text, only to be extracted by the most capable of readers, to an transactional or sociocultural perspective, where readers construct meaning in transaction with texts in a social context. Without this theoretical shift, the only things that will change in the reading workshop are the decorative features, the bells and whistles of how things are done.

It is no longer enough to say that one is using children's literature in the reading program, nor is it enough to fill the classroom with high-quality books and read aloud a picture book or two each day, although this may be a good place to start. Reading aloud and creating a literate environment that contains an extensive amount of high-quality children's literature are necessary but insufficient practices for implementing a workshop approach to reading instruction.

It has become apparent through my observations of classrooms and my interactions with numerous classroom teachers and school administrators that we need to increase the integrity of our teaching. That is, we need to raise the quality of discussions in our classrooms. We need to have more intellectual rigor in the learning experiences we provide and the assignments we construct. We need to challenge students to make robust, not superficial, connections and to pose questions of texts that are worthy of investigating. We need to respect the literature we read as a piece of art first, and find effective ways to use it as an instructional resource second. We need to promote intellectual conversations about literature that expand our understandings of the texts we read, our place in society, and what it means to be a human being.

Every experience we provide must be analyzed for its effect on readers and whether it is supporting their becoming lifelong readers or making them not want to read. Mark Twain wrote, "The man [*sic*] who does not read good books has no advantage over the man that can't read them." It seems that in our fervor to ensure that children are able to read, we are creating a society of people who are unwilling to engage in reading for pleasure and information. Having the ability to read, but not exercising that ability because of one's experiences in schools, does not lead to an informed citizenry, the cornerstone of our democratic society.

CHAPTER 2

September—Inviting Students into the World of Reading and Literature

The truly literate are not those who know how to read,
but those who read: independently, responsively,
critically, and because they want to.
—GLENNA SLOAN, *THE CHILD AS CRITIC*

SEPTEMBER CHAPTER OUTLINE

September Lessons and Learning Experiences
❖ Building a Community of Readers
❖ Organizing Classroom Space for Reading and Discussion
❖ Establishing Procedures for the Reading Workshop
❖ Helping Readers Make Appropriate Choices for Independent Reading
❖ Moving Beyond "I Like the Book" in Our Literature Discussions
❖ Introducing the Concept of "Thinking-Talking"
Featured Lesson in Comprehension for September: Approaching a Text
Literacy Assessments
❖ Reading Response Notebooks (used throughout the year)
❖ Daily Reading Logs (used throughout the year)
❖ Oral Reading Analyses (used throughout the year)

Introduction

Advertisements for back-to-school sales in the newspaper and on television serve as signals for teachers to begin reorganizing their lives to accommodate the upcoming challenges of a new school year. The quiet, relaxing days of reading novels and traveling to exotic places quickly disappear, and in their place emerge concerns about where to find appropriate resources for instruction, which literacy lessons will be the most engaging for a new group of students, and how the classroom environment should be organized to support a community of readers, writers, mathematicians, and scientists.

Each September, twenty-five or more students wander into our classrooms, hoping to be greeted by a teacher who will respect who they are, make learning enjoyable, and guide them through the rewards and challenges of another school year. Their hopes and expectations parallel our own as we wonder about the learners who will enter our classrooms, invade our dreams, and make their way into our hearts. There will be tremendous challenges and unanticipated celebrations in the upcoming year as teachers and students come together in the crowded space of a classroom for approximately 180 days.

The school year has a rhythm. September is different from January, which, in turn, is different from April. The reading workshop has a rhythm as well. The reading workshop does not begin the year in the same way it will end. As each month progresses, we'll add new components to the reading workshop, building upon the theoretical and pedagogical foundations we have established during the previous months. Each component of the reading workshop is introduced at a specific time during the school year and requires a different amount of student involvement and responsibility. The various components of the reading workshop offer teachers different ways of scaffolding students' learning experiences and transactions with literature.

The essential components of the reading workshop, including reading aloud with children, comprehension strategy lessons, and literature study groups, add to the complexity

❖ Reflection Logs (used throughout the year)
❖ Parent Information Request Letters (September only)
❖ Reading Inventories (September only)
Connections to the Writing Workshop
❖ Building a Community of Writers
❖ Understanding Genre

RECOMMENDED COMPREHENSION STRATEGIES FROM *LESSONS IN COMPREHENSION*

❖ 1.2 Choosing Appropriate Texts for Independent Reading
❖ 1.5 Constructing a Classroom Library
❖ 1.6 Understanding Genre
❖ 1.7 Becoming a Member of a Community of Readers
❖ 1.8 Establishing a Readers' Bill of Rights
❖ 3.3 Approaching a Text

and variety that are necessary for addressing the needs, interests, and abilities of a diverse group of students. Along with being a challenge, this diversity of students' abilities is what makes the reading workshop successful. Without a diversity of perspectives and interests, our literature discussions would not be rich and engaging, our readers would be not be able to learn from more capable others, and the teacher would become the only source of knowledge to draw upon.

The procedures and expectations that are established throughout September, October, and beyond will help the reading workshop become a structured instructional space that allows the teacher to work alongside students, instead of always standing in the front of the room, delivering lectures, or sitting behind a big wooden desk, waiting to correct students' worksheets. This is the difference between a structured classroom and a controlled classroom, which I discussed in Chapter 1.

September is a time for sharing responsibility, supporting students to take charge of their learning and make appropriate choices about what they read and discuss. It is important to remember that this sense of shared responsibility is something many students have never been asked to be part of in their previous years in school. Because of their lack of experience with being responsible for many decisions in the reading workshop, it is important to remain patient and flexible as the reading workshop unfolds.

I have to be careful not to expect everything to come together during the first week of school. All too easily, I can recall the ways the previous year's reading workshop ended the year, operating with minimal directions and teacher monitoring. This high level of student involvement and responsibility allowed me to work alongside readers instead of directing every student's decision about what to read and her engagement with various texts. I often forget that this was not the case when last year's class arrived in September. I forget about the setbacks, the restarts, the continuous explanations of expectations, rights, and responsibilities that went into getting last year's class to the level we were at when we parted company in May.

Unlike the months to follow, September has only the previous school year to build upon, and except in multiage classes, none of the students from the past year are still around. A new teacher, new classmates, and new expectations all provide a bit of tension as the first weeks of school unfold. I sometimes think if I could only teach these new students everything they need to know about the reading workshop by the end of the first week of school, I could get back to where we were when last year ended. But this is not possible. The sophisticated nature of the literature discussions I had with the previous class hinged upon the time I spent exposing readers to new books and authors, setting expectations for becoming a sophisticated and proficient reader, establishing an atmosphere where shared contemplation could take place, and getting to know the members of our classroom community. We need to be sure that we provide each new group of students the time, patience, and support to grow into the type of sophisticated readers we said good-bye to last year.

The September chapter is the most elaborate and lengthy chapter in the book because so many structures, components, and procedures are introduced and established during this month. In the same way that the month of September in my elementary classroom is the most challenging because of a lack of shared experiences among students and teacher, writing about what occurs in September is challenging because you and I, author and reader, have not established a relationship to build upon yet. We have just begun to establish a common language, a theoretical foundation, a set of expectations and understandings for sharing the essential components and instructional practices that are presented in each subsequent chapter. In other words, I have to introduce and explain things in this chapter that I will refer to for the rest of the book. In the same way, I will use the expectations, structures, and components I establish in the reading workshop in September as the foundation for the rest of the school year in the reading workshop.

September Lessons and Learning Experiences

Building a Community of Readers

Before students arrive on the first day of school, I send each of them a postcard from somewhere during my travels over the summer. A simple gesture, but one that sets the tone for the upcoming school year. As soon as rosters are created, I ask my principal for a list of addresses for the students who are scheduled to be in my class in September. Throughout the summer, I drop a postcard in the mail welcoming each student to our classroom and telling him or her how much I am looking forward to meeting and working with him or her. Each and every year, most of my students arrive at our classroom door holding up their postcards, as if I sent out only one and they were lucky enough to get it.

The first day of school is the most exciting and also the most unpredictable day of the school year. Children wander around the school grounds searching for their classrooms. There are assemblies to attend, paperwork that needs to be filled out, and student names that need to be learned, quickly. In order to reduce the tension of the first day, I keep things very simple. On our first day, we spend some time reading, listening to each other's life stories, playing educational games, reading aloud some picture books and a specially selected chapter book, and arranging the classroom to fit our needs.

Unlike the teachers in many traditional classrooms, when children arrive at my room on the first day of school, I do not have the bulletin boards neatly decorated with snappy borders and posters of celebrities extolling the virtues of being a reader. I do not have all of the desks lined up in neat little rows; in fact, I prefer not to even have desks. For me this sends the wrong message. If the room is completely organized and decorated by me before the first day of school, it sends the message that it is *my* room and my students are just visitors.

When I moved into my new house, believe me, Sharon and I arranged our furniture together. If I had set everything up, she would have just moved it around anyways. We shared the responsibility for how our space would look and how it would operate together. We talked about where things would go and what to put on the walls. I use the same procedures and give the same considerations to my students when setting up our classroom.

In addition, referring to our classroom by its assigned room number, for example, "room 306," rather than as "Mr. Serafini's room" signals to students that it is *our* room and we will make decisions together about how it will be set up and how things will operate. It is important to let students know that we will share responsibility for the procedures, organization, and expectations; rules won't simply be posted on the wall and dictated to students upon arrival. It may take more time to establish expectations and procedures this way, but I find it's well worth the effort to develop a sense of shared responsibility with my students as the year unfolds.

A community of readers is a group of people who share the common goal of reading and discussing literature and becoming literate human beings. This community is built upon mutual respect and a willingness on the part of each participant to listen to and consider the merits of each member's ideas and interpretations. In effect, this community of readers is a model of the kind of world I want to live in.

All interactions and responsibilities in a community of readers are based on democratic principles, allowing each member's voice to be heard and respected. Louise Rosenblatt's (1978) transactional theory of reading, which provides some of the theoretical foundation for the reading workshop, had as much to do with democratic principles as it does with literary criticism. It's not enough to create an appealing physical space for readers. The social dimensions of the reading workshop are as important as the way we arrange the furniture.

In order to establish the social dimensions that support readers and discussion, I use the following learning experiences during the first few weeks of the school year:

❖ *Shoe-box autobiographies.* I invite students to find a container, approximately the size of a shoe box, and fill it with artifacts that represent who they are—their interests, culture, and heritage, life experiences, and future goals. We share these boxes during the first few weeks of school, featuring one student each day until we have allowed everyone, including me, to share his or her shoe-box autobiography with the class.

❖ *Reading wall.* Every time I finish reading a book aloud with my students, I make a copy of the cover of the book and display it on a wall of the classroom for us to refer to as the year continues. By the end of the year, the wall is filled with the covers of books we have read. During the our literature discussions, students often refer to these displays to remind them of particular books we have read and discussed.

❖ *Community circle.* I begin each day of the year by inviting students to share with the other members of the class happenings from their lives outside of school. The more we know about each other, the more we will be willing to listen to and understand each other's ideas and interpretations. This sharing time is more than show-and-tell. It is a way of letting others know who we are, where we came from, what is happening in our lives, and where we are headed in the future.

❖ *Zero-tolerance policy.* The best way to get sent out of my classroom is to tell another student that her ideas are dumb. There is no place for this behavior in our community. I cannot allow it to happen, or my students will quickly stop sharing ideas. I have no tolerance for disrespect, and my students are made aware of this on the first day of school. I can't change the world my students live in, but I can do everything I can to make our classroom a place where ideas can be shared honestly and interpretations are open for negotiation, not unwarranted criticism.

There are other things I do, as I am sure there are ways in which you create community in your classroom, that are not included here. Some were described in *The Reading Workshop*, while new ones will be featured on my literacy website. The purpose of these learning experiences is to create a space for readers to read and discuss literature in a supportive community of readers.

Organizing Classroom Space for Reading and Discussion

I spent a great deal of time explaining my top ten physical arrangement suggestions in *The Reading Workshop*. This time around, I would like to explain how I try to bring real-world structures and physical dimensions into the classroom world of the reading workshop. Bookstores, libraries, and other businesses use marketing techniques and physical arrangements to promote the sales and circulation of their products that can also be used effectively in the reading workshop. My focus is teaching and learning, but some helpful techniques can be found in the ways literacy and reading are marketed in bookstores and advertisements.

Access to Literature

Most bookstores display their recent releases and bestselling books in a separate display with the covers showing, not the spines. Marketing research has shown that potential buyers (or readers) will pick up books more frequently if they can see the covers of the books being displayed. In one classroom I visited, a teacher used rain gutters she purchased at a home improvement store to display picture books for her readers. The gutters were positioned low enough on the wall so that the young readers in her classroom had easy access to her collection of books. Providing shelves and spaces for books where students can easily access them is an important consideration.

Book Displays

Bookstores and libraries display specific titles or the work of a particular author to call customers' attention to these featured books, setting them apart from the rest of the library or store collection. In our classrooms, we can use display shelves to feature specific authors or titles for a particular unit of study. By featuring specific books and authors, we can entice readers into trying new books and authors. These featured displays can be changed easily as the units of study change during the year.

Reading Areas

Many bookstores have special reading areas for reading aloud to parents and their children during store hours. In much the same way, our classrooms should have a specific area designed for reading aloud and gathering readers together to share literature and ideas. This should be a well-defined space, signaling to students what is expected when they are called to listen to a selection. In the same way sacred places like cathedrals or temples elicit certain behaviors when we enter them, the defined space used for reading aloud signals to our students how to behave when they arrive. Some teachers turn on a special light or have other rituals to signal the start of read-aloud time. These rituals help readers enter the moment and remember what is expected during read-aloud and discussion time.

Teacher Desks and Areas

When I walk into a classroom, I want to see children involved in relevant learning experiences, not standing in line in front of a desk that serves as a wooden monument to the teacher. In some traditional classrooms, the line of students extending from this desk, waiting to see the teacher so he can correct their seatwork, seems longer than the line waiting for a roller coaster at Six Flags on a holiday weekend. Teachers need their own space, I agree, but it can be off to the side and not take up one-third of the classroom. Space is a limited commodity in contemporary classrooms, and we need maximize what is available to us.

When we go to a video store, bookstore, or public library, videos and books are organized into categories or genres to enable patrons to find what they are looking for and to allow them to browse titles they are not aware of. Our classrooms need to be organized spaces to provide easy access for students to get the materials they need for the learning experiences we provide. Classroom libraries are essential to effective reading workshops. In some schools, most of the books are stored in a central library. They often go untouched simply because students have limited opportunities to check books out. I would like to see the majority of books in public schools housed in the individual classrooms where students can get to them. This would require a major shift concerning the role of the librarian, but I think it is well worth investigating.

Establishing Procedures for the Reading Workshop

During the first weeks of the school year, I focus on establishing three essential components of the reading workshop: (1) reading and exploring literature independently and in pairs for an extended period of time, (2) read-aloud and discussion as a daily ritual, and (3) an accessible, organized classroom library that includes a wide variety of reading materials that are appropriate and relevant to the students in my class (this includes procedures for maintaining the library and checking out books for home reading).

Other components, for example, comprehension strategy groups, literature study groups, book clubs, response to literature experiences, and inquiry projects, are introduced as the year progresses. However, none of these other components will be successful if I cannot get students to work independently and make appropriate decisions about what to do next without interrupting me when I am working with an individual or a small group of readers. Students are required to assume more responsibility in a reading workshop approach than in a traditional approach, and my procedures, components, structures, and expectations must support them in doing so.

Developing Students' Ability to Read and Explore Literature Independently and in Pairs

During the first few weeks of school, my goal is to have students read for an extended period of time, approximately twenty to forty minutes, each and every day. In order to do so, readers need to know where to find things to read, how to make appropriate selections for their reading, where to sit, and how to share ideas without interfering with other readers. One of the primary considerations during the beginning of the year in the reading workshop is establishing procedures that allow students to work independently, freeing up the teacher to work with individuals or small groups. Teaching students how to find and select an appropriate text is an important consideration in allowing this to happen.

Many primary-grade teachers use centers to organize their reading workshop for younger readers. These centers create predictable structures that scaffold individual readers' learning and provide clear guidelines for what readers are expected to do. I have no problem with the use of centers as an organizing device as long as the things that are happening at each center are worthwhile learning experiences, not "ditto dumps" containing worksheets designed to simply keep readers busy and in their seats. Only activities that are worth doing as a whole group are worth doing at a center.

Two examples of centers that I have used for years in my intermediate classrooms and found to be quite successful are (1) the listening center, featuring audio books and copies of the text for shared reading, and (2) the featured author or illustrator center, where readers can explore the work of a selected author or illustrator, including author interviews, biographies, and other information about that person. I introduce each of these centers during the first few weeks of school to the whole group. Once everyone understands what is expected of them in that center, we establish a sign-up sheet or procedure for students to use it independently. My goal is to provide more and more choices, enlarging the options available to readers as the year progresses.

Each day during the first week of school, I spend time talking with my students about how to select a book and find a place to read. In addition to the tables and chairs provided, I usually include a couch, floor pillows, and other comfortable seating options for students in our classroom. I do so because that is where I would like to sit and read if I were a student in the class. People read in comfortable places outside of school for extended periods of time. The same courtesy should be offered to our students.

The class discusses who gets to use these seating options each day and how to resolve conflicts about the limited spaces we have available. The decisions about how to deal with limited resources is an important one for students to address as the year begins. This won't be the only time this year when there are more people wanting to use something than can be accommodated, given our limited space and budget. Some years we used sign-up sheets and other times we assigned days of the week for certain groups of people to use the couches. In other years, it was a more open, first-come, first-served arrangement. The decision is made by the group and is open for revision as time goes on.

Many of my students in the intermediate and middle grades have experienced a reading and writing workshop before they arrive in my classroom. Because of this, many of them are quite capable of maintaining independent and paired reading for an extended period of time beginning on the first day of school. Other students have never been given this much choice and voice in their educational experiences. For those students, I spend more time talking about how to select an appropriate text, how to find a place to read, or how to read with a partner. I demonstrate to the whole class how to read alongside someone and share a book without disturbing other readers. Everything that I expect students to do is demonstrated in a whole-class setting before I set expectations for independent work. What happens in small groups is always demonstrated in whole groups first.

I have been spending time observing where people outside of school read and under what conditions they engage in the act of reading. I have found that mass transportation, for example, airplanes, trains, and subways, provides time and space for people to read. People read on the beach and waiting in line at the motor vehicle department. After observing people reading in many settings, I asked myself, "Why do people read in these places, and what do these places have in common to support so much reading?"

First, I noticed that people read when they want to pass time, they have a comfortable place to sit, and reading materials are readily available and free of charge, like in the dentist's or doctor's waiting room. Some people read when they have nothing else to do. Others go to places specifically to read, like coffee shops, libraries, bookstores, and universities.

I found that these spaces for reading have the following three things in common: First, there is access to a wide variety of reading materials and no one is pressuring people to read. People choose to read in these places; no one is forcing them. Second, there is an ample amount of time available to engage with a text. In fact, people say they read when they are on vacation because that is the only time they get to read what they want. And finally, there is no expectation for readers to do something after they read. We don't give quizzes in the dentist's office after someone puts down a magazine. We don't walk up and down the beach handing out book report forms. When most people are finished reading, they read another book or do something else. It's their choice.

Clearly, the conditions in which people choose to read outside of schools can be brought into the reading workshop. During the reading workshop, we must provide ample time to read and easy access to reading materials. We must consider carefully the types of activities we require readers to do after reading. We must allow readers to talk to other readers and share their ideas. We need to make our physical settings as comfortable as possible to support extended time for reading. And most of all, we must be available to help children find a place for reading in their lives by serving as their literary docents.

Establishing Reading Aloud as a Daily Ritual

They say that everything that happens in Las Vegas stays in Las Vegas. Fortunately, everything that happens during a read-aloud and discussion does *not* stay in the read-aloud and discussion! The read-aloud and the subsequent invested discussions are the foundation of the reading workshop. It is where I demonstrate how to approach a piece of literature, how to make an appropriate selection, how to read aloud with intonation and fluency, how to talk about a text, how to negotiate meanings with other readers, and how to evaluate and respond to the things being read. The things that happen during the read-aloud will support the things that individual readers will do with texts as they read independently and the types of discussions that occur in small-group literature studies.

In my second book, *Reading Aloud and Beyond: Fostering the Intellectual Life with Older Readers*, I tried to provide a rationale for the importance of including reading aloud in the intermediate grades and beyond. In that book, I discussed setting the stage for reading aloud and how I conceptualized reading aloud as a performance. At the beginning of the year, my focus is on establishing the read-aloud as a daily ritual and setting the expectations for students during this period of time each day.

Following are the features of reading aloud and discussing literature that I will introduce, demonstrate, and focus on during the first few weeks:

❖ *How to gather together for the read-aloud.* This includes where to sit, how to get there, when the read-aloud will occur during the day, and what to bring. I create an area in the front of the class with enough room for everyone and a special chair, low enough so that the person in it can see everyone and be seen by everyone, that will be used for our read-aloud sessions. I play a two-minute song on a tape recorder to signal that read-alouds are about to begin. Students are expected to put down what they are doing and find a spot in our reading area where they won't be distracted by other students. I allow students to make the decision about whom to sit next to themselves until they demonstrate that they need help in choosing a better location.

❖ *How to listen to a read-aloud and when to share ideas.* I expect my students to listen and attend to the story being read and to be ready to discuss the book at appropriate times. For example, when I am reading a page from a picture book, I expect students to listen and not interrupt the reading. When I have finished reading a page, and we are looking more closely at the illustrations, I invite students to offer ideas aloud before we move on to the next page. I don't expect my students to wait until the book is finished before telling each other what they think. However, I do expect them to listen when I am reading and be polite when someone else is offering an idea.

❖ *How to listen to other readers' ideas and interpretations.* Depending on the number of students in the class, during our discussions I try to have students face each other in a circle so they can see and hear each other when discussing a book. This shift in seating arrangements helps signal that students are sharing ideas with each other, not just with the teacher. We talk about what good listeners do and practice this procedure a great deal in the beginning of the year. If we are going to take each other's ideas seriously, we need to begin by listening to each other effectively.

❖ *The literacy notebook.* Many times, I have my students bring their literacy notebook, used for collecting writing and responses to literature, to the read-aloud and discussion. I have them use this notebook to take notes on the reading lessons I conduct and to respond to the books we share. I cannot allow this notebook to interfere with the primary goal of reading aloud, namely, engaging with the read-aloud. However, the notebook is a place for readers who are reluctant to share ideas aloud to write them down and share them later in a different setting. I talk more about this notebook later in the book.

When the read-aloud is over, we move into independent reading, paired reading, and eventually strategy and literature discussion groups. Each of these components is introduced one at a time and procedures are established for each component as the year progresses.

Creating an Accessible, Organized Classroom Library

In addition to public and school libraries, a classroom library can have a tremendous impact on the lives of readers in our classrooms. Well-designed and well-stocked classroom libraries provide access to a wide range of reading materials and are the cornerstone of a literature-based reading workshop. Research has shown that students who have access to a well-stocked classroom library engage in reading more frequently, know more about different genres, authors, and illustrators, and take books home for pleasure reading more often. Subsequently, we spend a great deal of time organizing the collection to provide easy access to a wide variety of reading materials and analyzing the collection so students know what is available to read. Librarians are assigned as one of our classroom jobs to help keep the collection organized and help readers check books in and out of the library.

In *The Reading Workshop*, I detailed the procedures I used for organizing the classroom library at the beginning of the year and will not go into that level of detail here. However, each day for the first few weeks of school, we spend about thirty minutes opening boxes of library books that I packed away from the previous year and investigating what is in each box. We create lists of the kinds of books we discover in the collection, organize those lists into categories, and use those categories to structure our library shelves and displays.

An effective library collection should have a wide variety of reading materials, including easy and complex picture and chapter books in a large assortment of genres and formats; nonfiction or expository texts; magazines; comics; pop-up books; audio books; series chapter books; song lyrics; poetry anthologies; short-story collections; reference books including almanacs, atlases, writing resources, and phone books; student-authored publications; plays; newspapers; and computers for Internet access. It takes a long time and many resources to amass a quality classroom library. Over the years, I have spent a great deal of my own money at used bookstores, garage sales, book warehouses, and reading conferences to add to my collection. Every year I wrote grants for money for books, asked my administrators for any spare funds available for books, and peddled book clubs to my students to add to our library. It isn't easy to find monies for books, but a literature-based classroom cannot exist without a large selection of literature. My goal was to provide at least one hundred books per child. This meant my library needed to house approximately twenty-five hundred books. A library of that size provides access to a wide range of books and makes a statement about what is important in the life of a classroom.

Helping Readers Make Appropriate Choices for Independent Reading

Helping readers make appropriate choices for what to read during independent and paired reading is one of the most important lessons I teach in the beginning of the school year. Many students come into my classroom making appropriate selections and need very little assistance to continue doing so. Others need lots of help and monitoring to find reading materials they can make sense of. In my experience with intermediate-grade students, about 50 percent of my students will make appropriate selections for their independent reading with little support from me. For them, my job is to get new books into their hands, to challenge them to try new genres and expand their reading repertoire. Another 25 percent of my students will listen to our discussions about the criteria for making an appropriate selection and will begin to make better choices for independent reading. The remaining 25 percent will need more monitoring, and we will have conversations about why they choose to read what they select. How will I know who makes appropriate selections and who does not? By using some of the classroom-based assessments that I describe throughout the book.

Making appropriate selections is contingent upon understanding that the purpose of reading is understanding what you read. Once readers internalize the fact that they are expected to make sense of what they read, they will begin to make better choices. Rather than focus on making choices for students, leveling and labeling texts, and creating book bins for students to limit their selections, I spend more time ensuring that my students are reading for meaning and making sense of what they read. This takes time, but shortcuts like leveling and labeling texts do not guarantee that students will make better choices. In addition, when we level texts we are taking away the responsibility readers have for choosing appropriately. Putting books in designated book baskets is all fine and dandy, but it will have little effect on students' reading and selections until readers learn to read for meaning.

Additionally, if students are going to be asked to make appropriate choices, they need a wide range of books to choose from, time to browse, and exposure to new titles, authors, genres, and topics. It's difficult for readers to make appropriate choices when there are only a few books to choose from. My classroom library includes books that range in difficulty from simple picture books, like *Green Eggs and Ham*, by Dr. Seuss (1960), to complex novels, like *The Giver*, by Lois Lowry (1993). The range of materials in my library is wide because so is the range of abilities of my readers.

One of the featured lessons from *Lessons in Comprehension: Explicit Instruction in the Reading Workshop* describes the discussions that I have with my students about making appropriate selections for independent reading. From these discussions I have created

FIG. 2.1
Choosing a Book to Read

- ❖ Open to a page and see if you can read and understand what is happening in the story.
- ❖ Read the blurb on the back cover.
- ❖ Ask friends for book recommendations and ideas.
- ❖ Look at the suggested age level.
- ❖ Read more books from the same author.
- ❖ Ask Dr. Serafini for some suggestions.
- ❖ Stop after reading a page and see if you can talk about what is happening.
- ❖ Be honest with yourself and pick a book you can read; it will be a more enjoyable experience.
- ❖ Remember that books will be available when you are ready for them.

classroom charts to remind students of some of the tips and techniques we can use to make better selections (see Figure 2.1).

Whether a selection is appropriate depends on the reader's purpose for reading a particular text. Why we read something influences how we read it. When readers are making selections for independent reading, their purpose is primarily to enjoy a story. This means that a reader has to be able to understand enough of the story to engage with it. Knowing every word is not necessary to enjoy a story. However, when reading expository texts for information, knowing important vocabulary words is very important. Browsing or skimming a text requires different selection criteria from reading for information or to complete a task.

When we select books to use in strategy groups, we select books that we know will pose a certain level of challenge for the students we have identified for these lessons. These strategy groups provide an opportunity for teachers to see what particular readers will do when they are challenged during their reading. When readers are reading to practice their oral fluency, for example, to read aloud a poem in front of the class, they should select a book that is relatively easy for them to read. In all of these examples, purpose plays an important role in determining what makes an appropriate choice. It is more complex than leveling books and sorting them into bins for students to choose from.

Moving Beyond "I Like the Book" in Our Literature Discussions

Students in my intermediate classes, much the same as the students in my graduate children's literature courses, initially respond to many of my read-alouds with the comment "I like that book!" I love it when students say that. I am glad to hear that I chose a book that they enjoyed. However, I cannot allow the discussion to simply stop there. I have to acknowledge their honest initial reactions while at the same time inviting them to expand on their ideas, to further articulate what they liked, why they liked it, and how the text made them respond the way they did.

The quality of the discussions that take place in the read-aloud set the stage for the quality of the discussions we will have in our literature study groups when they begin sometime around November. The level of sophistication of our small-group literature studies is contingent upon the quality of the whole-group discussions we have after a read-aloud. The demonstrations, both intended and unintended, that we offer students during our read-aloud and discussions support the quality of the thinking-talking that will occur in other settings.

Throughout the year, I introduce students to a variety of invested discussion strategies designed to help readers move beyond their initial responses into what Robert Scholes (1985) calls interpretation and criticism. During the first few weeks of school, the two strategies that I try to establish during the read-aloud and discussions that take place using picture and chapter books are (1) turn-pair-share, where each student shares with another student before sharing with the entire community, and (2) sharing without raising hands.

In the turn-pair-share strategy, students turn to a partner in the group and share their ideas after a book has been read. This strategy allows more voices into the conversation and supports those students more reticent to share ideas in front of everyone. It is essential for students to know that what they think is important and that I am not the hub through which all discussion flows. I want my students to learn to talk to each other, not just with me. I want them to know that their ideas are valued whether I hear them directly or not. Many students who are reluctant to share their own ideas are more than willing to talk about what their partner has shared with them. It is a form of literary gossip that is highly supported in my classroom.

This leads to the second invested discussion strategy, talking without raising one's hand. I attempt to get students to enter a conversation without raising their hands because I have found that many students can simply raise their hand and then check out until they hear their name called. Once they hear their name, they attend to the group discussion, have their say, and then check back out. Conversely, in order to join an ongoing conversation without raising one's hand, one must pay attention to the conversation and wait for an appropriate pause to share one's thoughts. Getting students to share ideas without raising their hands is not easy. Even in my graduate classes, students raise their hands to get my attention and share some thought. It is one of the most ingrained, established norms in all of schooling. However, the benefits make this strategy worth the effort. Once students begin to listen to each other in order to know when to enter the discussion, they will continue to do so in literature study groups and other settings.

Introducing the Concept of Thinking-Talking

I begin our yearlong journey into literary criticism by inviting students to tell me more about what they are thinking rather than asking them why they liked a particular book or part of a story. I first encountered this idea in Aidan Chambers' (1996) book *Tell Me: Children, Reading, and Talk*. Chambers went to great lengths in this text to explain how some questions can be perceived by students as adversarial and that asking students "Why?" does not help them articulate what they are thinking. He suggests that readers need to learn to share three types of responses to texts: (1) enthusiasms, or what they like about a text, (2) puzzles, or what confuses them about a text, and (3) connections and patterns, or how they relate particular texts to other texts and their lives. He wants readers to care about what they read and learn to participate in what he describes as "shared contemplation." Talking about literature is a form of shared contemplation, a way of giving form to thoughts and emotions stimulated by a text.

Learning to talk about books, to generate, articulate, negotiate, and revise meanings in a community of readers, is achieved through an apprenticeship with other, more experienced readers. Frank Smith (1988b) called this "joining the literacy club." Readers learn what to attend to and how to share ideas by watching what other readers attend to and how they share ideas. My grandmother told me, "You learn from the company you keep." In this instance, I want novice readers to keep company with more sophisticated, experienced readers.

The literate environment that I am establishing in my classroom has to allow students to offer half-baked ideas. That is, I cannot wait for students to get all their thoughts in order before they offer them in our discussions. I want to hear students say, "I was thinking that maybe this character was mean." This is what I mean by thinking-talking. This type of talk allows students to work through their ideas aloud and in the company of other readers. It is important to create a space where it is OK to share half-baked thoughts, to work through what you are thinking, and to get ideas out in the air in order to negotiate and revise meanings. All of the invested discussion strategies that I describe in this book have this sense of thinking-talking as an integral part of the experience.

Four additional strategies or components I use to develop students' abilities to generate and articulate interpretations are (1) reading aloud and discussing a poem each day, (2) reading aloud and discussing a chapter book or novel each day, (3) singing songs and discussing the lyrics each day, and (4) providing time at the end of the reading workshop to share ideas and reflect on our learning experiences.

At the beginning of the year, I introduce the *poem du jour* to my students. I select a poem each day to read aloud and discuss, and at the end of the week, I provide a copy of the five poems we read that week for students to put in their notebooks to revisit. Parents have reported that their children have come home and shared many of these poems with them, often reciting them at family get-togethers. Poems can be interpreted and discussed along with picture books and novels.

In addition to the poetry we share, I also choose a novel to read aloud that coincides with the particular unit of study we are involved with. I try to choose novels that students will enjoy and that relate to our discussion in the unit of study. Students are expected to sit back and relax on the floor and pay attention to the story as I close our day with a read-aloud of one of the chapters in the novel. We have a brief discussion before adjourning for the day.

As a singer and guitar player, and a member of many different bands performing in bars and on stage for many years, I bring some musical talent into my reading workshop. However, not being able to play an instrument does not exclude you from using the following strategy. I make copies of the lyrics for our song of the week and begin on Monday by playing and singing the song for my students. I select songs from a variety of musical genres—folk, rock, ballads, bluegrass—to share with my students. You could certainly play a song on a CD player instead. On Tuesday, I pass out the lyrics, sing the song while students follow along, and discuss what the song means for us. By Friday, students are singing along, and we talk more extensively about our developing interpretations. This is a fun way to bring the arts into the classroom, and I have had no problems getting adolescent boys and girls to sing along with carefully selected tunes.

At the end of the reading workshop, I gather the students together into a circle to share our experiences in the workshop that day. We talk about the books we found and read, their connections to the unit of study or what we discussed in the read-aloud, and the connections we made to the comprehension lessons I demonstrated. In much the same way that the author's chair closes my writing workshop, the readers' circle closes my reading workshop.

Summary of Lessons and Learning Experiences

The reading workshop is about creating space for reading and providing opportunities for children to become sophisticated and proficient readers. In order to do so, the reading workshop must provide time to read, opportunities to share ideas, opportunities to investigate texts, and opportunities to choose what one wants to read. Opportunity in the reading workshop is based on four components: (1) time, (2) access, (3) choice, and (4) response. The procedures we establish and our role as literary docent must enhance our students' opportunities to become literate, not limit them.

In the reading workshop, engagement is the key. Creating an accessible library helps students find a book to read and engage with. In order for all readers to engage in reading, each must be able to find a text she can read and make sense of, which means our collection must contain reading materials that come in a wide range of levels of complexity. Readers need to find a purpose for engaging with literature and other texts and do so in a nonthreatening environment. Brian Cambourne (1988) has suggested that these are the elements necessary for engagement to occur: exposure, demonstrations, and no negative repercussions for participating. I have to do my best to bring these elements to each and every reader in my classroom. Each child will need to be approached differently and will require different things to find his way into the world of reading and literature. This is what makes teaching such a challenge.

Featured Lesson in Comprehension for September: Approaching a Text

In each chapter I focus on one particular comprehension strategy that I weave into the unit of study that I am working on that month. For September, I focus on helping readers learn how to approach a text. In this comprehension strategy, I do a think-aloud in front of my students, explaining the things I attend to when I approach a text. I offer this strategy at the beginning of the book because thinking aloud is something that I will continue to do throughout the year. It is also one of the most effective ways to demonstrate what a proficient reader does when his is comprehending what he's reading.

I choose a picture book, poem, short story, or chapter book that will allow me to discuss the things I do when I pick up a book. I like to use a book that has an extensive peritext, that is, one that contains a lot of information in the front and back of the book. The *peritext* is all of the front matter of a book, the book-jacket blurb, the copyright page, the dedication, and other elements not part of the actual story. Some good examples of picture books that contain extensive peritextual elements are *The Stinky Cheeseman and Other Fairly Stupid Tales*, by Jon Sczieska (1992), *Black and White*, by David Macauley (1990), *Voices in the Park*, by Anthony Browne (2001), and *The Discovery of Dragons*, by Graeme Base (1996). For this lesson, I will use *Starry Messenger*, by Peter Sis (1996). This complex picture book depicts the life story of Galileo Galilei during the Italian Renaissance.

I begin by explaining to my students what I am going to do. It doesn't do much good to conduct a lesson before we are sure students know there is a lesson going on and why it is being given. A comprehension lesson should not come as a surprise to students. I think we should conduct what I have described elsewhere as full-disclosure lessons. We should explain why we are doing what we are doing and how we are going to do it. Then we are ready to begin the lesson.

I explain to my students that I am going to show them what I do when I pick up a new picture book to read. I show them how I look at the covers, front and back, and read the title and other information contained therein. I talk aloud about what I see, what it reminds me, of and how I am connecting to the text before I open the book. With *Starry Messenger*, I explain that I love to read about the Italian Renaissance and that my father's family all came to America from Italy. I tell my students that I have read a great deal about Galileo and bring extensive background knowledge of this man to the reading of this book.

As I open the book, I spend time looking at and investigating the content of the end pages and the title page. In contemporary picture books, authors and illustrators have begun to use this space to add information and provide readers with clues about the upcoming text. I want to demonstrate to my students that I do not just skip this stuff to get quickly to the first page of the story. I continue to think aloud about what I see and what interests me. I talk about the author and the illustrator; in this case, Peter Sis wrote and illustrated the book. I talk about the dedication and what I notice about the use of fonts and design elements of the text.

For this comprehension lesson, I do not read the entire text. I read about five or six pages into the story and stop. I will go back later and finish the story, because no one likes to be left hanging like that. But for now, I want my students' attention to focus on what I did as I approached the text. We discuss what I did and I provide a series of books for my students to try what I did in pairs around the room. I explain to them that I want them to take their time and approach a text in the same manner I did, thinking aloud with each other about what is on the covers of the book I gave them. I want them to make connections to the text, to anticipate what might be included in their story, and to attend to all of the peritextual matter that is included in their selection.

While students are working in pairs with the books I selected for them, I roam around the room, stopping with each group and observing what they are doing. I want them to feel comfortable trying this strategy with a partner so that they will feel comfortable using this strategy in their independent reading time. The lessons that I demonstrate and provide guided practice with focus on those strategies that I want readers to assimilate into their own reading repertoire. Before the lesson is finished, we circle back together and talk about how the strategy worked for each group. This opportunity to reflect on what we do as readers brings closure to our reading workshop and allows students to voice any concerns that may have arisen during the lesson. These comprehension lessons are based on an emerging expertise model, where students learn through demonstration, guided practice, and independent application those strategies that readers use to comprehend text.

Literacy Assessments

Classroom assessments should be used to help inform teachers about what readers in their class are capable of doing and what strategies they need more help with. The assessments that I have used and will be sharing with you are the ones that have helped me to understand whether readers are making sense of texts, in other words, assessments for comprehension. I am aware that there are other assessments available that focus on phonics skills and knowledge, but I have found that assessments that focus on comprehension are not as readily available and tend to limit the assessment of comprehension to literal recall of textual information. The assessments I describe here are those that help me understand whether readers are constructing meaning in transaction with texts. I find these to be the most valuable assessments to use in the intermediate grades and beyond.

Some of the assessments that I share in this chapter are those that I introduce early in the year and use throughout the year. I use others only in the month of September. I begin with those that I use for the entire year and continue with those that are specific to the beginning of the year.

Ongoing Literacy Assessments

Reading Response Notebooks

One of the most valuable, yet challenging assessments to use effectively is the reading response notebook, or literature response log. I required students to read each night for approximately thirty to forty minutes and write in their response notebook about what they have read and are thinking. I demonstrate how to respond in this notebook during whole-group discussions after a read-aloud early in the year. During the first two months, students are required to list the title, author, date, and genre at the top of each entry and then spend 25 percent of their time and space retelling what happened in the story and 75 percent reacting to what they read.

As the year progresses, the form we use for the reading response notebook will change to accommodate the growing sophistication of my students' responses. Students share their response notebook entry each morning with a reading response partner, and once a week they turn the notebooks in so I can read them. Providing students with response to these entries is essential for their continued success. The challenge is not to allow these response notebook entries to turn into glorified book reports. For September, my goals are to get students writing in their response notebook on a regular basis and sharing it with their reading partner each day. I also want them to spend more time reacting to what they read than retelling what happened. In order to support students' responses, I need to provide examples of quality entries and discuss what they might contain.

Daily Reading Logs

The daily reading log is a simple little form used to keep track of each student's daily reading. This form includes title, author, number of pages read, genre, and a few brief comments (see Figure 2.2). The purpose for keeping track of our daily reading is to look back and see what patterns and omissions appear in our selections. These logs help us learn about ourselves as readers.

Oral Reading Analyses

Whether you use running records or more elaborate miscue analyses of oral reading, you need to listen to readers read and attend to what readers are doing and not doing when they read. Yetta Goodman describes this as developing a "miscue ear" for reading and readers. Through our close observations of individual readers, we learn about the reading processes of individual readers and about reading processes in general.

There are numerous publications that provide more substantial accounts of oral reading analysis: *An Observation Survey of Early Literacy Achievement*, by Marie Clay (1993), *Miscue Analysis Made Easy*, by Sandra Wilde (2000), *Knowing Literacy*, by Peter Johnston (1997) and *Miscues Not Mistakes*, by Ruth Davenport (2002). I try to conduct an oral analysis on every child within the first two weeks of school, and once a month thereafter, especially for those readers that I am most concerned with. I collect the

FIG. 2.2 *Daily Reading Log*

Daily Reading Log

Title/Author	Genre	# of Pages Read	Comments

analyses in my assessment notebooks and use the information collected to select students for comprehension strategy groups and individualized instruction.

Reflection Logs

At the end of the first day of school, my students and I reflect on what we learned and experienced throughout the day. We talk about what happened, what was important for each of us, and what we might share with our parents when we get home. I then give my students a form (see Figure 2.3) to fill out and include in their reflection log, a three-ring folder that is used to keep these forms intact.

Each Friday, this reflection log will go home for parents or guardians to read, sign, respond to, and return by Monday. I provide a space for parents to write to me about specific concerns or comments. Like the response notebooks, the reflection log must be demonstrated and modeled for it to be effective. The more we talk about it, the more of a daily ritual it becomes. When I began using the reflection log, it was designed to get students to think about their day and reflect on their learning. Over the years, parents have found it valuable as a prompt for getting their child to talk about their day in school when they get home. Some parents have even requested that the reflection log go home each day for them to review. I did not foresee the value for parents when I began the reflection log, but continue using it primarily because of the positive responses I have received from parents.

September Literacy Assessments

Parent Information Request Letters

In Lucy Calkins' book *Living Between the Lines* (1991), she described the letter she wrote to parents each September requesting information about their child to help her teach more effectively. I have used a revised version of this form (see Figure 2.4) to elicit information from parents and guardians at the beginning of each year. I explain to parents how they are their child's first teacher, and the more information they are willing to share with me, the better I will get to know his or her child and be able to support their learning in my classroom.

Reading Inventories

In order to help students become better readers, I need to know more about their likes and dislikes as readers. I have adapted Carolyn Burke's reading inventory to use to interview my students as readers at the beginning of the year (see Figure 2.5). The questions are designed to help me understand how each child views reading, what she likes to read and does like to read, and how I can help her become a better reader.

I keep all of these classroom-based assessments in a series of three-ring notebooks with a section designated for each child. I begin each section with a student information sheet (see Figure 2.6). I use five separate notebooks, one for each set of students that I try to attend to each day of the week. By doing so, I am able to add information about every child once a week in my records. It's not a perfect system, but it works for me. The best assessment system is the one that helps you gather information that you will actually review and use to plan instruction.

FIG. 2.3 *Daily Reflection Log*

Daily Reflection Log
Reading:
Writing:
Math:
Sciences:
Special Areas:
Miscellaneous:
One thing I did well today:
One thing I could have done better:
May be copied for classroom use. © 2006 by Frank Serafini and Suzette Serafini-Youngs from *Around the Reading Workshop in 180 Days* (Heinemann: Portsmouth, NH).

FIG. 2.4 *Parent Information Request Letter*

Dear Parents and Guardians,

As mentioned during our open house, the more I understand the needs, interests, and abilities of your child, the better I will be able to help develop his or her academic abilities. Please take a few moments to fill out this questionnaire so that I will get to know your child as quickly as possible.

Thank you.

Child's Name: _____

1. What hobbies or special interests does your child have?

2. What does your child like to read or write at home?

3. What things has your child struggled with in the past at school?

4. What would you like to see developed more this year in your child?

5. What other things as a parent do you feel I should know about your child?

FIG. 2.5 *Reading Inventory*

Reading Inventory

1. What are the names of your favorite books? Why are these good?

2. Who are your favorite authors? What do you like about them?

3. Who is a good reader that you know? Why is (that person) a good reader?

4. What do you do when you come to something you don't know or understand in a book you are reading?

5. How would you help someone who was having trouble learning to read?

6. Do you think you are a good reader? Why or why not?

7. Why do you think people read?

8. What was reading like at school last year?

9. What did you like about reading at school?

10. What did you dislike about reading at school?

11. What can I do to make reading this year more enjoyable and successful for you?

FIG. 2.6 *Student Information Sheet*

Student Information Sheet

Student Name: _____

Birthday: _____ Age: _____

Parents' or Guardians' Names: _____

_____

Phone #: _____

Address: _____

_____

Brothers and Sisters: _____

_____

Pets: _____

_____

Favorite Things to Do: _____

_____

Connections to the Writing Workshop

Throughout the school year, I try to establish a two-and-a-half- to three-hour block of time for literacy instruction. This means that most days an hour to an hour and a half is dedicated to both reading and writing workshops. There are obvious connections between reading and writing throughout the year, and I use this section of each chapter to share a few of those connections with you.

The most important connection during the beginning of the year is to establish a community of writers in much the same way as we are establishing a community of readers. I want students to have a voice in their development as writers like they have as readers. I need to ensure that writers receive considerate responses to their writing so that they will be willing to share their pieces of writing and so the author's chair does not become a hot seat.

As we are developing an understanding of the concept of genre through the experiences I provide around analyzing and organizing the library collection, it is important to call students' attention to these insights when we are discussing the requirements and boundaries for writing in a particular genre in the writing workshop. Like the reading workshop, my writing workshop is organized around units of study that have a central focus and a series of learning experiences. Oftentimes when we are studying a genre in reading, we are working on writing the same genre in the writing workshop. I don't want to force the idea of integrating the curriculum; rather, I try to find natural connections that exist between the two workshops.

In order to teach students how to read and write, we must get them to engage in the acts of reading and writing. Once they engage, we will have a context to teach them about reading and writing. If they don't engage in these experiences, it is hard to teach them in meaningful contexts.

Things I Hope to See, Hear, and Have Established by Month's End

In order to know if we are making progress in our reading workshop, we have to know what we expect by certain dates. These dates are certainly flexible and will vary with every group every year. However, as part of establishing a preferred vision for my reading workshop, I create benchmarks—visions of what I hope will be in place by the end of each month. These benchmarks are not used to punish myself or my students if we have not attained them by a particular time, but they do serve as an evaluation point to understand how the procedures and components of the reading workshop are coming along.

By the end of September, I hope to begin to see, hear, and have established the following things:

1. Most students are choosing appropriate reading materials, based on their comprehension abilities, for independent and paired reading. I am aware that I will need to consistently monitor some readers' choices, but many of my students are choosing appropriate materials by the end of the month.

2. Students are willing to offer ideas when I am finished reading aloud a picture or chapter book without being asked. I want students to know that it is their responsibility to generate and articulate their interpretations without being asked after every reading what they think.

3. The classroom library is organized and being used regularly by all students. We spend a great deal of time on the classroom library in September and I expect students to know what is available and how to find it, check it out, and return it to its appropriate place.

4. Students are writing most every evening in their literature response log. Although the lit log will include longer and more sophisticated responses as the year progresses, it is essential that students immediately accept the responsibility for completing it every night.

5. Students know the basic procedures of the reading workshop and are in the right place, with the right materials, ready for instruction to begin.

6. Students sing along with me during our shared singing time. I begin the year playing the guitar and singing songs with my students. I try to choose songs they like, but the expectation is that everyone will participate.

7. My student assessment forms and notebooks are organized and I have begun to include various assessments in them. September is a time to get to know my students and for them to get to know me. It is important for me to set up my assessment files so I have a place to keep students' work samples and assessment forms organized.

8. Students are beginning to understand the concept of genre and to use terms like *science fiction, mystery, realistic fiction,* and *fairy tales* to describe the books they are reading.

9. Students are beginning to listen to each other in group discussions. The concept of thinking-talking is based on one's ability to articulate one's ideas *and* one's ability to listen to other students' ideas.

10. The classroom is noisy but not unruly; engaging but not intimidating; challenging but thoroughly enjoyable. Above all, the reading workshop is a place for people to read and revel in the joys and wonders of reading and literature. I need to create a space where every student, regardless of his reading experiences and abilities, can find enjoyment engaging in the act of reading.

Ideas for Further Reflection

❖ Draw yourself a classroom map and take an inventory of the physical spaces and arrangement of the classroom. Have you established defined spaces for student interaction and quiet spaces for reading and working?

❖ Spend a week watching one reader during the reading workshop and write detailed observations of what he or she does. How does this child handle the expectations and procedures that you have established? Are there any procedures that would better support the child?

- ❖ Analyze the materials included in the classroom library. Is there a wide range of reading levels available to support all students in the class?
- ❖ Keep a literature response log yourself and share your entries with your students.

Closing Thoughts

September is a busy month, full of invitations to enter into the world of reading and literature and opportunities to share ideas and interpretations. The procedures and components we set in motion in September serve as a foundation for the reading workshop throughout the school year. The time spent establishing these procedures, rituals, and expectations is vital for the life of the reading workshop and cannot be overlooked. One must be patient in September as things come together.

The reading workshop is a space for readers, a community where ideas and interpretations are generated, articulated, negotiated, and revised. The more consistent and transparent we can make the procedures in the reading workshop, the more they will fade into the background, allowing reading and discussing literature to assume its rightful position in the center of our instruction. Procedures are established to help us go about our daily work, but they should not be the focus of our attention. We don't want the procedures of the reading workshop to distract us from finding a place for reading in our lives.

When asked about my classroom management plan, I tell teachers that the first rule of classroom management is to cultivate an engaging curriculum, rather than develop a finely tuned set of rules to control their students. Children who are genuinely engaged in what they do in the reading workshop are simply better behaved. If an engaging curriculum doesn't help, I recommend a well-developed sense of humor. We cannot forget we work with children. Some days, it seems their job is to test the boundaries we set for them. Like the procedures we establish in our reading workshop, if our classroom rules and expectations for behavior are consistent, fair, and transparent—in other words, if students know what is expected of them and consequences are consistently and fairly applied—we will have a better chance at engaging more students in the lessons and activities we present and decreasing our students' desire to misbehave.

I would be lying to you if I said that every child who has ever spent a year in my classroom emerged as a lifelong reader, loved to read, and decided to engage in the act of reading for the rest of his or her life. I don't know the long-term effects of our time spent together. I have had students who began the year hating to read and left feeling much the same way. There was little I could do to change their well-established feelings and responses, although I tried each and every day to do so. On the other hand, I have had students who didn't like to read when they began the year and who by year's end had found favorite titles, authors, and illustrators and engaged in the act of reading almost every day. It is my hope that as time passes all of my students find a place for reading in their lives and discover the comfort and rewards in reading a quality piece of literature.

An Introduction to the Windows on the Workshop

Before describing September's Window on the Workshop, I (Suzette) would like to provide a context for the vignettes that you will be reading throughout this book. In these vignettes, I describe the learning environment my students and I create each year and illustrate some specific workshop components unique to my classroom. Although the essential components in my workshop align with what Frank has described, I have created my own vision of the reading workshop. Each Window on the Workshop will demonstrate how I have made Frank's ideas work for me, to give you some idea of how to make them work for you.

Each Window on the Workshop will take you through a complete unit of study that was conducted in my intermediate-grade classroom. Transactional units of study are learning experiences that focus on a particular topic, genre, theme or author and vary in length, purpose, and complexity. Some units of study were developed in conjunction with ideas from Frank's first book, *The Reading Workshop: Creating Space for Readers*, some were aligned to the state standards I was required to address, some came from common interests among my students and me, and a few emerged from interesting field trips and issues that arose in our community during the year.

Children's literature provides the foundation for each transactional unit of study. Literature is selected to meet the needs of the children in my classroom and the goals and objectives for that particular unit. When gathering resources for each unit of study, I use my knowledge of children's literature, ask for suggestions from colleagues, talk to Frank, and explore websites that offer suggestions for quality literature. Each book or resource is selected for its alignment with the focus of the unit of study and its relevance to the experiences, backgrounds, and cultures of my students.

Texts are selected for two primary purposes: to be read aloud and to be explored independently by students. Read-aloud texts are selected based on their alignment with the central theme of the unit. In particular, I choose a cornerstone text to introduce the topic and provide the foundation for the unit of study. The order in which I present the books depends on what happens during each day's discussions. I choose each subsequent text to take our discussions in different directions, adding complexity to our unit of study.

I also provide appropriate texts for students to explore independently. Students are expected to read and explore various titles in small groups as well as select titles for their independent reading. Some books are mentioned specifically in each Window on the Workshop; other titles are provided in the extensive children's literature reference list at the end of the book.

Establishing routines is an important consideration in my reading workshop. My reading workshop usually takes place for about an hour and a half. There are five essential components to my reading workshop time: (1) opening ceremonies, (2) read-alouds, (3) lessons in comprehension, (4) workshop experiences, and (5) share circle. The time devoted to each component depends on the unit of study, my students' responses, the complexity of the group discussions and learning experiences, and the featured lessons.

Opening Ceremonies (Twenty Minutes)

Each morning as students enter the classroom, they put their stuff away and gather on the carpet for our opening ceremonies. Our opening ceremonies set the stage for the entire school day. We share and listen to each other's stories. There are four components to these opening ceremonies: (1) sharing personal stories, (2) reading news articles, (3) sharing poetry, and (4) adding to the literacy expedition wall. Each of these components connects us to our particular unit of study.

Each morning, I ask students to share personal stories that add to our unit of study. These personal stories become a way for the children to connect the learning that is occurring in the classroom to their lives outside the classroom walls. In addition, I choose news articles from our local paper or national magazines that go along with our unit of study. These articles connect our unit of study to current events. As the school year progresses, students come in early to preview the newspaper and magazines and select some articles that go along with what we are studying to share with the class. There are many occasions when students and parents read the paper at home and students bring in articles to discuss. We post all relevant articles on a bulletin board in the room to refer to throughout the unit of study.

Poetry plays an important role in our opening ceremonies. I read aloud poetry in the beginning of the year and then invite students to read selections as they become more comfortable sharing and reading aloud. Students find or create poetry to fit every topic and concept we study. I require students to practice reading the poem before reading it to the whole class and to explain the connections to our unit.

Another way that we connect to our unit of study is through our literacy expedition wall. Just as Frank copies the covers of all the books he reads aloud, we copy the covers of the books we read, but we also write a two-sentence explanation about how each piece of literature connects to the unit. We add these explanations to the literacy expedition wall throughout the year. This visual representation of our connections among the units of study helps students apply them to other discussions throughout the year.

Read-Aloud and Comprehension Lesson (Twenty Minutes)

After our opening ceremonies, I read aloud a particular book selected for the unit of study. After the read-aloud, students move into a circle so they are all looking at one another to share ideas. I stand on the outside and record all of their interpretations and responses on chart paper. We record our ideas so we have a trail of our thinking and can easily refer to these ideas during subsequent discussions. After each day's read-aloud and discussion, I reflect on the content of our discussions and make a choice for the next day's read-aloud.

After the read-aloud, the students and I engage in an explicit reading comprehension lesson. Each lesson in comprehension is designed to support the unit of study and address the needs and abilities of each student in the class. I record each lesson on chart paper while students record ideas in their reader response notebooks.

Workshop Experiences (Fifty Minutes)

After the read-aloud and comprehension lesson, I invite students to transition to guided reading groups or independent practice. During this time, I conduct reading conferences, comprehension strategy groups, and literature study groups or meet with various readers to support the lesson I presented. The texts used during various small-group and individualized instruction connect directly to the focus of the unit of study. The explicit lessons I conduct address aspects of the unit of study and strategies proficient readers need to adopt.

While I meet with small groups of students, other students are provided with a selection of learning experiences to choose from during the workshop time. These learning experiences help students engage with the literature and the unit of study at their own level. Before students leave the carpeted area after the whole-group lesson, we discuss the learning experiences that are available so students can make decisions as to how they will schedule their time in the reading workshop. Learning experiences in the reading workshop can include independent reading, paired reading, the listening center, the poetry center, working in their reader response notebook, reading to support a writing project, and other experiences.

Share Circle (Ten Minutes)

At the end of every reading workshop, the students and I gather on the carpet to talk about our experiences. Some students share titles they are exploring and information they discovered that may add to the unit of study. Other students discuss their independent practice of a particular reading comprehension strategy. The sharing time gives closure to our workshop and helps us transition into the next curriculum area for the day.

I am eager to share with you these units of study from my classroom experiences in the Windows on the Workshop. My teaching experiences began in a rural town in Colorado, where I taught a multiage fourth-, fifth- and sixth-grade classroom. I spent one additional year teaching fifth grade at a charter school in northern Nevada. Both settings provided opportunities and support for a workshop approach to reading instruction. My goal for these Windows on the Workshop is to make a strong connection between theories and practices and to help you visualize what these ideas might look like in your own classroom.

Building a Community of Readers

In September, one of the most important objectives in the reading workshop is to establish a supportive and collaborative community of readers. One of the biggest challenges in beginning each school year is getting a diverse group of students to respect each other's ideas and listen to the various interpretations offered during a literature discussion.

Focus

In order to help create a supportive environment for reading and discussing literature, I begin each year with a unit of study focusing on building a community of readers in our reading workshop. I begin by reading books that address issues of community, respect for individuals, the importance of being an individual, and respecting differences and similarities among human beings.

Goals and Objectives

❖ provide opportunities to discuss who we are

❖ learn to accept differences

❖ learn to listen to each other's ideas

❖ create a space for readers to share ideas

❖ learn to "live together, differently"

Opening Ceremonies

In the beginning of the year, students shared personal stories and we used these stories to add to our discussions on building community. Asking students to connect their personal stories to the unit of study requires them to look for events in their life that relate to the unit's theme or focus and helps them understand how their own family functions like a community as well.

We began our discussions by choosing news articles from our local paper and national magazines that depicted people trying to build community in various ways or that described how some people worked against building community. The stories we shared paralleled what we were attempting to create in our own community of readers. In addition, poetry played an important role in these opening ceremonies. We began with selections from Langston Hughes, Emily Dickinson, Ralph Fletcher, and Byrd Baylor. I read poetry and invited students to read aloud selections they had chosen.

Cornerstone Texts

The cornerstone picture book I chose for this unit of study was *The Straight Line Wonder,* by Mem Fox (1997). In this book, three straight lines get upset when their friend stops being straight and begins jumping, creeping, and twisting around. The straight lines are concerned about their friend's behavior and turn their backs on him because of the choices he has made. This book has led to many interesting discussions and sets the tone for other discussions during our unit of study.

In addition, I used the novel *The View from Saturday*, by E. L. Konigsburg (1996), as a cornerstone novel for this unit of study. This complex novel, with four interdependent story lines, shares the preparation for a trivia contest through the eyes of four students that come together under the guidance of their teacher. Konigsburg uses the perspectives of four distinct students as main characters, along with their teacher, to describe the challenges they face in their lives and in school.

Launching the Unit of Study

On the first day of school, I discussed with students how we were going to begin the year year thinking about our community of readers. I began by putting the words *building* and *community* on the whiteboard and asking students to discuss what these words meant to them. We investigated the origins of these two words to create an understanding of what the two words meant individually before we defined them together. These discussions helped us create an understanding of what it means to establish a community of readers.

The discussions on building community helped us organize the classroom, establish procedures for the reading workshop, and develop our classroom rules and expectations. Since I had developed expectations for my students, they felt it would be important to develop expectations for me as well. Our discussions led to the creation of teacher expectations, which were posted on the wall next to the classroom rules.

On the first day, we discussed *The Straight Line Wonder*, focusing mainly on the differences between the characters and how the characters wouldn't stand by their friend until after he became famous. We spent a few days discussing the actions of the characters and the themes of the text before we read and discussed other picture books I selected for the unit. After discussing *The Straight Line Wonder*, I selected *Piggybook*, by Anthony Browne (1986), to build upon our discussions about being different and supporting friends.

Piggybook tells the story of a father and two sons who don't appreciate the work their mother does for them at home. I chose this book because the boys in *Piggybook* took full advantage of their mother and learned to appreciate her only after she walked out, leaving them to fend for themselves. Much of the discussion focused on how the mother fixed the car at the end of the story. Many boys in the class did not find the ending of the book feasible. This led me to read *Horace and Morris but Mostly Dolores*, by James Howe (1999). I wanted a text that challenged stereotypical portrayals of boys and girls. In this story, three best friends who have played together forever face societal pressures associated with gender expectations as Horace and Morris join a boys-only club and Dolores joins a girls-only club. The students began to think about the roles and expectations of boys and girls in our own classroom. Students shared ideas on what boys would do in a girls' club and vice versa. Students questioned the scene at the end when the characters went exploring together. The students considered the act of exploring to be a stereotypical activity for boys.

That discussion led me to choose *Tea with Milk*, by Allan Say (1999). This story addresses family and societal expectations of Japanese women in both the United States and Japan. We also read and discussed how male stereotypes were challenged in Mem Fox's picture book *Tough Boris* (1992) as well as in Charlotte Zolotow's book *William's Doll* (1972). Although I had gathered the titles prior to the beginning of the unit of study, the content of our discussions and the interests of the students determined the order in which we read and discussed them.

We documented our responses to the literature we read by creating two types of charts. The first chart was created to record ideas generated from individual book discussions. Each day I began a new chart for the read-aloud book and recorded the ideas that were specific to that text. These charts eventually included sections for impressions, connections, and wonderings. As we learned about the dynamic characters in each new book, we learned a great deal about each other and ourselves.

The second type of chart was an ongoing cumulative chart to record ideas about building a community of readers. This chart contained our thoughts on the building community theme. This cumulative chart also served as a way to compare titles and how each individual text contributed to the focus of our unit.

I organized students into small groups to investigate, for three to four days, other texts I had selected on building community. Each group decided how they wanted to read the selections and then recorded ideas about the text and building community on sticky notes. I gave each individual two to three sticky notes and asked the student to record his or her responses and any connections to our building community theme. Each student was responsible for generating his or her own ideas before meeting with the group to share ideas. I asked each group to read and discuss books for approximately twenty-five minutes. Depending on the complexity of the texts and depth of the discussion, the groups read up to three books during this time.

At the end of the investigation time, I asked students to bring their notes to the carpet so that we could share our ideas. We discussed the contents of each reader's notes and began to organize them into categories on a bulletin board. The categories we created emerged from our discussion about what individuals had written. As students shared the ideas from their notes, categories focusing on setting, plot, characters, personal connections, literary connections, and questions emerged. Throughout the next two weeks, I invited students to add to this bulletin board at any time. The use of sticky notes was very successful, so we used a bulletin board like this as a way to organize our ideas in future focus units.

| **Explicit Instruction** | Through a series of reading comprehension lessons, students were able to come to their own understanding of community and negotiate ideas about community with their classmates. The following is a description of various lessons that I used to support our investigations in this unit of study. |

Elements of Literature   We discussed the elements of character and theme throughout this unit. The books in this unit were selected for their strong and unique characters. Children began to attend to character traits and the themes that were intricately woven into the story lines. This led to a series of lessons on character and theme. For many students this was their first exposure to the term *literary elements*, so I demonstrated what these various elements were, how to identify elements in a work of literature, and how to use these elements as tools for analyzing what they read.

For *Tea with Milk, Tacky the Penguin* (Lester 1988), *The Straight Line Wonder*, and *Chrysanthemum* (Henkes 1991), we discussed the strength of the main characters, how each character dealt with diversity, and how the characters overcame the challenges they faced. Students began to understand the role the main character played in a story and the importance of the minor characters in the text. They asserted that the minor characters gave depth to the main characters in the stories we read. We recorded all these ideas on chart paper and created a character section on the wall devoted to literary elements for students to refer to at any time. Each student also received a personal copy of these charts to glue into his or her reader response notebook for future reference.

Think-Alouds   I conducted a series of think-alouds with our chapter book *The View from Saturday*, which I read after lunch each day. I demonstrated how to attend to changes in characters' perspectives, follow changes across settings and time, follow flashbacks, identify and analyze foreshadowing and symbolism, make connections between characters, use a graphic organizer to understand relationships among characters, and connect this chapter book to our theme of building community. Through these demonstrations, students were able to see and hear how a proficient reader attended to a complex, nonlinear text in service of meaning.

Teacher Conference Groups   During the first weeks of school, I asked small groups of children to meet with me with a book they were reading for independent reading. I gathered them together in alphabetical order. Students shared interesting titles they had read about community, discussed the ideas that were emerging in their reader response notebooks, and helped each other with difficult or confusing parts in their texts. We discussed, in a more intimate setting, new ideas on building a community of readers.

Workshop Experiences

In the beginning of the year, I introduced students to a variety of response strategies. I asked students to respond to the books they were reading independently and in pairs and to the books I read aloud. It was important for these response strategies to be an avenue for constructing deeper understandings of individual texts and the unit of study. For this unit, I used two response strategies: (1) a "Building Community" graffiti wall and (2) paired reading with an art extension.

"Building Community" Graffiti Wall   A graffiti wall is a space on our classroom wall covered with butcher paper where students can write "graffiti" that corresponds to our discussions and readings during the unit of study. Students loved using the graffiti wall. They

got to write all over the wall and share their own ideas about building community. The conversations that took place at the wall were as compelling as what the children wrote on it. Many students drew pictures of characters or wrote quotes from the books we were reading. Personal stories were also included as students shared what community meant to them and drew symbolic representations of building community in their world. At the end of the unit we took the paper down and analyzed the changes that occurred in students' understanding during the unit.

Paired Investigations   I asked students to work with a friend and draw or paint pictures to extend their interpretations of the texts to show their understandings of the building community theme. Students shared their drawings during the workshop sharing time. The discussions of the pictures helped us understand our collaborative interpretations of community as well as individuals' ideas of community. This investigation lasted two days, and I hung their pictures from the ceiling in our room.

Culminating Experience

To bring the unit to a close, we conducted an in-depth study of all the books we had used and created a comparison chart to represent our connections. The chart included six books for each small group, and the categories used for comparison included plot, setting, character, theme, and personal, literary, and worldly connections. We also included how the books helped students consider differences, the challenges characters faced, how characters dealt with their challenges, and our own differences and uniqueness. We spent three days completing these charts in small groups. Each group presented their ideas and we discussed what these meant for our theme of building community.

To close the unit, each group chose one book and created a presentation for the class. The purpose of the presentation was to use the dramatic arts to respond to one of the texts they had read. Students performed readers' theatre for *Tacky the Penguin*, made interpretive collages for *The Table Where Rich People Sit* (Baylor 1994), created murals depicting characters from many of the books we read, wrote a play based on *The Straight Line Wonder* (Fox 1997), and made a soundtrack to go along with *Smoky Night* (Bunting 1994b) as it was read aloud. We invited parents to attend the presentations, and students shared the class' interpretation of a community of readers and their plans for maintaining this community throughout the year.

Closing the Window

The Building Community unit became a vehicle for us to discuss what we wanted our classroom to look like and how we wanted to be treated by each other. Students began to realize their voices were heard, valued, and respected in our community. The biggest challenge for me was to help those students who were quiet and reserved find an avenue for sharing their ideas with the whole class. Each year, I added new titles to this unit, the order of the read-alouds changed, and the discussions were different based on the visions students had for our community of readers.

CHAPTER 3

October—Coming to Know Ourselves as Readers

All readers bring to their experience of reading a complex set of expectations, desires, prejudices, and prior experiences, or what I call their reading repertoire.
—KATHLEEN MCCORMICK, *THE CULTURE OF READING AND THE TEACHING OF ENGLISH*

OCTOBER CHAPTER OUTLINE

October Lessons and Learning Experiences
❖ Investigating What Successful Readers Do
❖ Reading Strategies Bookmarks
❖ The Walking Journal
❖ Selecting Quality Literature
❖ Establishing Book Clubs
❖ Reading Buddies
❖ Author/Illustrator Studies—Chris Van Allsburg
❖ Exploring Design Elements of Literature
❖ Introducing Primary Elements of Literature—Character, Setting, and Plot
Featured Lesson in Comprehension for October:
Visualizing Literacy Assessments
❖ Treasuries
❖ Weekly Reading Conferences
Connections to the Writing Workshop
❖ What Writers Do

Introduction

The desert Southwest relinquishes its summer much more slowly than other areas of the United States. Nonetheless, come October, cooler evenings provide opportunities for eating dinner on the patio and reading outside in a comfortable chair. I have lived and taught elementary school and university classes in the Southwest deserts of Arizona and Nevada for the past twenty years. In this part of the country, October is one of my favorite months because it is the month farthest away from the stilting heat of the next summer.

Unlike the reading workshop in September, October's workshop has one full month of shared experiences to draw upon—one month of reading aloud and sharing ideas, one month of getting to know each other as readers. By October, the components and procedures introduced in September are beginning to take hold. The changes made to the weekly schedule and routines subside; in fact, the schedule has become quite stable, and many children understand how to operate within our structures and procedures.

Plato wrote that literature is a force exerted upon the world and that experiencing this force motivates our desire to read. October is a time to come to know ourselves as readers, to understand the force literature has upon us, and to investigate what motivates us to read. In other words, we begin to interrogate what Kathleen McCormick referred to in the epigraph as our "reading repertoire." In October, we talk openly about what types of books we like and don't like, what kinds of texts we choose to read and not read, and how we respond to the texts we have read. The instructional experiences in September focused on getting students to read, generate

RECOMMENDED COMPREHENSION STRATEGIES FROM *LESSONS IN COMPREHENSION*

- ❖ 1.1 Setting Expectations for Readers
- ❖ 1.3 Understanding Purposes for Reading
- ❖ 3.1 Reading Strategies Bookmarks
- ❖ 4.1 Think, Pair, and Share
- ❖ 4.3 Illustrated Quotes
- ❖ 4.6 Walking Journals
- ❖ 5.1 Visualizing What We Read
- ❖ 7.1 Literature Response Logs
- ❖ 7.5 Responding to Our Responses
- ❖ 7.7 Reader's Chair

interpretations, and share ideas with other members of our community of readers. September was about inviting students into the world of reading and literature and getting students to engage in the act of reading. In October, we begin to investigate the types of responses and interpretations we have generated. In September, we wanted to *get* readers to engage with, and respond to, texts. In October, we want to understand *why* readers respond the way they do.

In addition to the learning experiences that focus on understanding ourselves as readers, we will investigate the processes we use to construct meaning with texts. One of the most important series of lessons, one that is featured in Suzette's Window on the Workshop this month, focuses on helping students understand what proficient and sophisticated readers do. During this series of lessons, we collaboratively construct a set of characteristics or criteria for the types of readers we want to become. We do this by reading and discussing a series of picture books and a novel that contain images of readers and reading and by investigating the types of readers that are traditionally created and supported in school settings. We look at the curriculum documents and reading guides found in our school's instructional resources and standards documents and discuss whether they portray the type of reader we want to emulate. In other words, through a series of readings, investigations, and discussions, we will construct a preferred vision for our future selves as readers.

In Chapter 1, I explained how I wanted teachers to develop a preferred vision for their teaching and the literate environment they would create and support through the reading workshop. In this chapter, I am suggesting we help our students develop a preferred vision for the kind of reader they want to be. Through a series of learning experiences, we generate a list of characteristics, a negotiated criteria, for what a proficient, sophisticated reader might look, act, and think like. It is important that these criteria remain open to revision so that they do not exclude particular children and favor mainstream reading identities. However, we are trying to make a platform statement about the expectations we hold for sophisticated and proficient readers.

The process of generating this list is far more important than the actual list that is produced. The learning takes place in the discussion about what successful readers do, not in the presentation of our list to other classes or other teachers. In Chapter 1 I listed some of the characteristics of readers I hoped to develop through time spent in our reading workshop. In this chapter, I describe how this list of characteristics is generated in the reading workshop and how expectations are constructed.

Paralleling this investigation into ourselves as readers, and the processes we use when we read, is an investigation of the structures and elements of literature and other texts. We begin with three primary elements of literature, character, setting and sequence of events (plot), before I introduce more complex elements, for example, point of view, theme, and symbolism.

In this chapter, our investigations of ourselves as readers and the elements and structures of literature are grounded in two units of study: (1) images of readers and reading and (2) the work of a particular author or illustrator, in this case, Chris Van Allsburg. What is important to understand is that our focus on readers and their reading processes, like the comprehension strategies we introduce and demonstrate, will always be contextualized within a transactional unit of study. The focus of the unit of study will *not* be the comprehension strategy itself, but an author, genre, central theme, or content area topic. If anyone asks one of my students what we are reading and discussing in the reading workshop, I want them to talk about the literature they are reading and discussing *first* and the comprehension strategies we are learning and assimilating *second*. The unit provides a context for the demonstration and instruction of particular comprehension strategies.

In addition, during the month of October we begin collecting evidence of our literate behaviors in our *treasuries*, more commonly referred to as portfolios, and continue adding to these treasuries throughout the year. I call them treasuries because they are places where things of great value are stored and preserved. Treasuries are composed of learning artifacts that matter to us as readers and writers, mathematicians and scientists. They are places to collect and represent our understandings and development as learners. Our treasuries will be shared with parents during our student-led conferences in the spring and will serve as the basis for student self-evaluations and negotiated reporting procedures. These assessments and reporting procedures are discussed in greater detail in Chapter 8 (March).

One of the challenges of a workshop approach to reading instruction is helping children make their literate abilities visible so other concerned stakeholders, primarily parents and administrators, can see growth in their development as literate human beings. In the reading workshop, there are no worksheets to collect at the end of the unit of study, no chapter quizzes to grade as we progress through a book. Worksheets and black-line masters that focus on one's ability to recall factoids from a single page of a particular text do not make children's literate abilities visible. They focus on memory, not thinking and comprehension, and provide teachers with a false sense of accountability about children's development. These inauthentic learning experiences do not provide quality information about a reader's ability to generate, articulate, negotiate, and revise meanings in transactions with a work of literature.

October is a transitional month. We rearrange and reorganize our workshop time to accommodate new components and procedures. We spend time getting to know each other as readers and human beings and continue to experience the wonders of reading and children's literature. During this month, my expectations are expanding, but not so quickly that I make students feel inadequate or uncomfortable. I want to slowly raise the ante so my students don't throw in their cards too early in the game. In the continuing balance between support and challenge, there is more support than challenge during the month of October. I am just getting my students to trust me. There will be plenty of time for challenging them as the year progresses.

October Lessons and Learning Experiences

Investigating What Successful Readers Do

Throughout the first two weeks of October, we conduct an investigation into what sophisticated and proficient readers do. During this investigation, we discuss what we ourselves do as readers, conduct interviews with more capable readers, often parents and siblings, read picture and chapter books about what readers do, and look at official statements about what readers are expected to do in our school district. We create a classroom wall chart listing what we consider to be characteristics of successful readers, which we will add to and revise throughout the year. I have provided an example of what this list has initially contained in past years (see Figure 3.1).

This chart represents our initial discussions about how successful readers think and act. We added things to the list that were included in our reading curriculum guides, from the discussions we had about the books about readers and reading, and from the interviews we conducted with other readers. As time went on, we added various items to the class chart: read a wide variety of genres, use comprehension strategies to make

Successful readers:

- ❖ *understand* what they read
- ❖ buy books of their own
- ❖ don't like to stop reading
- ❖ don't like to be disturbed when reading
- ❖ find a place where they can read
- ❖ read a lot in their spare time, at home and at school
- ❖ take care of books
- ❖ practice, practice, practice
- ❖ imagine they are *in* the book
- ❖ get a movie or images in their head when they read
- ❖ finish what they start reading most of the time
- ❖ write about what they read
- ❖ take their time
- ❖ read to others
- ❖ use the library
- ❖ share ideas about what they read
- ❖ recommend books to other readers
- ❖ use books to find information

FIG. 3.1
Becoming a Successful Reader

sense of texts, understand elements of literature, interrogate books from multiple perspectives, and understand that books are written by particular people, in particular times and places. Our goal was to create a shared vision of the kinds of readers we wanted to become.

During our reading and discussions of books containing images of readers and reading, language arts curriculum guides, and interviews with proficient readers, I wanted students to know exactly what would be expected of them as readers in our reading workshop. We needed to make our expectations clear and explicit so students would understand the types of readers we were trying to become.

Though not directly apparent in the discussion so far, the type of reader I am hoping to create and support is the type of reader necessary for a successful democratic society. I want to create readers who question what they read, become involved in civic matters, find a voice for the issues and causes they feel are important, and become members of what Thomas Jefferson called an "informed citizenry." No little task to be sure; however, I never said that teaching reading was easy or didn't aspire to lofty goals.

Reading Strategies Bookmarks

One important comprehension lesson that I use early in the school year is called a collaborative cloze procedure. In this lesson, I take a big book or oversized version of a picture book and carefully select words to conceal with sticky notes. I cover particular words to force readers to use other cues to predict what the word might be and to call attention to what readers do when they are reading. The collaborative cloze procedure forces readers to attend to cueing systems other than sound-symbol relationships, or the graphophonic cueing system, by not allowing them to see the word. If you can't see the word, you can't sound it out and are forced to use other strategies.

I initially cover up words that are relatively easy to predict and have few alternatives. As the lesson continues, I cover up words that are more ambiguous, usually adjectives or adverbs, that allow for multiple possibilities. The goal of this learning experience is not to predict each word verbatim, but to predict words that make sense and could have been written by the author. This lesson is about making sense, not guessing words correctly. I don't want this lesson to turn into an "I got it right and you got it wrong" competition. It is more important to be able to predict words that are possible and make sense than to guess the exact words the author chose to use in the text at that particular moment.

As students predict what the covered words might be, I also ask them to explain what cues or strategies they used to construct their predictions. We list these strategies on a class chart and add to the chart as the lesson continues. By the time we finish reading the big book, we have a substantial list of reading strategies. These are not strategies that were listed in a reading methods textbook somewhere or provided on a wall chart for students to simply memorize. This class chart represents the strategies we actually used to make sense of the text we read collaboratively.

Our list of strategies evolves over the course of the year as we discuss additional strategies that readers use to make sense of different types of texts. Later in the year, I repeat the collaborative cloze procedure using an expository text or other type of reading material to see what different strategies we draw upon when reading different texts. This class list of strategies is eventually made into a reading strategies bookmark that students keep in their selections for independent reading (see Figure 3.2).

Ask yourself three questions:

Does it make sense?

Does it sound right?

Does it look right?

Reread parts that are confusing.

Think about what you know.

Read ahead and go back.

Look at the punctuation.

Think.

Sound it out.

Look at the pictures.

Look for words in words.

Stop and tell yourself what the story is about.

Make connections.

Pay attention to unknown words.

Ask questions.

Listen to yourself reading.

FIG. 3.2
Reading Strategies Bookmark

Students use these reading strategies bookmarks to remind themselves of the reading strategies we have discussed and new ones I have introduced. The goal is for these strategies to become automatic in students' reading processes. Proficient readers flexibly orchestrate a variety of reading and comprehension strategies when they read. Our instructional practices should make these strategies visible so that readers can begin to assimilate them into their own repertoires.

The Walking Journal

In September, I spend a great deal of time introducing and demonstrating individual reading response notebooks. We use these reading response notebooks at school to hold our ideas and interpretations about books we read during the reading workshop and at home for the reading students do for homework. These notebooks also provide evidence of students' reading and individual development. However, they are used primarily as a way to generate interpretations for ourselves and share ideas with other readers. I keep my own reading response notebook and share my entries with students on a regular basis. As I mentioned previously, we cannot allow these response notebooks to become glorified book reports.

In October, I extend our response strategies by introducing the walking journal. In essence, the walking journal is a shared reading response notebook. I select a special notebook to use as our walking journal and write an entry about one of the books we read aloud and discussed. I begin by writing, "Dear Journal," and then I share my reactions and thoughts about a particular book. I write about things that matter to me and my impressions, connections, and wonderings about a particular text. When I finish, I *walk* the journal over to one of my students and ask him or her to read what I wrote and respond to my entry.

As the journal makes its way around our classroom, I explain that students have the option of responding to previous entries or starting a new discussion by posing a question or reacting to a different book. It is important for me to remind students to write in the journal each day and then pass it along to someone else. I collect the walking journal every few weeks, read through it, and make an additional entry of my own. I also use the walking journal to initiate discussions by sharing some of the entries written by students during our reading lessons. If I don't call students' attention to the walking journal, and show how it can be used to respond to what we have read, it will quickly fade away.

Selecting Quality Literature

My basic motto for literature discussions is "If you want to have a quality discussion, read quality literature!" However, this begs the question "What constitutes quality literature?" Do we consider only books that have garnered prestigious children's literature awards, like the Newbery or Caldecott Medals, to be of literary quality? What about the books that have been selected by children for the Children's Choices published in *The Reading Teacher*? Are the classics of children's literature, those that have stood the test of time, the best examples of quality literature?

I have been investigating whether there are, in fact, objective criteria that can be used for selecting literature that *all* children should read. Unfortunately, I have not found a definitive answer. Probably never will. Everyone has different favorites and different criteria for selecting what children should read. Some espouse a particular canon of texts to be read by all students; others try to include a wider range of literature to be experienced. Each literary critic brings his or her own values to bear on the selection process.

I have found that the selection of children's literature for the reading workshop depends on the children in the classroom, the role literature will play in the reading curriculum or particular lesson, the attributes and elements of the actual piece of literature itself, and the knowledge base of the teacher doing the selecting. When selecting literature for my read-alouds and classroom library, I try not to limit myself to particular award-winning books. I see many texts serving many purposes in the reading workshop. I may begin with award winners, but I'll include a wide variety of texts for my students to explore and consider.

Now, don't misconstrue my comments here. There are books that are so poorly written and illustrated that I would never include them in my classroom library. I can be a literary snob on occasion if I have to! However, I don't want my personal tastes and sensibilities to dictate to my readers their complete diet of literature. Too often, those books that I love are not those that inspire my students to read. I cannot allow my selection criteria to limit access to books that my students might enjoy or learn from. However, I cannot allow my students to pass through our time together without being exposed to certain classic texts and considering various criteria used to designate quality literature.

Selecting books that have won the Newbery, Caldecott, Coretta Scott King, or Orbis Pictus award is a good place to start. However, the literature we select for use in the reading workshop has to address a variety of purposes: reading for enjoyment, discussing social issues, motivating students to read, finding information, conducting research projects, and reading with our reading buddies. The books I select for literature study groups must have certain qualities, while books that are selected for my classroom library may have different characteristics. I want my students to recognize a quality story when they see one; however, the world isn't just *Wuthering Heights*. Students need a large selection to choose from to satisfy their many needs as readers.

After reviewing literature selection criteria and considering the books I include in my collection, I constructed the following criteria to guide your selection of books for your classroom. In general, books that I choose to read aloud and discuss with my students and use in literature study groups exhibit the following characteristics:

❖ *Attractive and appealing.* Books need to have visual appeal, especially picture books. I like books that are well illustrated and designed. With the expanded use of the computer in the publishing industry during the past thirty years, the reproduction and representation of visual images has dramatically enhanced the quality of children's literature. Books that have visual appeal are more frequently chosen by students to read. I know that you can't judge a book by its cover, but readers pick up and read more books that have immediate visual appeal than old books hiding few illustrations or visual components.

❖ *Tell a great story.* One primary reason we enjoy the books we read is the quality of the story being told. The first thing I look for in a book to read aloud or for a literature study group is the quality of the story. Stories that move us emotionally, surprise us, help us relate to our own experiences, and help us better understand the world are usually those that contain quality stories. If the story doesn't compel us to continue reading, we often give up on the book and look for a new one.

❖ *Provide opportunities for teaching and discussion.* I have adopted two roles as a literacy educator: one as an advocate for the inclusion of children's literature in the reading curriculum and one as an advocate for children's literature as an art form in and of itself. On one hand, I believe that a piece of children's literature should be enjoyed for the qualities it brings to the reader. It is a piece of art to be enjoyed and worthy of consideration in and of itself. On the other hand, children's literature can be used as a instructional device that creates space for discussions of significant topics, engages the reader's mind, and provides opportunities for readers to investigate topics and events in ways that textbooks and other resources do not. I choose books to read that connect to our topics in math and science. I draw upon the techniques writers use to create literature for lessons in the writing workshop. I try to maintain the integrity of a work of literature by reading and discussing it in its entirety before analyzing it or using it to demonstrate a particular comprehension strategy. There is a fine line between these two roles, and I walk it every day as I write about the reading workshop and make selections for the classes I teach at the university.

❖ *Conceptually appropriate.* I once had a teacher tell me that her third graders were having a difficult time understanding *The Giver*, by Lois Lowry (1993). I couldn't believe what she was saying. Of course they were having trouble making sense of that book—it isn't appropriate conceptually for the experiences and understandings those children in her class were bringing to the story. I am not an advocate of censoring books, but choosing books my students can connect to and understand has to play a major role in my selection process. Although I would include *The Giver* in my third-grade classroom library, I would not expect many, if any, of my students to be able to handle the challenges of this complex piece of literature at that age. There are so many wonderful books available to students; why force them prematurely into books beyond their experiences? Just because a student *can* read a book doesn't mean that she *should*. Reading is about understanding and enjoyment, not about collecting literary trophies. Books will sit patiently on the shelves in our libraries until readers mature and grow into them. We must guard against rushing readers into books that are too difficult for them. This can lead only to frustration and disengagement.

❖ *Relate to the lives of my students.* Not only do books have to be conceptually appropriate, but they need to be experientially appropriate. The literature that I provide for my students needs to connect to their experiences, background, race, ethnicity, gender, and social class. Too often, classroom libraries are full of books about middle-class white boys and girls while the classroom contains a diverse group of students from different socioeconomic, racial, and experiential backgrounds. I believe that readers should experience literature about people and places unlike their own community; however, they should also see themselves in some of the books they read. Our libraries should provide a mirror into ourselves as well as a window onto the world.

❖ *Memorable characters.* Most readers whom I talk to tell me that they like a book because they can relate to the experiences of the characters in the story. It is difficult to enjoy a book if we can't empathize with the characters and the challenges they face. Many young readers choose books that contain characters that appear across a series of texts—the Boxcar Children, Harry Potter, Junie B. Jones, Amber Brown, Arthur, Captain Underpants, and others. As an adult, I have found particular characters that have made an everlasting impact on me as a reader. From Odysseus to Travis McGee, from the Lorax to Robert Langsford, the heroes of literature that I have connected with may have changed, but they still remain in my memory. When selecting books for our classroom library, I am careful to choose books that contain a balance of male and female protagonists, have memorable characters, and have characters who are worth spending time with in another story.

❖ *Worth rereading.* One way to tell how well a book is accepted in my classroom is to watch how quickly students run to the display shelf to pick it up and read it themselves after I have read it aloud. Unlike many adults, children can listen to the same story again and again, especially young children. If I read a book aloud and no one goes over to pick it up after I am finished, I reconsider my selection. Experiencing books more than once is an important component of the reading workshop. There are significant, qualitative differences between the first and second readings of a book. The second time around we already know what happens and can spend more time studying the language and literary devices used by the author. We can dwell in the details of the illustrations, looking for things we missed the first time around. In our fervor to expose students to new authors, titles, and genres, we unintentionally demonstrate a read-it-once-and-move-on mentality. Stories that are worth sharing are worth sharing over and over. This leads us to one of my most important criteria for selecting literature.

❖ *Doesn't reveal itself immediately*. Literature that contains multiple layers of meaning and complex illustrations does not give up all of its meanings and possibilities during a first read-through. The novels that I choose for literature study groups *must* have this characteristic or I won't use them for intense literature study. There are times when I purposefully read a book two or three times in a row to demonstrate how we can build understandings from successive readings that we may have not grasped during an initial reading. The best novels for literature study are those that are complex enough to sustain intense investigation over repeated readings.

❖ *Quality writing*. The last criterion I will discuss, and one that has begun to influence my selections a great deal as I have matured as a reader, is the quality of the writing in a particular piece of children's literature. There is a quality to the writing in a story crafted by Cynthia Rylant, Jane Yolen, Laurie Halse Anderson, Natalie Babbitt, and Jerry Spinelli that does not exist in books written by less talented writers. I know that the qualities of writing I am referring to here are quite subjective, but I enjoy reading books by authors who can turn a phrase, can craft a literary passage in unique ways, more than books by those who cannot. The language of a story should not only tell the story but have an emotional impact on one's reading. It is not just the story but the way that it is told that makes for a high-quality piece of literature.

I have very specific reasons for every text I select to read aloud, discuss in a literature study group, or include in our classroom library. The reasons I select specific texts range from inducing enjoyment to providing opportunities to discuss a specific historical event or science topic. The important thing is that we don't just pick up any book to read and share with students for no reason whatsoever. I plan ahead for every read-aloud and literature study group I conduct. I carefully consider the characteristics I have just described as I make my selections for read-alouds or the classroom library. I carefully plan these literary exposures and experiences to ensure that students can connect to the books we read.

Most readers are what I consider simultaneous readers, meaning they are in the process of reading more than one book at any given time. Simultaneous readers have more than one purpose for reading; therefore, they require more than one text to fulfill their reading purposes. I read certain books, usually young adult novels, when I work out at my local fitness center in the morning. I take travel books about a particular location when I go on vacation. I read philosophy and literary theory when I am wide awake and have time to devote the level of attention needed for these texts. I read magazines when I have short airplane flights and novels when I have longer ones. As a simultaneous reader, I have different moods and interests; therefore, I require different books throughout my reading life. It is important that we explain the concept of simultaneous reading to our students so that they don't feel they must have only one book in process at a time. The types of readers that exist in the real world need to be able to exist and sustain their reading lives in our reading workshops as well.

Selecting books for use throughout the reading workshop is not a disinterested, haphazard process. Whether a book fits with a particular unit of study or is simply a new title that I feel my students would enjoy sharing, I have reasons for every selection I make. If I want to help students make connections to literature and across texts, also known as intertextual connections, I need to ensure that the books I share are connected. This takes foresight, an extensive knowledge of children's literature, and planning.

Establishing Book Clubs

Book clubs are different from literature study groups. However, they can serve as a bridge into intensive studies of particular texts. Book clubs are established by students when they want to read and discuss particular books with other students and do not want to include the teacher in their discussions. They are informal literary discussion groups that provide an opportunity for students to share common reading interests and ideas across the reading of a single text.

If my students haven't noticed already, I point out to them that there are numerous novel sets, usually containing four to six copies of a particular title, provided in our classroom library. These literature sets provide opportunities for small groups of students to share the experiences of reading a novel together. Basic rules for book clubs include the following: the book must be appropriate for all readers who join the group to ensure that they can make sense of it given the limited teacher support these clubs involve, the club must remain open to any interested student, the club must submit a request in writing before beginning their readings and discussions, and a sign-up sheet has to be posted in the class for a few days so everyone will know what book clubs are available.

Students choose books for book clubs that I would not necessarily choose for literature study groups later in the year. Throughout my years of teaching, series books have been very popular in book clubs. Series like the Baby-Sitters Club, Goosebumps, Animorphs, and Junie B. Jones are well liked. I am not overly concerned about what books kids choose for book clubs as long as students want to read them, enjoy their time with the story, and can make sense of what they are reading. I monitor the membership of these groups and check up on them from time to time to ensure engagement and productivity. Book clubs, in general, do not play a prominent role in the reading workshop, but I want students to know that this opportunity is available if they choose to take advantage of it.

When a book club is completed, I require students to make a brief presentation to the class about their experience. They are required to do a book talk about the book, without giving away the ending, and share some of the important issues that arose throughout their discussions. These are three- to five-minute presentations designed to get students used to talking in front of their classmates and to entice other readers into reading books selected for book clubs. Most students take recommendations from their classmates seriously, and many new favorites have been discovered by my students during these presentations.

Reading Buddies

Every year that I have been an intermediate-grade teacher, I have paired up with a primary-grade teacher to conduct reading buddies. Once a week, my students select books to share with their assigned reading buddies, and we either go to their classroom, sit outside, or host them in our room for about half an hour. For many students, this is a special opportunity, a time when they are seen as an accomplished reader sharing their ideas with a younger, novice reader. Our younger reading buddies eagerly await the selections their older partners bring to share with them. Often the books I have read aloud to my students are those selected by my students to share with their reading buddies. Other times, my students choose books based on the interests of their reading buddies.

The first time we meet together, I have my students interview their assigned reading buddies to find out what kinds of books they like. Before that initial meeting, we brainstorm questions to ask and make a list of possibilities. My students select from this list some questions to pose to their reading buddies in order to get to know them as readers. In addition to conducting this reading interview, my students bring one of their favorite books to read aloud and use this selection to introduce themselves as readers to their reading buddies. Every year, my students love to read with their reading buddies. It is an event at which all of my students can be successful, and many of them list it as one of their favorite experiences of the entire school year.

Author/Illustrator Studies—Chris Van Allsburg

One of the easiest ways to organize a unit of study is to create an author or illustrator study. Obviously, the common thread in these units of study is the work of a particular author or illustrator. Text sets are easily created because many libraries organize their collections by author or illustrator. I like to choose authors who have a large body of work in order to sustain the unit of study across a couple of weeks and to ensure that there will be more books available than I can read aloud and share. I want students to do some exploring of an author's work on their own. There are numerous authors and illustrators who have large bodies of work, including both chapter and picture books, who make excellent choices for an author or illustrator study. You can refer to the booklists on my website for some of my favorite authors and illustrators.

Throughout the school year, I feature the work of numerous children's authors and illustrators on display in our classroom library. I want to draw my readers' attention to the writing styles and illustration techniques of these famous and talented artists. I also want my students to discover favorite authors and illustrators for themselves. During our author studies, we explore the types of writing these authors do, the genres they work within, the illustration techniques the artists use, and the ways their publications have evolved over the course of their careers. I also use particular authors and illustrators to focus on design elements and elements of literature that I want to introduce to my students.

I use a type of chart for supporting our discussions that I have called an Impressions-Connections-Wonderings (ICW) chart. This type of chart helps us keep track of our ideas across the various texts we read and discuss throughout a unit of study. ICW charts have three columns to display students' impressions, connections, and wonderings, respectively. Impressions are things that we notice in a text. They focus on the text more than an individual reader's responses. Connections can be either literary, connecting to another book, movie, play, poem, or image, or personal, connecting to one's life and experiences. Wonderings are questions that we are left with during or after our readings. Throughout a particular unit of study, I sometimes use different-color markers on the ICW chart to indicate the different books we have read by the featured author or illustrator. The ICW chart is the most frequently used chart format in my reading workshop. It supports our interpretations and discussions across texts and allows us to revisit what we have been thinking and talking about throughout the unit.

In an author/illustrator study focusing on the works of Chris Van Allsburg, I begin by collecting every one of his titles in my collection and the school or public library. I gather together any interviews, publishers' promotional materials, newspaper clippings, and articles available about Van Allsburg. Over the years, I have created notebooks full of any author and illustrator information I find in journals, books, newspapers, and at reading conferences. This information helps bring the authors and illustrators to life and gives us some insight into their personal life and artistic preferences.

Before I begin, I decide which books I will read aloud and which ones I will invite students to explore on their own. I select one particular title, possibly *Jumanji* (1981) or *The Polar Express* (1985), as our cornerstone text for this unit of study. We spend time intensively studying this one example of the author-illustrator's work before moving on to other titles. The time we spend with our cornerstone text will provide the foundation for the exploration of subsequent texts. I am unable to spend three or four days investigating every text in the unit, so I provide an example of how I explore the cornerstone text and invite students to go into depth with other texts on their own.

As a culminating experience for this particular unit of study, I have had students explore the illustration techniques that Van Allsburg uses in his various books. We try using pastels, charcoal, ink, and crayon drawings and develop a greater appreciation of his work by trying to work in the same media he chooses to work in. And then we move on. No quizzes, no exams. We have explored an author-illustrator's work, enjoyed reading and exploring his texts, and made his books available for further exploration. For me, that is a successful unit of study.

Exploring Design Elements of Literature

It is important for readers to learn various ways to approach a text. I discussed how the comprehension lesson on approaching a text might proceed in the September chapter. In October, I extend this lesson by introducing more elements and structures to my students through think-alouds. I use a think-aloud, a process where I think aloud while reading a text in front of my students, to call their attention to the specialized vocabulary used by publishers and literary critics to analyze and describe the elements, structures, and features of literature. This literary vocabulary is an important component of the reading workshop and is learned through participating in discussions where this vocabulary is introduced and used consistently. In addition, when I read aloud picture and chapter books with my students, I call their attention to particular design elements, for example, end pages, title pages, dedications, Library of Congress information, award stickers, book spines and gutters, book jackets, author blurbs, and so on, on a regular basis. By constantly using these terms in our book discussions, students begin to appropriate these literary vocabularies for themselves.

Mingshui Cai and Rick Traw (1997) have discussed the importance of developing students' "literary literacy." They suggest that literature is a discipline in and of itself, requiring a particular way of talking and thinking that students need to develop in order to understand literature in greater depth. This literary literacy is the focus of many comprehension lessons and learning experiences throughout the year in the reading workshop.

Introducing Primary Elements of Literature—Character, Setting, and Plot

While establishing reading aloud and discussion as a daily ritual in the reading workshop, developing students' vocabulary focusing on the design, elements, and structures of literature, and providing time for extensive and intensive reading and exploration of texts, I use our discussions to introduce three primary elements of story; character, plot, and setting. In general, most students are already familiar with these three elements; however, I want to get them used to using these terms during our literature discussions. As students appropriate this literary vocabulary through participation in our discussions, they begin to pay closer attention to the structures and elements of literature. This focused attention on the elements and structures of literature fosters reading comprehension and one's ability to discuss literature.

In order to keep these elements of literature visible during our classroom discussions, I create a series of wall charts to display the definitions that we have constructed for each of the elements. I don't hand out lists of definitions for students to memorize, nor do I require them to look up these terms in the dictionary. But I do consistently use these terms during our literature discussions and expect students to use these terms when they speak about texts. The charts are posted so students can see them from where they sit during our literature discussions, and they serve as mnemonic devices to help students remember what we decided each of these elements means.

When I introduce the elements of character and setting, I choose particular titles that feature interesting characters or richly descriptive settings as key components in the story. I choose examples of literature that draw heavily upon these two characteristics so that students can easily recognize their role in creating an effective story. Some of my favorite characters in children's literature are included in these selections; Max from Maurice Sendak's *Where the Wild Things Are* (1963), Sylvester from William Steig's *Sylvester and the Magic Pebble* (1969), the wolf from Becky Bloom's *Wolf!* (1999), Solomon from Cynthia Rylant's *An Angel for Solomon Singer* (1992), Flossie from Patricia McKissak's *Flossie and the Fox* (1986), and the princess from Robert Munsch's *Paper Bag Princess* (1980).

I repeat many of the same learning experiences when I am teaching students about setting. First, I explain that setting contains two dimensions: time and place. Then we read and discuss books where setting plays an integral part in the story, for example, *Owl Moon*, by Jane Yolen (1987), *Paradise Garden*, by Colin Thompson (1988), *Miss Rumphius*, by Barbara Cooney (1982), *What You Know First*, by Patricia MacLachlan (1995), and *Zoo*, by Anthony Browne (1992). The goal of these experiences is not to get students to simply identify these elements of literature in some sort of literary scavenger hunt, but to come to understand how these authors use various literary elements in the stories they tell.

Teaching students about plot, or the series of events or episodes in a story, requires more than having them cut up comics and reorganize them or fill in flowcharts with episodes of a particular story. When we teach about plot, we need to address this concept in the same way we would address story structures. Our focus should be on the big picture, the various ways a story unfolds, for example, the use of flashbacks, multiple perspectives, or parallel story lines, in addition to understanding what happens in the beginning, middle, and end of a story. I want students to recognize a cyclical story line from a linear one. I want them to notice when a story goes back and forth from the present to the past in each subsequent chapter of a novel.

Plot is bigger than sequencing skills. It is also about conflict and resolution. Authors create tension in order to get readers to continue reading the story. They introduce challenges the main characters must face and overcome, they leave readers hanging at the end of chapters, and they provide insights into future events that the characters don't even know about through foreshadowing devices. Sometimes the character is successful in his struggles—this is known as drama or comedy. Sometimes he is unsuccessful—this is known as tragedy.

Drawing on structuralist literary theories, William Labov and Joshua Waletzky (1967) have analyzed narrative stories to develop categories that can help us understand the structures and elements of narratives. The narrative elements they identified are: (1) *orientation*, used to orient the listener in respect to person, place, time, and behavioral situation; (2) *complicating actions*, a series of events that lead to the climax of the narrative; (3) *evaluation, significance, and meaning of the action*, which reveal the attitude of the narrator toward the narrative by emphasizing the relative importance of some events over others; (4) *resolution*, which follows the evaluation and explains what finally happened; and (5) *coda*, a functional device for returning the reader's perspective to the present moment.

In a traditional narrative structure, the narrative begins with the orientation as the reader becomes familiar with the setting and the characters. During the orientation, readers learn the who, what, when, and where of a story. The narrative cycle continues as the complicating action unfolds in a series of events that lead to the evaluation or climax, often considered the most important element of the story. After the evaluation has occurred, the story comes to a conclusion with a resolution and often a coda that brings the reader back to the present time.

This approach to defining and understanding plot and the structures of literature may be overly complicated to share with students without explicit examples, but Labov and Waletzky provide a heuristic device for understanding the ways stories are organized. Not all stories contain every element they described, but we can talk about the sequence of these structures and better understand the stories we read. The important point here is that there are many ways to help students see the big picture or structures of stories. Plot should be conceived of and described as something more complex than simply a number of disjointed events that happen in a particular sequence. As the school year progresses, I introduce students to other elements of literature, including point of view, mood, theme, and symbolism, building on the foundation established by our discussions of plot, character, and setting. I will also return to plot, setting, and character as we dig deeper into the literature we experience.

Summary of Lessons and Learning Experiences

As you may have noticed by now, picture books and poetry play a prominent role in my reading workshop and the instructional experiences I provide. My primary reason for using these texts in my instructional experiences is that most picture books and poems can be experienced in a single session and allow readers to discuss a complete work of literature in a short time. Second, picture books come in a wide variety of genres, formats, and content area topics. Although I read chapter books aloud to my students throughout the year, and investigate them in literature study groups, most of my readalouds and lessons in comprehension focus on poetry and picture books. This goes for all grades, kindergarten through college.

As we learn to talk about literature in a more sophisticated manner, our individual response notebooks and the entries in the walking journal will develop in turn. The whole-group read-aloud and discussion is the foundation for all of the reading workshop components and experiences. It provides support for what students are expected to do on their own. Fortunately, what happens in the read-aloud and group discussions does not stay there. It supports individual readers' responses in their response notebooks and independent reading. If students are unable to have rich discussions with the support of the whole class and the teacher, why would I expect them to be more successful when they are reading independently or in small groups?

For some units of study I conduct, I may focus on the topic, theme, author or illustrator, or genre for three days a week, Monday, Wednesday, and Friday, and other topics, for example, the basic elements of literature, during Tuesday's and Thursday's reading workshops. Other times, my students are so consumed by the unit of study that we focus on it every day of the week. I leave those decisions for when we are immersed in the unit of study, rather than make every decision before it begins. This is what differentiates a transactional unit of study from the traditional thematic units where teachers create all the learning experiences over the summer and plug the children into them come fall.

Reading aloud is not simply a way to get students to quiet down and relax after lunch. That is an *excuse* for reading aloud. Introducing students to new titles, authors, and genres, demonstrating fluent oral reading, and providing opportunities for discussions and explorations of literature are the *reasons* we read aloud, especially in intermediate- and middle-grade classrooms.

Featured Lesson in Comprehension for October: Visualizing

Sophisticated, proficient readers construct a series of rolling images in their minds as they read certain texts, in particular novels and poetry. We add details to the written text by creating images in our minds that go beyond the literal description. A dog in the text becomes a golden retriever with a bandanna for a collar. We use our imagination to fill in the gaps of the text, as Wolfgang Iser (1978) has described. Both Iser and Louise Rosenblatt (1978) have theorized that the text is only one part of the reading transaction. Rosenblatt explains that the reader draws upon her experiential reservoir or background knowledge to provide information that is not contained in the text when reading.

As adults, when we read novels we often picture characters in our minds in such detail that we envision which contemporary actor might be best suited to portray a particular fictional character should the book be developed into a movie. Some of the images of characters that we create are so powerful that we are sometimes quite dismayed when a director casts an actor in a role adapted from a book who does not fit with our images of the character.

Although we may not construct images in our minds as a primary comprehension strategy when transacting with all types of texts, for example, job applications, email messages, or a bus schedule, it is still a prominent comprehension strategy used by proficient readers when reading novels, poetry and other narrative texts, and therefore it warrants our attention.

The biggest challenge I find in demonstrating the process of visualization to my students is how to represent the images that I construct so that students can get a sense of what I am visualizing. It is no easy task to describe an image in one's head using oral or written language or visual arts. The media we choose to represent the images we construct also play a role in what can be represented. Even if I were a talented artist, I would still be challenged when trying to draw the complex images I construct in my mind as I read.

When I introduce the process of visualizing to my students, I sometimes conduct what I have called imaginary voyages with them. I ask my students to sit back and close their eyes as I explain to them we are going on an adventure in our minds. I begin by selecting a mode of transportation, for example, a car, bus, rocket, plane, or magic carpet, or I have them choose their own imaginary transportation, and then I describe what I am seeing on my adventure. I use descriptive language to evoke images in their minds, and then we talk about what images they created as I described my imaginary voyage. For instance, I might say that I am flying over a rain forest that contains a meandering river somewhere near the equator. I ask students to describe the images they used to fill in the gaps in my story and what they imagined as I was describing my adventure.

After conducting a few imaginary voyages, I read one of my favorite poems, like "Thunder Dragon," by Harry Behn. This poem contains wonderfully descriptive phrases like "up to his cave in the craggy walls," "dropped his scaly carcass down," and "crept over the mountain flashing flame." These phrases from the poem usually evoke powerful images in the minds of my students. We then discuss the images the poem has evoked for each of us, paying close attention to the similarities and differences in our images.

I then invite my students to choose one of poems that I have provided copies of, including "Thunder Dragon," and read through it a few times, paying particular attention to any images that are evoked during their reading. After a brief discussion, I ask my students to choose one particularly powerful phrase or stanza from their poem, cut it out or copy it onto a large piece of construction paper, and use one of several illustration techniques to represent what they visualized while reading. They can use images from magazines or newspapers to create a collage, draw pictures with charcoal, pastels, or paint, or use some of the visual art programs available on our class computers to represent their visualizations.

The goal of this series of lessons is to help students understand how readers visualize when they read, that different readers construct different images from the same text, and that those images help readers make sense of what they are reading by providing additional information not explicitly stated in the text. In other words, we are trying to understand how different readers fill in the gaps in a text when they are reading and that they do so in idiosyncratic ways.

I do not use picture books for comprehension lessons on visualization. I do not hide the illustrations from my students while reading picture books. That is not how a picture book is designed to be read. Picture books are created using the interplay of two systems of meaning: visual images and written text. When we hide the illustrations included in a picture book, we are privileging the written text over the illustrations. As with picture walks, the illustrations end up serving as prompts for guessing the words in the text. According to this line of reasoning, we should preview a movie with the sound turned down before watching it with the sound, yet that sounds rather ridiculous. Equally ridiculous would be a text walk, where we'd give students the written text and then make them guess what the images should be.

Picture books are created so that readers experience the text and illustrations simultaneously. Visual images and written texts in a picture book should be experienced together. The interplay of these two meaning systems is the focus of a series of comprehension lessons in a future month. For these reasons, I primarily use poetry and short stories like fables and fairy tales to get students to visualize. Texts with descriptive language and no illustrations tend to make the best texts for these comprehension lessons.

Literacy Assessments

In the September chapter, I introduced several literacy assessments that I began the year with to understand my students as readers. In October, we begin collecting artifacts of our learning in literacy portfolios, or treasuries. I also continue to add artifacts to my assessment files as the year progresses, including oral reading analyses, interest inventories, and retellings, when they are conducted with students.

Treasuries

To introduce treasuries, I have students from previous classes come to our class and share their treasuries. I also invite friends and university students who have created showcase portfolios in the real world to share their work with my students. I have had architects, interior designers, artists, and musicians come share their portfolios. These portfolios used in the world outside of school provide a variety of examples for my students when launching our treasuries.

To make these treasuries a vital part of our classroom, I need to provide some time each and every week for us to tend to our collections. Until time is provided each week, these treasuries won't become part of our classroom culture. I begin by having students decorate a file folder to hold examples of their work throughout our year. We will use these collections of artifacts to get a window into our growth as readers and writers. We will also use treasuries to demonstrate students' learning to their parents in March when we do our student-led conferences. I explain how I conduct student-led conferences in Chapter 8.

Students add samples from their reading response notebooks, reading logs, literature response activities, and reflection logs to their treasuries in October. There is little power in any one artifact that is included in a treasury. The power comes in seeing artifacts over time and reflecting on the growth they represent.

Weekly Reading Conferences

In addition, I conduct weekly literacy conferences with my students at the beginning of each day's reading and writing workshops. These are two-minute conversations with about five students per day so that I make sure I meet with every student once a week. I take notes about what they accomplished in reading the previous week and what they are working on for the upcoming week.

Two important things have emerged from these literacy conferences. First, I am able to keep track of students' progress and am able to suggest new titles, authors, and genres for them to explore. There is a modicum of accountability provided by these conferences. Second, and probably most important, my students quickly realize that I am going to ask them about their reading and writing every week. Consequently, they learn to attend to what they are reading and writing so they are prepared when I call them to the conference. I want students to be aware of what they are reading and writing, to notice patterns and trends in their literate activities, in order to become more reflective readers and writers.

Connections to the Writing Workshop

At the same time I am reading books about being a reader in our reading workshop, I am also reading books about being a writer in the writing workshop. In the same manner that we are investigating books with characters that read, we are investigating books with characters that write as well as biographies and autobiographies about famous writers. There is a booklist on my website that includes books about writers and writing for you to use in this investigation.

I want my students to understand what writers do as much as they understand how writers write. For example, every writer I have ever met keeps some sort of writer's notebook or place for gathering words, ideas, quotes, phrases, pictures, and anything else that might serve as an impetus for their writing. Most writers write every day and find a special place and time to write. I want my students to find a place for writing in their lives in the same way I am helping them find a place for reading in their lives.

After reading books about writers and writing, we create charts similar to the ones we did about successful readers. These charts help us create a preferred vision for ourselves as writers. Beginning the year with discussions about what successful readers, writers, mathematicians, and scientists do helps us unpack the criteria we hold for our students in these areas and makes our expectations visible and open for negotiation and revision.

Things I Hope to See, Hear, and Have Established by Month's End

1. Students are beginning to talk about the images they construct when they are reading. I expect my teaching to be taken seriously by my students and the lessons I demonstrate to be used in their reading.

2. The terms *character*, *setting*, and *plot* are being used in our literature discussions as we continue to focus on these elements in our read-alouds and invested discussions.

3. Students are able to talk about the design elements of a work of literature, in particular the work of any author or illustrator we have studied.

4. Students understand the nuances and styles of the authors and illustrators we have been studying and to continue read and explore their work. I also expect students to attend to who is writing and illustrating the books they read.

5. Students are attending to the characteristics of sophisticated and proficient readers that we have generated. If proficient readers check out books from the

library, make appropriate choices for their independent reading, talk about what they read, read to others, and take care of their books, I expect my readers to begin to do the same.

6. Students are using their reading strategies bookmarks and beginning to use reading and comprehension strategies in addition to sounding it out and asking for help.

7. By the end of the month, I expect every student to have made an entry in the class walking journal. I will check to see who has written in there and have a friendly chat with those who have not, reminding them of their responsibilities.

8. I hope to see a few book clubs established by the end of the month. I make sure students remember that this option is available, but I won't push it on them.

9. All of my students look forward each week to reading buddies. I want this to be an enjoyable experience and one in which they feel successful participating.

10. The books I have selected to read aloud and include in our classroom library are conceptually appropriate for the various reading experiences and abilities I have in my classroom. By mid-October, I will spend some time analyzing my library collection and get some ideas about books and reading materials I may need to include.

Ideas for Further Reflection

❖ The more we know ourselves as readers, the better we will be able to help children understand what it means to be a reader. One way to understand ourselves as readers is to keep a reading response notebook for ourselves and to use this notebook to demonstrate how we respond to our own reading when we are introducing reading response notebooks to our students.

❖ The list of characteristics we have developed with students about successful readers can be used as a rubric for evaluating the readers in our classroom. If the list describes the types of readers we want students to become, then it may also serve as an evaluation tool to measure students' progress toward these goals.

❖ The list of characteristics that we develop concerning successful readers cannot become a narrow, rigid set of expectations that few readers find themselves able to measure up to. This list should grow as our discussions provide more insights into ourselves as readers, but it should not be used to denigrate any one reader.

Closing Thoughts

When we read a piece of children's literature, we learn as much about ourselves as we do about the book. By attending to the types of responses we construct in transaction with a text, we learn about ourselves as readers, the types of books we find most comfortable, and when and where we tend to engage in the act of reading. These observations are without merit if they are not used to broaden students' understandings of themselves as readers in order to help them become better at reading.

Søren Kierkegaard once wrote, "Life can only be understood backwards; but it must be lived forwards." Thinking about ourselves as readers is not a navel-gazing activity. It is used to better understand what we currently do and don't do as readers so that we may improve our reading ability in the future. If we spend more time thinking about our reading lives than we spend actually reading, we may end up ignoring the one thing we are trying to become: readers.

Becoming a Sophisticated Reader

In October it is important for us as a class to understand what proficient and sophisticated readers do in order to develop a vision for the readers we want to become. This unit of study is designed to help children create and negotiate an image of proficient reading that all readers can emulate.

Focus

This unit includes a series of lessons and learning experiences to help students discuss what proficient readers do, gain confidence as readers, and develop comprehension and reading strategies to expand their reading and interpretive repertoires.

Goals and Objectives

❖ help students understand that reading is a meaning-making process

❖ support readers in choosing appropriate texts

❖ analyze images of readers and reading in literature and the media

❖ introduce various reading and comprehension strategies

Opening Ceremonies

In October we focused on images of reading and the reader. We investigated the role of reading in our families, our local community, and the literature we read. I asked students to share stories of how reading was important in their personal lives and how family members and friends used reading and texts to fix cars, cook food, buy houses, select movies, and find interesting locations for vacation on the Internet.

During the month of October, students took turns bringing our walking journal home each night to record what they wanted to be when they grew up. They were to then consider and research how reading would impact their career choices. Students responded to each other's entries and shared their ideas for the future.

In addition, students made connections on our literacy expedition wall between the books on reading and readers and the unit of study on building community. They discovered that reading had a lot to do with our classroom community, that we were not only a community but a community of readers.

Cornerstone Texts

I selected *Wolf!* by Becky Bloom (1999), as the cornerstone picture book for this unit. In this story, the wolf, lonely and hungry, happens upon a farm and goes there to get something to eat. He tries to scare the farm animals, but the pig, the duck, and the cow are not the least bit impressed. They explain that the farm is for educated animals. After time spent in school, a library, and a bookstore, the wolf becomes a reader and is accepted into the farm community when he reads with confidence and passion.

The cornerstone chapter book I selected was *Just Juice*, by Karen Hesse (1999). In this story, a young girl struggles with reading at school and prefers to stay at home and work with her father. The story takes place in rural Appalachia and weaves together issues of literacy and socioeconomic hardships. These two books created a space for students to discuss what reading is, what proficient and struggling readers do, and how reading and literacy affect one's place in the community.

Launching the Unit of Study

I began by creating an Impressions-Connections-Wonderings chart for *Wolf!* I asked students to construct reading autobiography boxes to share with their classmates. Students gathered artifacts that represented themselves as readers. This experience provided a window into the role reading played in my students' lives. It also provided an avenue for discussing the various images of reading and readers we had collected. After we finished sharing our boxes, I asked students to create two lists, one that defined what reading is and the second to describe characteristics of a proficient reader. We then used these lists to create a bulletin board titled "Images of a Reader."

We read *Wolf!* several times over the course of three days. At first the students thought I was a little crazy to read one book so many times. They soon began to realize they had new ideas about the text as they kept negotiating and revising their understandings during subsequent readings. I used a different-color marker each day to record their ideas so students could see how their thoughts built upon previous ideas and were becoming more sophisticated as the days went by.

On the third day of discussion, students offered opposing interpretations concerning *Wolf!* One group of children felt that the pig, the duck, and the cow created an exclusionary club and accepted the wolf only once he had become a reader like them. A second group argued that the duck, the pig, and the cow inspired the wolf to read. These discussions grew in complexity as we returned to the book and continued investigating the text.

Students were invited to write on sticky notes anytime during our investigations throughout the unit, share their ideas with the class, and then post ideas on the bulletin board. Numerous categories emerged as students attended to the various texts we shared throughout the unit. Some of these categories included what readers look like, what readers read, how readers act, treatment of people who can and cannot read, images of readers we agree with and images we do not agree with, and questions asked of readers.

Our experiences eventually led us to discuss our purposes for reading. I then selected *Read for Me, Mama*, by Vashanti Rahaman (1997). In this story a little boy enjoys being read to and eventually forces his mama to finally admit she can't read. This causes her to learn how to read. Next, I read *The Girl Who Hated Books*, by Manjusha Pawagi (1998). In this book, the main character, Meena, hates to read and hates having books all around her house. When the piles of books in her house fall over, animal characters come to life and spring forth from the books. Meena has to read all the stories in order to put the characters back where they belong. At the end of the first week, I read *The Wednesday Surprise,* by Eve Bunting (1989). In this story a young girl surprises her father by teaching her grandmother to read.

As we read each book, we continually revised our ideas of what sophisticated readers do. Students began to realize how important reading is and that it looked different in many contexts. During the second week of the unit, we continued to discuss what kind of readers we wanted to be, interviewed readers we thought were successful, and focused on specific reading strategies. I demonstrated many strategies using think-alouds and asked students to practice the strategies I demonstrated in small groups or independently.

Explicit Instruction

Explicit teaching is an important instructional component to help students become more proficient in their reading. As their teacher, I needed to model the reading strategies and literate practices I wanted them to develop. In the next section, I describe how I presented a series of lessons on choosing appropriate texts and using specific reading comprehension strategies.

Choosing Appropriate Texts   Children need to understand how to choose texts that are appropriate for their purposes for reading. We need to help them assume the responsibility for their choices and guide them to select texts they can read and understand.

To begin, I brought in a book that was easy for me to read, a text that was completely frustrating to read, and a book that I would need a little help to understand. I read aloud a selection from each text and asked students to describe for me what they noticed while I was reading. I read aloud and described my thinking as I read so students could understand what I was thinking.

I began with the easy text. Students observed that I read with fluency and style and had little difficulty pronouncing any of the words. Next I read the book that was frustrating for me to read. Students noticed I didn't know some of the words, I began to sound out words I couldn't pronounce, and I didn't understand what I had read. With the third text, students observed that I knew most of the words but had trouble comprehending what the text was about.

We talked about three kinds of texts—easy, instructional, and frustrating. That night for homework I asked students to identify an easy text, one that was at an instructional level, and one that was frustrating. I asked them to do this for homework so that no child would be embarrassed by telling the class which text was frustrating for him or her. As a class, we discussed the characteristics of each type of book we chose and created a bookmark for the students to use when choosing books. Our discussion did not include any specific titles, only students' reflections on the process of identifying these types of texts. These bookmarks helped children remember what to think about when selecting a text, which was a big step toward helping students select more appropriately.

Reading Strategy Lessons   In two different comprehension lessons, I chose a piece of poetry and an expository piece to demonstrate, using think-alouds, the types of questions

I ask before, during, and after reading. For these lessons, I chose the poem "Mother to Son," by Langston Hughes, and an article from Scholastic's *Super Science* magazine. I began with the poem "Mother to Son," thinking out loud to demonstrate the types of questions I had about the poem. I wondered about the context for writing it and about Langston Hughes himself.

I read and thought aloud with the expository text in the same manner. I selected an article about animal digestion. I read the piece and asked questions out loud for students. We then had a discussion about what they observed during my think-aloud. I asked them, "What kinds of questions did I ask? Were the questions different for the two kinds of text I read? When did I ask questions? Did I answer all my questions? Did asking questions help me think about the text in a different way? Did the reading strategy of questioning help me better understand each text?" My goal was to introduce various strategies to students as I felt they were ready for them. Throughout the year, we came back to the asking questions strategy and discussed when and how we were using it in our independent reading.

Workshop Experiences

Comprehension Strategy Groups   Much of what the students were doing during the workshop time in the second and third week of this study was an extension of the reading lessons I had conducted. I used the texts students had selected to read for independent reading and pulled passages out of them so we could discuss the strategies they needed to understand specific texts. In our reading response notebooks, we added a section for the strategies we had learned and used and how each strategy enhanced understanding. We shared these entries during the workshop share circle.

Culminating Experience

Class Book of Images   For our culminating experience we conducted an investigation of the kinds of images found in the media depicting readers and reading. We looked at images in magazines, newspapers, books, posters, and on the Internet. We also explored images presented on television. Students shared their findings, and we created a chart of the kinds of images of readers and reading we found. As a class we decided to create our own "image of a reader" book. Each student drew a picture of him- or herself in the act of reading and wrote one or two sentences describing the implications of the picture. Students drew themselves reading with friends, reading instructions to a game, reading an acceptance letter from a ballet school, reading under a tree, reading a medical text, reading a Nintendo guide, and reading other texts. The book was a wonderful culminating project, representing images of the readers the students were and the readers they were striving to become.

Closing the Window

This unit never truly came to a close because the strategies taught in these few weeks were revisited for the rest of the year with each new text and unit. In addition, this unit of study provided a foundation for students to rethink their own images of what a successful reader does. Students began to choose books they could read on their own and learned a great deal about each other as readers.

CHAPTER 4

November—Negotiating Responses to Literature

> Talking about literature is a form of shared contemplation, a way of giving form to the thoughts and emotions stimulated by the book and the meanings we make together out of its text.
> —AIDAN CHAMBERS, *TELL ME*

Introduction

By the time we get to November, students are settling into routines, and the complexity of our literature discussions is expanding. In November, I focus on adding two essential components to the reading workshop: literature study groups and comprehension strategy groups. Literature study groups, sometimes referred to as literature circles, involve the intense study of one particular piece of literature by a small group of students, with a more knowledgeable reader, usually the teacher, facilitating the discussions. Comprehension strategy groups, sometimes referred to as guided reading groups, involve the teachers selecting particular texts to teach comprehension strategies to a small group of children through demonstrations and discussions as the teacher and students work through the text together.

As Aidan Chambers states in the epigraph, the discussions that take place in literature study groups are a form of shared contemplation, a type of talk that promotes and leads to what Peterson and Eeds (1990)

Recommended Comprehension Strategies from *Lessons in Comprehension*

2.1 The Hero Cycle

2.2 Using Diagrams to Understand Story Structures

3.2 Investigating Fonts and Visual Design Elements

3.4 Rules of Notice

3.7 Previewing a Text

3.8 Reading Postmodern Picture Books

4.2 Disrupting a Text

5.6 Suspending Closure

5.8 Drawing Inferences

have called "grand conversations." Literature study groups are designed to help students delve into a selected work of literature, examining the structures and elements of the work along with the author's writing style and techniques. This intensive study of a single work leads to more sophisticated understandings of literature in general and of oneself as a reader in particular.

Comprehension strategy groups focus on particular comprehension and navigation strategies, where literature study groups focus on a particular work of literature. Although reading a work of literature in literature study groups helps students become better readers, the focus is not on particular reading and comprehension strategies per se, but the work of literature being read. In literature study groups, texts are selected that students can read independently or with minimal support. In comprehension strategy groups, texts are selected for the challenges they present to the readers, allowing teachers to help students develop strategies to deal with these challenges.

Comprehension strategy groups are an instructional approach where a teacher selects a particular text to demonstrate a specified comprehension or navigation strategy to a small group of readers. Although the text should present some challenge, the readers must be able to read the text to some degree independently for these groups to be successful. The teacher focuses readers' attention on what they are doing when they read and the new strategy she would like students to appropriate in their future engagements with text.

The assessments I conduct during the months of September and October provide a window into students' reading needs, interests, and abilities. This information supports the formation of small groups for comprehension instruction and literature study. In addition, these assessments allow me to provide individual students with focused instructional experiences at their point of need. Colleagues Barbara Taylor and P. David Pearson (2000) have conducted research studies on effective reading instruction programs across the United States. One key finding from their research is the importance of small-group instruction. They have demonstrated that teachers providing small-group instruction in reading comprehension strategies, based on the needs and abilities of individual readers, are more effective than teachers who provide instruction primarily in whole-group settings. During the months of September and October, most of my reading instruction and demonstrations occur in whole-class discussions or with individual students. In November, I begin to implement small-group instruction, introducing literature study and comprehension strategy groups, based on the needs of individual readers, into the reading workshop.

November is also a time to continue digging deeper into the responses we construct in transaction with literature and the elements and structures of the texts we read. During the first two months of school, I was primarily concerned with helping students generate and begin to articulate their interpretations of the literature we shared. We investigated the types of responses we generated through reading response notebooks and various invested discussion strategies. In November, we focus on negotiating these interpretations with other readers in literature study groups. I begin to challenge readers to defend their interpretations, providing evidentiary warrants for their assertions. As readers offer interpretations up for interrogation and discussion, we focus on how our ideas are negotiated and revised through our shared contemplation of a work of literature.

In the first two months of school, I pay close attention to the ways my students respond to the literature we read, if they listen to each other's ideas, how they respond to another student's comments, and how they incorporate the literary terms I have introduced into our discussions. I pay close attention to two parallel developments that signal whether students are ready for literature study groups: (1) an increasing respect for readers' ideas and interpretations, and a willingness to listen to, and negotiate, ideas with their classmates, and (2) an expanding level of knowledge of the elements and structures of literature necessary for progressing discussions beyond "I like the book."

There are numerous signals I look for that indicate that these two features are beginning to develop within our community of readers. I notice that students are responding to each other in our group discussions, not just directing all of their ideas toward me. Students don't interrupt each other as frequently, and they are listening to each other, considering alternative interpretations. Students begin asking each other questions and are discussing favorite authors, texts, and genres. The walking journal is progressing satisfactorily, with students frequently commenting on each other's ideas and adding new strands to the written dialogue. Students begin using appropriate literary terms in their comments and attending to the visual and design elements of what we are reading and discussing. Students become engaged in the author and illustrator studies we conduct, interrogating the writer's craft and illustrator's techniques in greater detail. And most importantly, students are able to sustain independent and paired reading for thirty minutes or so and are able to solve any challenges that arise during the reading workshop block, allowing me to work with small groups without being constantly interrupted.

These are important developments in our community of readers. Until I begin to see and hear these signals, I am reticent to establish literature study groups in the reading workshop. Some years I introduce literature study groups in October, sometimes not until January. However, in most of my years of teaching, I have introduced literature study groups around the beginning of November.

November Lessons and Learning Experiences

Poetry Discussion Groups

Reading a poem du jour, I have exposed students to a variety of poetry, both simple, humorous poems and more complex ones, throughout September and October. Our daily readings of poetry have provided students with an opportunity to hear poems read aloud and discover some favorite poems and poets. The poem du jour is used to immerse students in the world of poetry, calling their attention to the various forms, formats, and contents of poetry. Now I focus students' attention on a single poem in order to delve deeper into our interpretive processes.

As I notice more depth in our whole-group discussions, and more respect for the ideas offered, I begin our journey into literature study groups by launching poetry study groups and picture book study groups, before moving on to assigning full-length novels for investigation. The experiences we provide and the type of community of readers we have created form the foundation for literature study groups to be successful. If a solid literary foundation is provided long before we invite students into small groups to discuss a novel, our chances of having some of our conversations *turn grand* increase. The discussions that take place in small groups are directly affected by the quality of the discussions that take place in our whole-group sessions. Grand conversations usually won't happen in small groups until they begin to appear in whole-group literature discussions.

I begin by selecting poems to discuss that are written by some of my favorite poets, including Nikki Giovanni, Langston Hughes, Myra Cohn Livingston, Naomi Shihab Nye, Eloise Greenfield, Lee Bennett Hopkins, Georgia Heard, Harry Behn, Ogden Nash, and Judith Viorst. I select poems that have engaged my students in the past and have provided an impetus for in-depth discussions. Whatever poem I choose, it must have the following two characteristics: first, students must be able to read and construct a basic understanding of the poem during an initial reading, and second, the poem must be complex enough to support our subsequent readings and discussions. In other words, the poem I select must simultaneously provide a door into meaning and room to wander once we get in. For me, these characteristics of openness and complexity are crucial for supporting our discussions and investigations of a literary work.

After selecting a poem to launch our discussions, I read it aloud a couple of times, asking students to simply listen and enjoy the poem. Georgia Heard has spoken about the importance of hearing poetry from a variety of voices to see how it may be read differently. So, after my second reading, I ask a couple of students to read the poem again in their own voices. We listen to the differences each reader brings to the poem and then break into small groups to discuss the poem. I usually assign students to this first set of groups to avoid behavior challenges, but I will allow students to create their own groups as we get better at discussing literature. I provide copies of the poem with plenty of white space around the text for students to write comments and questions. I ask students to read the poem once again to themselves and write their reactions in the space around the poem before sharing ideas with the group. I want readers to assume responsibility for reacting to the poem as individuals before sharing their interpretations with other readers. Each reader is responsible for generating interpretations herself, not waiting for other readers to interpret the poem for her.

After each reader has made some comments on her paper, I invite students to share ideas with their group. During this sharing time, I walk around and listen in on each conversation, making some notes and listening for things that support and challenge the kinds of interactions I am hoping to establish. I am as concerned with students' interpretations of the poem as I am with their abilities to listen and talk effectively with other members of the group. At times, I will stop the discussions to make a particular point. These pullbacks are designed to help students focus on our processes for discussing as well as the poem itself. For example, if I notice someone leaning in to listen closely to another student's ideas, I will call the class' attention to the types of behaviors I want them to adopt. From these pullbacks and our discussions about small-group interactions, we create a chart that lists things that have helped us discuss the poem, and things that have blocked our discussions (see Figure 4.1).

Helpers

looking at each other when speaking

asking each other questions

listening and caring about what each other thinks and says

talking so everyone can hear

giving everyone a chance to talk

learning to politely disagree

Blockers

playing around in groups

being rude

constantly interrupting others

allowing one person to do all the talking

not coming to the group with your own ideas

not talking

saying you are done when there may be more to say

FIG. 4.1
Literature Discussion Ideas

I use these poetry groups to introduce students to small-group discussions. I want to make my expectations clear for students' discussions and behaviors from the beginning. Too often, teachers allow small-group work to become chaotic. This does not have to be the case. However, don't expect small-group discussions to begin without some challenges. By providing clear expectations for behavior, and support through whole-group discussions and demonstrations, we can make small-group work an important and successful component of the reading workshop.

Picture Book Discussion Groups

Poetry discussion groups are used to introduce the types of discussions and procedures we will be doing with picture books, and eventually novels, during our literature study groups. As we launch picture book discussion groups, more time is required for readers to read the work for discussion and prepare ideas to share. I need approximately five or six copies of various picture books for these discussions. If these multiple copies are not available, one copy of each book can suffice, but readers will have to share the text before they are ready to talk in small groups. I choose picture books using the same criteria I described for the poems I select: an openness for students to initiate understandings and a complexity that will allow students to dig deeper.

To begin, I give each student a copy of the book and a small stack of sticky notes to code passages in the text as they are reading. I demonstrate how to code passages readers want to share by writing a word or two on a sticky note to remind students of what they were thinking. I don't require students to use their reading response notebooks for these poetry and picture book discussions because I don't want writing to get in the way of their discussions at this point. Reading response notebooks, in particular book logs, will play a central role when we begin reading novels, but for these picture book and poetry discussion groups, I want students to focus on their oral discussion techniques and group behavior.

Unlike with poetry discussion groups, where I selected the poems and assigned the students to groups, I allow students to choose which book they would like to discuss for picture book groups. I provide six or seven picture books and ask students to choose one to read and discuss. Sometimes it is necessary to ask students to pick their top three choices and arrange groups myself to accommodate all students. Sometimes it is necessary to add new titles to the choices available if some of the books are not selected by anyone. I want students to enjoy reading the books they select and be able to understand what they are reading. I want these first small-group discussions to be very successful for all of my students so they will help support more intensive literature study groups.

After selections are made and groups are formed, I ask students to read the picture book and mark passages or images they feel are significant and would like to eventually share and discuss with the group. Students need to come to the group prepared to talk about what they have read. This means that they have read the book, have marked passages or images they want to talk about, have generated some interpretations for themselves, and are willing to listen to others' ideas.

Our first meeting usually lasts about ten to twenty minutes and generally consists of students sharing the parts of the story they liked and disliked, anything that was confusing, and any images that caught their attention. This informal conversation has to take place before students can move into more complex dialogue about a text. It's like going to a party. You have to talk about the weather before you can talk about life-altering events. I have watched this phenomenon with both fifth graders and graduate students at university. Both groups begin by sharing their likes and dislikes and then move into more complex topics and issues. The trick is to not let students think that once the informal sharing of likes and dislikes is over, so is the literature study. Our discussions are just beginning.

Over the course of the next few days, I meet with each group individually to talk about their selected text. I listen as they summarize their discussions up to that point, and I might ask a few questions to clarify certain ideas. After listening to their ideas, I suggest a particular topic or theme for them to pursue further. I send students back to the picture book to generate ideas about our selected topic or theme. I do this with each group to demonstrate the importance of returning to the text and images in a picture book during the interpretive process.

Each group will then do a brief self-evaluation, focusing on the group's discussions, behaviors, and interpretations (see Figure 4.2). I want them to attend to how the group worked together so we can improve our discussions as we get ready to launch literature studies on children's and young adult novels.

As I have suggested earlier, if you want to have quality discussions, read quality literature that connects to the lives and experiences of your students. You will find several booklists of my favorite books that I have used for picture book discussions on my website. I will continually update these booklists to provide teachers with lists of new favorites as well as classic texts that have been used successfully.

Supporting Picture Book Investigations

The read-alouds that continue each day before launching small-group discussions are used to call students' attention to the various elements and structures of the picture books we are sharing. As their literary docent, I call their attention to the characteris-

Answer and give examples for the following questions:

1. Did group members listen to each other's ideas?

2. Did members ask each other any questions?

3. Was anyone rude or impolite when talking?

4. Did you change any of your ideas after the discussions?

5. Did you go back and look at the book for ideas?

6. What big ideas did you generate from your readings and discussions?

FIG. 4.2
Picture Book Discussion Self-Evaluation Questions

tics of written texts and visual images they may have overlooked or did not understand. This is where my knowledge of children's literature, and its elements and structures, is so important. I cannot call students' attention to those things I don't know about or attend to myself. The more sophisticated a reader I can become, the more I will be able to support my students development as sophisticated readers.

In *Reading Aloud and Beyond: Fostering the Intellectual Life with Older Readers*, Cyndi Giorgis and I (2003) provide an in-depth discussion of artistic media and techniques used by contemporary illustrators along with a theoretical discussion of the relationships between text and illustrations. The information we provide in this book, or that can be found in any quality children's literature textbook, will help you attend to and understand the elements and structures of contemporary picture books. Taking a refresher course in children's literature, forming discussion groups with other educators to talk about picture books and novels, spending time at school and public libraries reading children's literature, and reading professional resources that help you understand literary theories and the elements and structures of children's literature will support your ability to teach in a literature-based reading workshop.

I now want to describe three examples of the types of learning experiences I provide during the reading workshop, in particular during our read-alouds and invested discussions of literature, before I begin to incorporate literature studies on novels in the reading workshop. One is a series of engagements I call disrupting a text, the second focuses on the interplay or relationships between written text and visual images in a picture book, and the third focuses on calling students' attention to one of the most common structures in children's literature, the home-away-home structure or hero cycle. These instructional experiences help readers attend to three important aspects of picture books: (1) the way illustrations and written texts are organized and designed, (2) the interplay between text and images, and (3) the overall structure of the sequence of events in a story.

Disrupting a Text

What I am referring to when I use the phrase *disrupting a text* is separating the visual images and written text in a picture book and discussing these two components separately. I have used two different ways to separate written text from visual images. One way is to type up the words of a picture book on a single sheet of paper, retaining the original line breaks from the book but simply omitting the illustrations. The second way is to make color copies of the visual images, or physically take a book apart, and display the images in storyboard fashion on a wall in the classroom.

Before disrupting a picture book, I spend time talking about the book in its entirety, reading it aloud and discussing the book in our usual way. Then I take away the written text and we discuss what we notice in the illustrations alone, and then we focus our attention on the written text alone. By disrupting various picture books, I have been able to help readers approach texts from different perspectives and notice things they didn't see when we read the story as a whole. I don't recommend this for every book as some wouldn't warrant this type of visual analysis. The three books with which I have used this instructional strategy quite successfully are *Where the Wild Things Are*, by Maurice Sendak (1963), *Voices in the Park*, by Anthony Browne (2001), and *Black and White*, by David Macauley (1990).

Interplay Between Written Text and Visual Images

The written text and images or illustrations contained in a text work in concert in a picture book to tell the story or convey information. Rather than disrupting the text, separating visual images from written text, in this instructional strategy we help readers focus on the relationship between visual images and written text in a picture book.

Research conducted by Perry Nodelman (1988) and Maria Nikolajeva and Carole Scott (2000) on the interplay between written text and visual images in picture books has suggested that the types of relationships between text and image fall into three general categories: (1) symmetrical, (2) enhancing, and (3) contradictory. In a symmetrical relationship, the information represented in written text and the visual image is basically the same. Although these two sign systems can never represent exactly the same ideas or concepts, in a symmetrical relationship, the written text and the visual images closely mirror each other. For example, there is picture of a green ball sitting in some grass, and the text says, "The green ball is sitting in the grass."

The enhancing relationship is the most common in picture books; in this relationship the written text enhances the visual images, and the visual images enhance the written text. Not only is it a green ball sitting in some grass, but it is a tennis ball sitting on a tennis court at Wimbledon. The text may remain the same, but the visual images enhance the meaning of the ball in the grass.

In a contradictory relationship, the visual images contradict what is represented in the written text. Perry Nodelman refers to this relationship as having a sense of irony between text and image. This relationship is not common, but it can be found more prevalently in postmodern picture books, or books that use metafictive devices.

During the lessons focusing on the relationships between written text and visual images, I provide numerous examples of each type of interplay in specially selected picture books. We discuss how the text and the illustrations work together to tell the story. I introduce the three terms, *symmetrical*, *enhancing*, and *contradictory*, and make a class chart so we can refer to these ideas as we continue with our picture book investigations. I want my readers to attend to the written text and the visual images in a picture book as a whole, separately, and in relationship with one another.

The Hero Cycle

The third series of lessons addresses the overall structure of a fictional narrative. Since ancient times, storytellers have used what has been referred to as the hero cycle or a home-away-home structure to construct their tales. *The Odyssey* is one of the oldest examples of this type of narrative. In a basic home-away-home structure, the main character leaves home on an adventure, meets challenges in the world, adapts and learns from these experiences, and returns home a changed, but wiser, person. The hero cycle is very common in children's literature, especially fairy tales. In most fairy tales, the main character, usually a child or a fictional animal, is sent out into the world to run an errand or seek her fortune, meets evil characters and faces other challenges, vanquishes her foes with the help of magical powers or her own cunning, and learns the lesson "There's no place like home."

Getting novice readers to understand the overall structure of a story is a challenge. They generally have been asked to retell or sequence events rather than focus on the overall structure of a story. Using examples where the structure is quite apparent helps readers attend to stories where the structure is more nuanced and complex.

The three learning experiences I have just described occur during our morning read-aloud and discussion, or with the picture book discussion groups during the reading workshop. As students meet to discuss their selections in literature study groups, focusing on novels or picture books, I am continually calling their attention to the elements and structures of literature during read-alouds and invested discussion times. Some days of the week, I introduce a literary concept in a short, explicit lesson and have students engage in their discussion groups almost immediately. I wander around and teach into these groups throughout the reading workshop time. Other days, the learning experiences I provide are longer and require students to engage in common experiences for the whole workshop block of time.

The Goldfish Bowl

Before launching literature study groups that focus on contemporary children's and young adult novels, I conduct a learning experience known as the goldfish bowl. The goldfish bowl experience is where I have one group of students discuss a picture book in front of the other students while we pay attention to what they say and take observational notes. This can be a daunting experience for many readers, and I am very careful about which students I select to be part of the featured group in the goldfish bowl. I want the group sharing their ideas to be successful and provide a positive model of literature discussion.

I explain to the students not in the goldfish bowl that they are going to be literary researchers conducting observations to understand how quality literature discussion groups operate. I ask students to bring a pencil and notebook with them so they can take notes about what they observe. I ask the group doing the discussion to try to forget we are even there. I want them to simply talk about the book as they would if they were off in a corner of the room doing their regular literature discussions.

As the featured group discusses the book, the other students and I take notes about what we notice and then we discuss what we have seen. We may add new ideas to our "Helpers and Blockers" chart or talk about the ways each student participated. The goldfish bowl experience gives students an opportunity to watch an actual discussion and make the experience of being in a literature study group more concrete for every student. It is my hope that this experience will help us conduct better discussions as we move into literature study groups.

Launching Literature Study Groups

As the discussions focusing on picture books and poems become more sophisticated, and children begin living up to the expectations we have created for the social interactions in small groups, I begin to think about what novels I will choose for our literature study groups. I am very picky about the books I use for these lit study groups. These books must be wonderfully engaging stories and complex enough to foster extensive discussions. As I suggested earlier, if you want grand conversations, read grand literature.

It is important for me to state that I do not believe that independent reading levels should keep children out of literature study groups. By utilizing books on tape, parents as reading partners, or peer helpers, or reading along with students myself, I am able to help all children understand the stories they select and participate in our discussions. I want any child who desires to be involved in a particular group to have the opportunity to participate. Over the years, students who have not been able to read a book by themselves have made significant contributions to their literature study discussions. It can be challenging finding support for all readers to participate, but it's the only option I can consider. If teachers decide that a student is too slow a reader to be given a chance to experience a great book, they do a serious disservice to another human being.

I begin by selecting seven or eight books of which I have multiple copies and introducing each book during a book talk with the class. A book talk is a short presentation designed to help students understand what the book is about and entice them into reading it. I may read information from the back cover of the book or from a review I have found or share a few thoughts from my own experience with the book. I post sign-up sheets for every book I will be offering and invite students to sign up for a book of their choice. If this process gets too chaotic, I have students write down their top three choices and I form the groups myself.

I have read every book that I offer for literature study at least once, and I will read it again before the group convenes. In order to facilitate discussions, I read the book along with my students to experience the book once more and prepare for our upcoming discussions. This may be time-consuming, but it better prepares me for our discussions than trying to remember a book I haven't read in two years. The literature study cycle allows me to have to read only one book at a time, another advantage of this literature study cycle.

I may make certain books available all year so that more than one group can read them. Other books that are not immediately selected can be taken down and new ones offered in their place. Students are not required to sign up for one of the first books, but if they wait too long they will get a visit from their friendly teacher reminding them that membership in literature study groups is expected from every student. I may ask these reluctant readers what books they might like to read and provide several new choices to help get them involved.

Theoretically, the books themselves create the groups. Children see a book that they really want to read and sign up for that book. However, some students will wait and see what books their friends sign up for; I watch for this and talk with students about the importance of selecting a book they *really* want to read. I give students a few days to look over the books available and make their selections. I choose one group that I feel will be successful as my first literature study group. I want the discussions and literature study experience to go well with the first group so that other groups look

FIG. 4.3 *The Literature Study Contract*

The Literature Study Contract

I agree to read the book _____.
(insert title of book here)

I will finish the book by the time the group decides.

I will take notes in my book log and use them to help me in our discussion of the book.

I will bring my book and book log to class *every day*!

I will *participate* in the discussion of the book.

I agree to help other students to better understand the book we have read.

I agree to work together in a group to celebrate finishing the book by creating a presentation for the class.

Date: _____

Student Signatures:

1. _____

2. _____

3. _____

4. _____

5. _____

forward to their discussions. Once I've selected a group, I ask them to read a few pages of the book overnight to make sure they like the book and can make sense of it. Afterward, I require members of the group to sign a literature study contract (see Figure 4.3).

Being a member of a literature study group demands commitment, not only to read the book but to engage in discussions and negotiate and revise meanings with other members. These responsibilities are not to be taken lightly. It should be an enjoyable experience, but is an intensive one as well. The contract signals to students the level of commitment necessary for the group to be successful.

I allow students about two weeks to read the average chapter book. Most children's and young adult novels range from 125 to 175 pages. If students read a page every two minutes, which is slow compared with most proficient intermediate-grade readers, they will be able to read fifteen pages each night for homework. If they read for thirty to forty minutes, as required, they will be able to finish the book in approximately seven to ten days.

Some groups take a bit longer, some shorter. I meet with some groups each day while we read the book, and for some groups I wait until the book is finished before we meet. I check up on each group during the reading of their novel to ensure there are no major misunderstandings, but the bulk of our discussions take place when the reading is completed. How much teacher support is required depends on the experience of the readers and the complexity of the book. I don't want students to become frustrated or confused at the beginning of a novel because the rest of the book may not make sense to them and will become more frustrating.

To support my students as they are reading the book, I have created a book log each student can use to take notes and bring ideas back to the group. I have included a list of headings for sections of the book log that I have used in the past (see Figure 4.4). I want the book log to support students' reading and interpretations, not to turn into a book report. For each heading that I have listed here, I provide about a page or half a page of space for students to write. When we meet as a group, students are required to bring their copy of the book and their book log to the discussion.

These book log categories are closely related to the headings and topics that I have been using on our class discussion charts so that students are familiar with them and able to respond appropriately in the book logs. I want students to write in their book

FIG. 4.4
Book Log Categories

Book Log Categories

Ideas About the Main Character

Ideas About the Setting

Impressions

Literary Connections

Personal Connections

Wonderings

Notes About the Story Structure

Big Ideas to Share

logs each time they read, adding notes to help them share ideas in our group discussions. I also provide sticky notes for readers to code pages in much the same way we did during our picture book studies. I want to capture students' initial reactions with the sticky notes, and their reflections with the book logs.

As our class discussions become more complex, so will the book logs. As students are made aware of other elements and structures of literature, for example, mood, symbolism, tension, irony, and theme, and begin to use these in our discussions, I will expand the book log categories to include them. In other words, the book logs we use in November are less complicated than those we use in April.

Literature Study Discussions

The first day the group meets with me, I begin by asking, "Well, what do you think?" It is my hope that students come to our discussions ready to share ideas and interpretations. Our first discussion is very informal. I invite students to talk about anything that interests them about the story or any connections they made with the book. I listen carefully to their discussions and take notes to reflect on the major points of interest they address. I will use these notes to offer suggestions for where the discussion may go in subsequent meetings.

As a literary docent, my role in these discussions is to help readers notice things they didn't notice for themselves and to help them experience the work of literature in greater detail than they could on their own. To do so, I offer my ideas later in the discussions and then quite tentatively. I often begin my comments with "I was thinking . . ." or "What I thought before was . . ." I use this language to help children see that I am only *one* voice in the group, not *the* voice. I want my expertise to sneak into these discussions, not come charging in through the front door.

The Literature Study Cycle

In *The Reading Workshop*, I presented my version of the literature study cycle. In the chapter titled "Investigations," I explained the organizational framework I used to allow me to work with *one* group at a time so that I could facilitate each literature study group's discussions. Let me repeat myself: *one* group at a time. As good a teacher as I think I am, I know I can't facilitate seven group discussions at any one time successfully. I believe that literature study groups are more successful when a more experienced, capable reader is part of the group, adding to the discussion in subtle ways but not dominating the proceedings. Because of this, I want to be part of each literature study discussion, and so I created the literature study cycle and rotated students through the various phases, allowing only one group to be discussing their book with me at any given time.

The cycle begins with a pool of readers reading independently and in pairs during the reading workshop. Time and procedures for independent reading, literature explorations, and paired reading are established during September and October and can take a variety of forms, as discussed in previous chapters. From this pool of readers, one group is selected to begin the cycle and launch a literature study group. I meet with this group to discuss their selections and responsibilities, and then I let them begin reading the novel. As this group finishes the book and begins the discussion phase, I can launch a second group. I meet with the first group each day and participate in their discussions as the second group prepares for their discussion. When the first group finishes their discussions, they move on to create a presentation for the class, while the second group moves into the discussion phase. I can launch a third group at this time if I choose, and the cycle continues. Eventually, six students may be preparing for discussions, six may be in a discussion group with me, and six may be working on their literature presentation. As this cycle progresses, there aren't as many readers left in the pool as when we began.

The pace at which readers progress through these phases varies. Some literature discussions go on for a week or more, while others seem to finish in a few days. With the literature study cycle, this doesn't matter. I don't have to worry about one group finishing before another and needing a new book to read. Also, the membership in the various groups changes based on the next book to be read, not who is in the previous group. Because of the intense nature of the preparation and discussions in these groups, I want students going back to their independent reading and literature explorations between literature study groups. I expect every student to be involved in at least one group per semester, or approximately four or five per year. It is important to understand that literature study groups are only one small, but extremely important, component of the reading workshop.

Some Final Thoughts on Literature Study Groups

As reading workshop teachers, we have to have faith in our students that they will be willing to talk about their ideas, generate interpretations, and make connections to their personal experiences. We must also have faith in ourselves as teachers that we will be able respond appropriately to students' questions, interpretations, and ideas. The more we know about children's literature and about ourselves as readers, the better prepared we will be to meet these challenges.

As literature study groups evolve in the reading workshop, I require students to make presentations to the class demonstrating what they learned and experienced during their readings and discussions. These presentations take many forms, including skits, posters, models, and oral presentations. Students have used a variety of artistic media to extend their understandings of a work of literature. When this is all finished, we celebrate our hard work by sharing lunch and some specially selected desserts together. After all the hard work that goes into a literature study discussion, dessert seems a just reward.

Some of you may be asking about the assignment of roles during literature study groups. I simply don't do it. I have written a few articles detailing my decisions not to use role sheets, and you will find these on my website. I don't think assigning roles supports the kinds of discussions I am trying to conduct. I feel they distract students from the piece of literature.

I respect other educators' positions on assigning roles and using role sheets, but I feel that students worry about their assigned roles rather than the piece of literature. Roles can reduce literature discussions to a set of procedures, where students blindly follow their roles without thinking about connections, wonderings, and impressions of a text. I think that assigning roles is more of a crutch for teachers, a way to bypass the often difficult work of deeply knowing a piece of literature and supporting students' unpredictable discussions, than it is a support for students. Usually when literature study groups are not working, it is because of the lack of a solid foundation established during read-alouds and invested discussion strategies. Not all conversations will turn grand, but assigning roles won't guarantee it will happen, either. Without an extensive knowledge of ourselves as readers and the elements and structures of literature, and our willingness to listen and to negotiate meanings with other members of a community of readers, conversations will never turn grand.

Launching Comprehension Strategy Groups

Along with the introduction of literature study groups, I introduce comprehension strategy groups in November as well. However, before I form comprehension strategy groups, I have already been meeting with individual readers, especially those I have observed struggling with their reading and comprehension, and worked with them on various reading strategies to support their comprehension of text. I don't wait until November to help readers read, I just wait to form comprehension strategy groups until I know my readers better.

All readers will be included in comprehension strategy groups, based on their needs, interests, and abilities. Readers who struggle to make sense of texts will get more focused attention than readers who are choosing appropriately, making sense of what they read, and monitoring their comprehension. But *all* readers will take part in these groups.

Early in November, I form comprehension strategy groups based on my continuing assessments of readers. The primary focus of the comprehension strategy groups, hereby referred to as strategy groups, is to demonstrate reading and comprehension strategies to small groups of readers during the act of reading actual texts. Explicit comprehension strategy instruction requires purposeful selection of texts at various levels to provide appropriate amounts of support and challenge for each reader, setting objectives based on readers' needs and abilities, and providing opportunities to apply these strategies in guided practice and independent reading. Although many of the comprehension lessons presented in my book *Lessons in Comprehension: Explicit Instruction in the Reading Workshop* are conducted in whole-group settings, all of the lessons can be used in comprehension strategy groups.

In Chapter 1, I discussed five critical dispositions that readers need to adopt before explicit comprehension strategy instruction is successful. Some of the readers in my strategy groups have not adopted these dispositions; therefore, the focus of my instruction with these students will be these dispositions. For example, if some students are not choosing texts appropriately for independent reading, they may not understand that reading is about making sense. Teaching these struggling readers to simply predict more often or visualize in more detail would be a waste of time. The lessons I conduct with struggling readers may be about selecting appropriate texts, understanding that the goal of reading is to make sense, and helping them be able to talk about what they have read. Once these five dispositions are firmly established, lessons in various comprehension strategies would be appropriate.

In general, the types of lessons I conduct in strategy groups fall into one of the following categories: cognitive, literary, and sociocultural perspectives. Many educational publications regarding comprehension strategy instruction focus almost entirely on the cognitive aspects of comprehension. The "seven magnificent strategies" of summarizing, visualizing, predicting, inferring, determining importance, monitoring comprehension, and asking questions seem to dominate most discussions on comprehension instruction. These cognitively based comprehension strategies are touted as based on scientific reading research, which generally means they have been proven to raise test scores. However, reducing our instruction to only these strategies, limiting one's definition of comprehension to finding meaning *in* the text (see the section "Literary Theory 101" in Chapter 1 for a fuller discussion of this distinction), may do a disservice to our struggling readers. What I am trying to point out here is that comprehension is about more than discovering the main idea that resides a priori in a text, and reading is as much a social process as it is a cognitive operation. Because of this orientation, limiting my readers to the seven magnificent strategies may be dangerous.

In addition to the seven scientifically based cognitive strategies I have mentioned, readers need to be able to empathize with a character, question the authority of an author, and understand how various texts position readers according to race, gender, and social class. Readers need to be able to deal with the ambiguity inherent in a work of literature, remaining open to multiple perspectives and interpretations. These literary and sociocultural strategies are worth demonstrating as well, even if their research base isn't recognized by the powers in charge at the moment.

Some Final Thoughts on Comprehension Strategy Groups

I need to be careful that the comprehension strategies I demonstrate and teach do not become an end in themselves. That is, getting good at predicting does not necessarily mean you are understanding what you are reading. The instruction I provide in my strategy groups must always demonstrate how various comprehension strategies are used to make sense of texts. Our goal is comprehension; therefore, our instruction must always be *in service of meaning*.

Featured Lesson in Comprehension for November: Drawing Inferences

Readers need to understand that meaning comes from sources inside and outside the text as they are reading. The process of using sources outside the literal text is often referred to as drawing inferences. In this series of lessons, I want readers to understand that when they read, they attend to the text, the experiences they have had in their lives, and their knowledge of the world outside the text in order to understand what they are reading. It is not just attention to the text itself that supports comprehension. To conduct this series of lessons, I draw on some Impressions-Connections-Wonderings that we previously created during an author study or literature discussion.

I display the ICW charts we created earlier in the year on the wall and ask students to closely examine them. I ask students to explain whether an entry referred to information in the text, info from an individual's experiences, or someone's knowledge of the world. I use three symbols: a book, for textual sources; a brain, for individuals' experiences; and a globe, for world experiences. I want to call readers' attention to the various ways we connect and respond to texts and the sources of information we use to construct meaning.

Another way to address this issue is to take some reading passages from a standardized test and ask students to tell me, considering only the types of questions being asked, whether the answers would be found in the text itself, could be constructed from a blend of textual information and readers' experiences, or should be answered by thinking about the world outside of the text. Questions that ask for literal details can be answered by looking directly in the text. Questions that ask you to take information from the text and draw conclusions or inferences require readers to attend to the text and infer from their thinking what an appropriate answer would be. Questions about what kind of genre the passage represents require readers to think outside the text about what they know about literature in general and the text itself. If readers can identify the different sources of information needed to answer these questions, maybe they will get better at answering these questions.

Using either strategy, we examine the types of questions or the entries on ICW charts to discuss the three sources of information available to readers. The goal of these lessons is to help readers understand how we draw on sources outside the text in order to comprehend the text.

Literacy Assessments

Expanding Reading Response Notebooks

Even though students have become more comfortable with the format used for their reading response notebooks, I introduce them to a new format designed to expand their response repertoires in their independent reading time. The response notebook format I introduce in November is directly related to the Impressions-Connections-Wonderings charts we have been using during our read-aloud discussions. The new format requires students to react to the text, discuss the connections they make to other texts and their experiences, and ask questions as they read (see Figure 4.5). I want students' homework to be related to what we do in our literature discussions in class.

For students to be successful with this new format for their response notebooks, I must demonstrate how to respond on these forms the same way I introduced the first version of the response notebook. I provide students with an outline of my expectations for this new notebook form, and send a note to parents so they are made aware of what is expected of their children for homework (see Figure 4.6).

Literature Study Discussion Notes

With the introduction of literature study groups, I begin to collect information about the ways in which students participate in these discussions. Using a literature discussion notes form (see Figure 4.7), I keep track of the ideas each member of the group shares and the elements and structures of literature that he is attending to. At the bottom of the assessment form, I list all of the elements, structures, and other literary devices I have been introducing during read-alouds and invested discussions to remind myself what to listen for.

Literature Study Group Self-Evaluation

I want students to be involved in assessing their own performance and growth as readers. One of the assessments I introduce during November is a self-evaluation focusing on members' preparation, participation, and behavior in the literature study group. Each member fills out one of these forms after finishing a literature study group (see Figure 4.8). I read through these self-evaluations and use them to understand how students are perceiving the literature study group format and expectations.

FIG. 4.5 *Expanded Reading Response Notebook*

Reading Response Notebook

Title: _____

Author: _____

Genre: _____

Impressions: _____

_____

_____

Personal Connections: _____

_____

_____

Literary Connections: _____

_____

_____

Wonderings: _____

_____

_____

Additional Ideas: _____

_____

_____

FIG. 4.6 *New Expectations for the Reading Response Notebook*

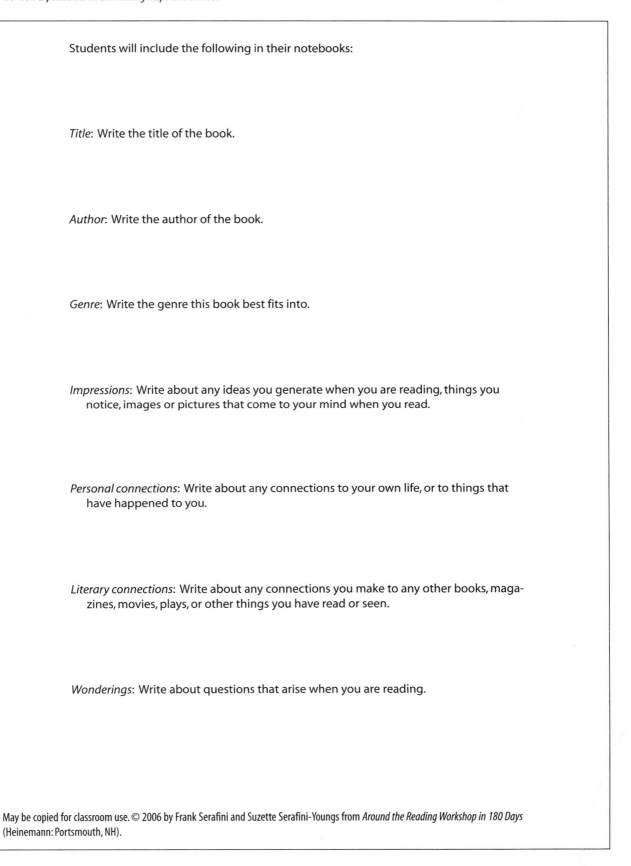

Students will include the following in their notebooks:

Title: Write the title of the book.

Author: Write the author of the book.

Genre: Write the genre this book best fits into.

Impressions: Write about any ideas you generate when you are reading, things you notice, images or pictures that come to your mind when you read.

Personal connections: Write about any connections to your own life, or to things that have happened to you.

Literary connections: Write about any connections you make to any other books, magazines, movies, plays, or other things you have read or seen.

Wonderings: Write about questions that arise when you are reading.

FIG. 4.7 *Literature Discussion Notes*

Literature Discussion Notes

Book Title: _____

Date: _____

Group Members	Comments Offered
1.	
2.	
3.	
4.	
5.	

symbols – emotional response – justifications – character – themes – setting – metaphors – mood – point of view – episodes – tension/resolution

FIG. 4.8 *Literature Study Self-Evaluation*

Literature Study Self-Evaluation

Name: _____

Date: _____

Book Read: _____

1. What did I do to help my group work together?

2. Did I use my book and book log to discuss the book?

3. What ideas did I share with my group?

4. How did I help others understand the book we read?

5. What did I do to help with the presentation?

6. Anything else that should be mentioned?

Connections to the Writing Workshop

Units of study focusing on particular authors, genres, what it means to be a writer, and the writer's notebook have helped organize the writing curriculum. As expectations rise in the reading workshop, so do the expectations we hold for our students as writers.

As we spend more time studying an author or illustrator in the reading workshop, I also focus on particular authors in the writing workshop. We use authors as mentors throughout the writing workshop, encouraging students to extend their study of a particular author to examining that author's writing style and the craft elements he or she uses to construct works of literature. In the reading workshop, we teach students to read like proficient readers; in the writing workshop, we teach them to read like talented writers.

Reading like a writer focuses the reader's attention on elements and structures from a different perspective. Not only do we want students to be able to read and understand personal narratives, but we want students to write personal narratives of their own, drawing on the craft and techniques of quality authors. Reading books about writers, using authors as writing mentors, using the literature we read to stimulate ideas for our writing, understanding the characteristics and boundaries of genres, and investigating the craft and techniques of quality writing are just a few of the connections between the reading and the writing workshops.

Things I Hope to See, Hear, and Have Established by Month's End

1. Students are using and discussing the reading comprehension strategies I have been teaching. These strategies are not an end in themselves; they need to be used to make sense of what is being read.

2. Instruction is conducted in a variety of settings and groupings, including whole group, small groups, pairs, and individuals.

3. Language arts standards are being read and used to help guide curricular decisions. Standards are one part of the negotiation process when developing reading instruction experiences.

4. I want to have completed at least one literature study group by the end of the month. So much time has gone into getting them set up and started that I want to have a few students experience the full literature study cycle by the end of the month. It is my hope that the completion of one group, and their presentation and enthusiasm, will entice others to participate in literature study groups.

5. I am using think-alouds to demonstrate my own reading strategies to my students. Finding language to explain what happens in our minds when we read a text is a challenge. I hope to have some common language established for describing various strategies by the end of the month.

6. Students are beginning to see me as only *one* voice in our literature discussions, not *the* voice. I want students to feel comfortable telling each other what they

think. My favorites are just that, mine. My students must find their own favorites for themselves.

7. I have been able to share my own reading life with my students, and they have begun to share their reading lives with me. In becoming a community of readers, we have to share what we read, why we read, where we read, and when we find time to read. Inviting students to read and experience literature is a noble gesture, but it's the acceptance of those invitations that makes the reading workshop successful.

Ideas for Further Reflection

By the time we get literature study and comprehension strategy groups up and running, we tend to focus on what students are doing, not just what we are teaching. I recommend tape-recording a literature study or comprehension strategy group every once in a while, maybe one day a month, to listen to your role in these groups. I take these tapes home and listen to them, jotting down a few notes for myself about what I notice about my participation in the group.

Closing Thoughts

It is important to keep in mind that literature study and comprehension strategy groups are simply two components in the reading workshop. They may be important components, ones that we spend a great deal of time working on, but they are only two of the many components in a reading workshop. Their success depends on the foundation and procedures that have been established in October and September. The more we support readers' interpretations and sharing of ideas in our whole-group discussions and read-alouds, the more of these behaviors will trickle down into independent reading and small-group discussions.

Exploring Postmodern Picture Books

Introduction

In November, I wanted students to investigate a selection of picture books that contained postmodern or metafictive elements. Postmodern picture books, with nonlinear structures, surrealistic images, and self-referential text, challenge readers to interact with the written text, illustrations, and elements of design and ask readers to play an active role in the construction of meaning during the reading process.

Focus

In this six-week unit, I introduced students to twenty picture books that contained postmodern or metafictive elements. Postmodern picture books:

❖ expand the conventional boundaries of picture book formats

❖ contain nonlinear structures and story lines

❖ contain new or unfamiliar structures

❖ offer multiple perspectives or realities to the reader

❖ contain elements of ambiguity or irony

❖ contain surrealistic images

Goals and Objectives

❖ attend to textual and visual elements to construct meaning

❖ negotiate meaning within a social context

❖ introduce students to a variety of reading strategies to enhance their comprehension of postmodern texts

❖ learn to navigate postmodern texts

Opening Ceremonies

The amount of time needed for reading and discussion of these books was greater than in other units; therefore, we briefly shared what was happening in our lives, adding to the expedition wall, and immediately began reading the series of postmodern picture books.

For this unit we relied heavily on a walking journal, providing students with opportunities to respond to literature and one another's ideas. We called it the "weird book walking journal." To launch the walking journal, I recorded my thoughts on *Voices in the Park* (Browne 2001) and passed it along. Each student was then required to make an entry at least once a week. I read the journal each night and then shared ideas with the students during the next day's discussion. I used the journal as an impetus for reading lessons, an assessment tool, and a place for students to negotiate ideas and interpretations.

Cornerstone Text

The cornerstone text for this unit was *Voices in the Park*, by Anthony Browne. It is a picture book telling the story of an outing to a park from four perspectives. Anthony Browne tells this story through four distinct voices: a mother and her son and a father and his daughter. The voices are presented separately, yet they are intricately connected to tell the story of how class, prejudice, control, hope, and friendship determine the perspectives of four different people. Anthony Browne uses detailed illustrations to not only support the story structure but extend it as well. *Voices in the Park* contains a nonlinear text structure, multiple perspectives, ambiguity, a sarcastic tone, surrealistic imagery, unique treatment of time, hidden images, symbolism, antiauthoritarian language, and a juxtaposition of unrelated visual images.

Launching the Unit of Study

To launch this unit, I began by thinking aloud to introduce students to the idea of navigating through postmodern or nonlinear texts. Students were familiar with some of the titles, yet they weren't used to attending closely to both visual and textual clues to make meaning. Before I presented the first book to the class, I read and responded to the text on my own. I paid close attention to how I navigated through the text so I could call students' attention to features and structures within the text.

Next, I conducted a think-aloud with *Voices in the Park* in front of the class. I described how I was attending to various features of the text and the interplay between the text and the illustrations. In addition, students offered ideas while I read. After I read the text aloud, we discussed the book at length. We created an ICW chart and continued our discussion about *Voices in the Park*. During their independent reading, students read some of the postmodern picture books I had provided.

On the second day, we read *Voices in the Park* again. This time, I used different-color markers to highlight the progression of my students' thoughts. The day before, some students investigated the hidden and unrelated images in the book and had ideas to share. After reading it aloud, we passed the book around and shared our observations of the illustrations with each other. We added these ideas to the ICW chart.

On the third day, I introduced students to an invested discussion strategy called *disrupting the text*. The purpose of the strategy is to separate the text from the illustrations to investigate each in turn. Students were attending to the illustrations more than the textual features during our discussions. Because Browne uses his illustrations to expand the story, I wanted to provide an opportunity to investigate the illustrations by themselves.

First, I made a colored copy of each illustration from the book, removing the text. Then I placed the color copies of the illustrations up on a board in storyboard fashion. I asked students to make observations in their literature response logs. This was a full-hour activity; students worked in pairs and rotated around the illustrations. As students discussed the illustrations, I made notes on the conversations that were taking place and the kinds of strategies students were using to make sense of the illustrations. I eventually discussed my observations with the students.

On the fourth day, students attended to the text only. I typed the text on a couple of sheets of paper and made copies for every student. I had students pair up and I gave them time to investigate how the textual features added to their interpretations.

The next day we read the book in a readers' theatre performance, using four student volunteers who had taken the text home to practice their voices. They used their voices and intonation to represent their interpretations of the text. Students read their parts as if they were the characters speaking.

Each day's discussion was different. By attending to the complete book, then just the illustrations, then the text alone, I invited students to interpret the book from a variety of perspectives. By disrupting the text, students attended to various components of the book to varying degrees.

Explicit Instruction
After reading the cornerstone text, I read a new postmodern picture book each day for the next four weeks, completing ICW charts and making connections across various titles. I began by reading and responding to each of the postmodern picture books myself prior to reading it aloud to students. I made notes and considered what would be an appropriate selection to continue and extend the discussion from the previous day. With each new book, I determined what would be an appropriate strategy or comprehension lesson to present. I have included two examples in the following sections.

Attending to the Front Matter   Authors and illustrators of postmodern picture books use every part of the book to convey meaning. As I became familiar with these books myself, I realized how much information the authors and illustrators presented in the front matter, for example, the book jacket, the dedication, the title page, and the end pages. During my read-alouds, I noticed I was not attending to all of these features and that most of my students were skipping over the front matter as well. My own understanding of these texts was greatly enhanced once I began attending to these peritextual features.

When I noticed this in my own reading, I had already read eight of the twenty books aloud with my students. So, we divided into eight groups and students went back and looked at all the front-matter features in the books we had read, and then we shared any new information or ideas generated from this investigation. Students made connections between David Macaulay and David Wiesner based on their dedications, and we used the front matter to help us understand the book *Black and White* (Macaulay 1990) a little better. Attending to the front matter became an important reading strategy for all of us. I began to observe students attending to these features in many other kinds of texts even after the unit had concluded.

Inferring   It became apparent that teaching the strategy of inferring would be very important, as postmodern picture book authors and illustrators leave many gaps for the reader to fill in, requiring readers to infer meaning from the text and their experiences.

I used this opportunity to discuss, model, and practice with students inferential thinking as a reading strategy. I used the ICW charts of many of the texts we'd previously read and had students discuss how they had already used the strategy in many places. We discussed how we came to various ideas and the differences between literal recall and inferential thinking.

I modeled how a reader fills in the gaps with background knowledge, with information from the text, and with ideas about the world around her. In their reading response logs I asked students to make special note of each time they inferred meaning. I also asked them to analyze what knowledge they used to fill in the gaps and to substantiate their inferences with evidence from the text or personal experiences.

Many of the reading lessons I presented were spontaneously created, relating directly to what the students were attempting to do with these texts. I met with small groups and individuals as they worked their way through these texts so I could scaffold their reading practices.

Workshop Experiences

During workshop time, students were invited to reread any book that I had read aloud, research information about any text, author, or illustrator, record ideas in the walking journal, or read and discuss a different postmodern picture book independently, in pairs, or in small groups.

Many students formed their own groups to investigate particular authors, illustrators, and texts. For example, one group spent four days with the book *Bright and Early Thursday Evening,* by Audrey Wood (1996), even looking through her website for further clues to the text. Some students investigated how Anthony Browne created symmetrical designs in many of his illustrations. Other groups became intrigued with various illustrations and researched how to use visual clues to interpret picture books. Students soon realized that their understanding was enhanced by these connections to the authors, and thus more students began to investigate as well. Students researched, responded in their reading response logs and then shared with the group at the end or beginning of each reading workshop. These groups were organized by students based on their interests and interpretive repertoires.

To tie the unit together we decided to create a comparison chart. We began by discussing possible categories to compare across titles. The categories we selected were ambiguity, sarcastic tone, treatment of time, hidden images, surrealistic imagery, multiple perspectives, characters, setting, language, and symbolism. Once the chart was created, students formed small groups and proposed five books they would be interested in comparing and then explained why they chose those books. Students completed their comparison charts and shared their interpretations and understandings of postmodern elements with their classmates, their families, and our principal.

Culminating Experience Postmodern Writing Piece

As students researched particular authors and books, they discovered tips on how to write their own postmodern picture books. For example, Audrey Wood provided tips on her website about how to create a tangled tale. Students requested to write their own postmodern pieces as a culminating project. Students worked alone or in pairs and chose one of the books in the unit to be their mentor piece. Students created tangled tales like Audrey and Don Wood's, circular stories like David Macaulay's, and multiple-perspective pieces like Anthony Browne's. Students realized how difficult it was to create these stories and came to a greater appreciation for the authors and their work.

Closing the Window

This unit was exciting and challenging for all of us. Many students enjoyed the texts, while others found them weird and too difficult to interpret. The textual and visual features of these picture books required readers to interact with these texts in ways that students were unaccustomed to. I found myself learning about how to read and interpret these texts along with my students. We investigated the nuances of postmodern texts and developed a passion for them. We developed a greater appreciation for the writing and artistic talents of these authors and illustrators as we took an in-depth look at the techniques and elements employed in creating postmodern picture books.

CHAPTER 5

December—Exploring Expository Texts

Ninety percent of answering questions is anticipating which ones will be asked, having a sense of what's important, and being interested enough in something to pose the questions for yourself in advance.
—RICHARD RUSSO, *STRAIGHT MAN*

Introduction

As autumn gives way to winter, most of the major components have been introduced into the reading workshop. From here on through the end of the year, it is more about fine-tuning our instructional repertoire and challenging students to attend in different ways to the texts they read than it is about adding new components and procedures to the reading workshop.

Most intermediate-grade readers spend as much time with expository texts as they do with fictional narratives. As people get older, expository texts become a larger percentage of their daily reading. In fact, most school librarians will attest that at least 50 percent of their library's circulation is nonfiction or expository texts. It is for these reasons that I focus this entire chapter on the uses of expository texts in the reading workshop and content areas. I describe how I get students to attend to and understand the various elements and structures of expository texts, discuss various expository text formats, describe appropriate reading strategies for expository texts, and talk about how we use expository texts differently from fictional literature.

DECEMBER CHAPTER OUTLINE

December Lessons and Learning Experiences
❖ Selection Criteria for Expository Texts
❖ Challenges of Comprehending Expository Texts
❖ Types of Expository Texts
❖ Expository Text Structures and Components
❖ Approaching Expository Texts
❖ Rules of Notice, Significance, and Credibility
❖ Reading Images, Diagrams, Charts, and Graphs
❖ Building Vocabulary
Featured Lesson in Comprehension for December: Asking Quality Questions
Literacy Assessments
❖ Reader Response Notebook Checklist
Connections to the Writing Workshop
❖ Expository Texts as a Genre

I fear that I may have unintentionally demonstrated or suggested that up until December I read only fictional narratives with my students. Although I have focused on the reading of fiction and comprehension strategies that support the reading of literature during my discussions of the reading workshop so far, I have also been reading and discussing expository texts in other areas of the curriculum with my students.

Reading and reading instruction take place in a variety of contexts throughout the school day. The experiences provided in the reading workshop include literature and expository texts, but expository texts and literature are also used to introduce mathematical concepts, explore historical events, understand topics in science and health, and make us aware of current events in social studies. In other words, literature and expository texts are used across the curriculum each and every day in my classroom. In the reading workshop we work to develop students' literary literacies, while in other times of the day, literature and expository texts are used to support content area literacies.

I have chosen to use the term *expository texts* rather than *nonfiction* for the following reasons. First, using *nonfiction* versus *fiction* refers to the truth value of the information provided in the text rather than the structure of the text or the style of writing used to present information. Nonfiction versus fiction is based on the relationship between reality and the way reality is represented in written text. Second, nonfiction texts often contain elements of fiction, and fictional texts, for example, historical fiction, contain factual information about historical events. Third, the distinction between fiction and nonfiction focuses on elements of the text, not the stance a reader assumes. Louise Rosenblatt (1978) described how readers assume different stances regardless of the type of text they are reading. Readers can approach an informational text aesthetically, enjoying the lived-through experience of reading the text, or approach a work of literature efferently, attending to various bits of information to take away from their reading.

I prefer to talk about the differences between *expository* texts, texts that are written to convey information, and *narrative* texts, those that are written to tell a story. In general, expository texts do not contain characters or a plot, whereas narrative texts do. Narrative texts employ setting, plot, and characters to tell their story and create tension in order to keep the reader reading. Authors of informational texts write texts to convey information about a particular topic.

Chapters in narrative texts usually end in tension, whereas chapters in expository texts usually end in a summary. We continue reading expository texts because we are interested in the topic, not because we need to find out what happens next to the main character. An author's intentions and the structures of the text, including written text and visual images, are different when used in narratives than in expository texts, regardless of the stance the reader assumes.

Of course, there are numerous examples of texts available today that are blurring even these distinctions. For example, books in the Magic School Bus series contain factual information, presented in sidebars and other components, in addition to a narrative story line concerning Ms. Frizzle and her students. Readers are required to navigate both narrative and expository writing in order to comprehend these books. Some students read Magic School Bus books because they are looking for information to take away, assuming an efferent stance; others read them because they want to follow the adventures of Ms. Frizzle and her students, adopting more of an aesthetic stance.

In addition to the different characteristics of expository texts, there are different reasons teachers use these texts in the classroom and different reasons readers engage with expository texts. Readers read them to get information while teachers may use them to awaken curiosity. Teachers may introduce students to expository texts because they know that a majority of the passages students will confront on standardized tests are expository in nature. Teachers also use expository texts as models for the research papers and projects they will require students to create in content area subjects.

There are numerous characteristics of expository texts that need to be brought to students' attention in order to help them comprehend and use these texts more effectively. Most expository texts contain a variety of genres in a single text. In one expository text, there may be short biographical pieces, graphs, captions, narrative sections, visual images, diagrams, charts, sidebars containing informational text, characters, and glossaries. Helping students navigate the challenges of expository texts is the focus of this chapter.

December Lessons and Learning Experiences

Before we can begin to read and study expository texts in the reading workshop, we must select texts for our classroom library and various units of study. I have studied numerous criteria for selecting quality expository texts, and I present a brief review of this research for you to consider as you begin collecting expository texts for your classroom.

Selection Criteria for Expository Texts

❖ *Accuracy of information.* A primary consideration in selecting expository texts is the accuracy of the information provided. Books that are outdated or provide misleading information should be reconsidered for inclusion in one's collection. Providing multiple sources for the information presented, being tentative when presenting conflicting theories, and providing alternative resources to check on the accuracy of the information (e.g., websites, phone numbers, brochures) are important aspects of this criterion.

❖ *Authority of authors.* Authors of expository texts need to do in-depth research to obtain current and factual information about their subject matter. When an author or illustrator has established a reputation for accuracy and depth of research, for example, Russell Freedman, Jim Murphy, James Cross Giblin, and David Adler, it is easier to count on the information he or she provides.

❖ *Appropriateness of material.* Controversial topics are often presented in expository text formats. Books on sexually transmitted diseases, the Holocaust, violent criminals, and natural disasters may not be appropriate for younger audiences. Although I believe that an accomplished, discerning teacher can present controversial material in an appropriate context and help readers with the challenges inherent in many topics, I still feel that some content may not be suitable for specific audiences. Teachers need to read through and review the materials they gather for their classroom libraries and units of study before providing these materials for students.

❖ *Organization of information.* Expository texts that are confusing to read are often confusing because of the way the information is presented and organized. Chapter titles, headings, and reading guides help readers navigate the information in expository texts. Most quality expository texts are logically organized and provide resources like indices, glossaries, tables of contents, chapter summaries, and graphic organizers to make reading easier and information more accessible.

❖ *Quality of images and visual design.* The quality of the visual images presented in expository texts has increased tremendously with the advances made in digital imagery and computer publishing. Computers used to publish expository texts allow diagrams and photographs to be reproduced in exacting detail. The quality of the visual elements presented in expository texts has come a long way from the How and Why Wonder Books of my youth.

❖ *Quality of written text.* Not only have the images contained in expository texts improved dramatically, but so has the quality of the writing. The writing in contemporary expository texts does not sound like an outdated encyclopedia anymore. Texts are written by talented, skillful writers, drawing on rhetorical techniques to present information. Original sources of information, for example, diaries, journals, letters, and news reports, are included with the author's commentaries and analysis. When expository texts contain better writing, readers read more, learn more, and return to these texts more frequently.

Selecting expository texts for the reading workshop has been made easier by the variety and quality of expository texts being published. Using the criteria just described does not guarantee a book will be well loved or chosen by students more frequently. But by attending to these criteria, teachers become more critical consumers of expository texts. Unfortunately, poorly written and organized texts are still being published. It takes a discerning teacher, one who spends time reviewing the variety of expository texts published and made available in libraries and bookstores, to find quality materials to provide in her reading workshop.

Challenges of Comprehending Expository Texts

For many young readers, expository texts can be challenging to read and comprehend. Expository texts have unique structures and components, qualitatively different from the narrative texts that many young readers have been repeatedly exposed to. Expository texts require readers to call forth background knowledge from the content areas during the act of reading in order to comprehend what is being presented. Students' lack of experience in reading expository texts and limited knowledge of content area subjects present readers with unique challenges.

In addition, the specialized vocabulary of content area subjects requires students to become familiar with the concepts of science and math in order to comprehend expository texts. For example, the vocabulary used in expository texts often demands closer attention than the vocabulary used in narratives. Misreading the word *gravy* for *gravity* in a story may not matter, but in a science text, it would confuse even Sir Isaac Newton.

In the same manner that literature is introduced and shared with readers, expository texts need to be read aloud with students and made accessible in the classroom library. However, most classroom libraries tend to include more fictional literature than expository texts. In most cases, unless a particular content area topic is being studied, expository texts are rarely read aloud and discussed. This presents several implications for instruction focusing on expository texts.

First, teachers need to familiarize students with the structures, components, and writing styles of expository texts. This is accomplished by reading aloud and discussing these texts with greater regularity. We can't expect readers to become proficient readers of texts they rarely encounter. Second, the vocabulary used in expository texts requires extensive background knowledge to understand the concepts presented. Teachers need to be aware of the vocabulary presented in expository texts and provide additional support for readers new to these concepts and words. Finally, when we read expository texts during a science or social studies unit of study, the focus is usually on the content of the text, not its structures or components. We need to teach readers how to approach an expository text as a genre and format in and of itself, regardless of the topic being investigated. Teachers who teach in a departmentalized approach need to remember that they are not just teaching science but teaching students to *read* science.

Types of Expository Texts

Within the wide-ranging format of expository texts, there are many types of texts that are appropriate for intermediate-grade readers. There are concept books, focusing on a single topic or subject, question-and-answer books, alphabet books, magazines, reference materials, photo-essays, newspapers, how-to books, recipe books, instructional manuals, activity and experiment books, informational storybooks, biographies, and autobiographies. Each of these texts may contain several different structures, components, styles of writing, visual images, diagrams, and design features. Unfortunately, there is not enough space in this book to describe all of the structures and writing styles that are contained in expository texts. Instead, I will address a few of the prominent structures and components of expository texts to help you get started.

Expository Text Structures and Components

There are numerous ways that expository texts can be organized. Here are some of the most common organizational structures:

❖ *Question and answer.* This is a simple, yet highly effective way of organizing information, in which a question is posed and highlighted, and subsequently an answer is given. The question-and-answer format makes finding information easy and provides a basic structure for students to organize their own research information.

❖ *Sequential or chronological.* Historical information is often organized into time periods or chronologically sequenced. This allows readers to contextualize particular events and understand what came before and after important dates.

❖ *Cause and effect*. In addition to historical events, science concepts are often organized into cause-and-effect relationships. An effect is listed and causes are posited. A direct relationship is often assumed in this format, where one event directly affects another. While this may reduce the complexity of some relationships, it does organize information for readers to access easily.

❖ *Descriptive writing*. Most expository texts are written in straightforward descriptive language. The narrator's or author's perspective is made transparent. In other words, facts are simply presented as facts. Although most authors of expository texts work hard to present truths, all facts are subject to interpretation and perspective, and readers of expository texts should be taught to read with this in mind.

❖ *Blended structures*. Most expository texts are actually blends of many of the previously mentioned structures. A single book may contain biographical information, time lines, descriptive paragraphs, questions and answers, and cause-and-effect relationships. Each section of these texts must be addressed individually, drawing on various strategies and information to comprehend the text. One of the most important strategies to be learned by readers of expository texts is how to identify these various structures and approach them in ways to comprehend what is being presented.

In addition to the various ways that expository texts are structured, there are numerous components that teachers need to call students' attention to when reading for information. Some of the most common components of expository texts are:

1. titles and covers
2. sidebars
3. tables of contents
4. author's notes and introductions
5. glossaries
6. indices
7. reading guides
8. chapter summaries
9. graphic organizers
10. diagrams, maps, charts, and graphs
11. visual images
12. headings, labels, and subheadings
13. captions

In some ways, each of these components can be thought of as a separate sub-genre. Captions, for example, have distinct characteristics that make them different from headings and labels. In order to teach students how to approach and comprehend information presented in these components, I make overhead copies of examples of each component and talk with students about how information is presented, what is important to attend to, and what strategies will help readers make sense of the information. I call attention to the features of each component and provide numerous examples from books, newspapers, magazines, and textbooks. We discuss how information is presented in each component and how to approach reading it.

Approaching Expository Texts

Through the use of think-alouds, I demonstrate how I approach an expository text, explaining my purposes for reading a particular text and what I attend to as I read it. I demonstrate how I attend to the peritextual information and scan the entire text before reading any one section. I show students how to approach a reading guide or table of contents. Each of the lessons I conduct focuses on a particular component and demonstrates what proficient readers of expository texts do when approaching such a text.

Rules of Notice, Significance, and Credibility

All visual elements of a piece of literature (text, images, illustrations, headings, chapter titles, epigraphs) do not provide the same amount of information to the reader. Peter Rabinowitz, in his book *Before Reading* (1997), suggests that readers follow certain rules when reading literary texts. Taking his ideas and adapting them for use with expository texts, I introduce three categories of rules that will help students understand how to make sense of expository texts. The three categories of rules I discuss are (1) rules of notice, (2) rules of significance, and (3) rules of credibility. I have taken some liberties with Rabinowitz's literary theories, and any discrepancies that may arise should be entirely blamed on my ignorance.

The first category of rules, rules of notice, implies that certain words, phrases, and visual elements of a text are privileged over other words and images, and that readers should attend to particular portions of text more than others when reading. Novice readers often give equal attention to all elements of an expository text. We need to demonstrate how we dedicate our attention to particular elements in an expository text over other elements. For example, subheadings and particular vocabulary words are often italicized or in bold print, signaling to the reader their importance in a section of text. Readers need to know that these words are highlighted for a purpose and deserve special attention. In discussing rules of notice, I teach students to attend to how information is presented, what part of the text is more important, and what may be skimmed over. This is not a purely objective process, where rules of notice can be simply stated and applied; rather, these rules are contingent upon the reader's purpose for reading.

Rules of significance take what we have attended to or noticed and construct significance or attach meanings to those components. In other words, we realize that the things we noticed play a significant role in the construction of meanings. Once we have attended to historical events, dates, and characters, we must interpret them and discuss and negotiate their meanings, or significance.

Rules of credibility was not one of Rabinowitz's original categories, but is actually an amalgam of several ideas he presented. In addressing expository texts, rules of credibility focus on the value placed on particular statements or images presented in the text. Multiple sources of information, presented from a variety of perspectives, should be given more credibility than a single source or uncorroborated statement. The reputation of the researcher or author also lends credibility to what is presented. The final decision about what to believe and what to attend to is the reader's. Based on their knowledge of the world, readers play a part in deciding what is worth taking away from their transactions with particular expository texts.

These three categories of rules help readers approach an expository text not as a container of facts to be memorized, but as a presentation of perspectives and information to be interpreted and evaluated. Reading expository texts is as much a process of interpretation and comprehension as reading literature is. Even though the nature of the texts may vary, the meanings constructed remain open for negotiation and revision.

Reading Images, Diagrams, Charts, and Graphs

We read and interpret the diagrams, charts, maps, graphs, and other visual images in an expository text in much the same way we make sense of the written information. We look at information, represented in words, symbols, numbers, or images, and make sense of it based on our prior experiences, linguistic knowledge, and knowledge of the world. Outside of school, in the activities many adolescents engage in, visual images and hypertext play a prominent role. We can capitalize on their knowledge and experience with these images and representations when teaching them to approach the various visual components of expository texts.

There are many authentic examples of charts, graphs, diagrams, and visual images available to draw upon for instruction. I use the charts and graphs found in many newspapers, especially *USA Today*, to call students' attention to how information is represented in these texts. I make overhead copies of numerous charts and diagrams to share with students. After an initial examination of a particular component, image, or diagram, we look at the chart or graph and try to answer the following questions:

1. What is the subject of this component?
2. Why do you think the publisher put it in there?
3. What can you learn about the subject in this component?
4. What is challenging about reading this component?
5. What strategies would you suggest for other readers approaching this component?

By presenting this series of lessons, I am trying to demonstrate to readers that we interpret texts, visual images, and other components in much the same way as written text when we are exploring expository texts. These lessons provide a shared experience to call readers' attention to the various components and structures of expository texts.

Before moving on to the featured comprehension lesson for December, I want to discuss the role of vocabulary instruction and how this fits in the reading workshop, especially within a unit of study on expository texts.

Building Vocabulary

When reading either expository texts or literature, one's vocabulary knowledge plays an important role in comprehending. Before making specific instructional suggestions for teaching and developing vocabulary, I would like to briefly present some of the research on vocabulary development and instruction.

Research suggests that vocabulary instruction done through inquiry projects in content area reading and meaningful contexts is more effective than isolated memorizing or defining of predetermined targeted words. Teachers call students' conscious awareness to particular vocabulary words in the context of reading, writing, and content area instruction, actively involving them in the processing of new words. Classroom discussions pertaining to particular vocabulary words is used to establish relationships to and among words. It is the process of constructing and discussing word meanings, not simply memorizing dictionary entries, that helps readers expand their vocabularies. When specific purposes for acquiring particular vocabulary words can be demonstrated and students understand the reasons for studying particular words, explicit vocabulary instruction has been shown to be an effective instructional strategy.

Common sense holds, and contemporary research demonstrates, that there is a strong correlation between the amount of reading a person does and the depth and breadth of one's general vocabulary. The more a person reads, the larger his sight and working vocabularies. Classroom discussions calling attention to environmental print, written language demonstrations, and opportunities to read extensively have all been shown to contribute to readers' vocabulary development.

Readers are able to infer meanings of many words through the context in which they appear. However, this assumes readers are actively making sense of what they read and are attending to vocabulary in doing so. Reading for pleasure exposes readers to new vocabulary words but does not guarantee that readers will attend to new words or seek out their definitions.

If instruction focusing on developing readers' vocabularies assumes prominence over constructing meaning in transaction with texts or responding aesthetically to what has been read, we may distract readers from the primary objective of reading, namely, comprehending and enjoying what is read. We don't want readers to spend so much time defining or memorizing individual words that they no longer pay attention to what they are reading. However, as educators we must remain cognizant of the fact that without an extensive vocabulary, comprehending expository texts can be challenging.

So, you may ask, what does this mean for the reading workshop? As stated earlier, there is a difference between instruction that focuses on teaching *specific* vocabulary words and instruction that tries to expand one's *general* vocabulary. Steven Stahl (1986) described three principles of vocabulary instruction: (1) include both definitional information and contextual information about each word's meaning, (2) actively involve children in attending to and investigating new vocabulary words, and (3) use discussion to teach word meanings. New vocabulary words are learned in meaningful contexts and purposeful activities. The more we can contextually ground vocabulary instruction on specific words, for specific purposes, the better our efforts will be rewarded.

From my review of the research and past experiences in elementary classrooms, I believe extensive reading of texts and using new words in classroom discussions are the two best ways to develop *general* vocabularies. Explicit instruction does not have as much impact as reading and discussion for developing general vocabularies. However, explicit instruction that focuses on *specific* vocabularies may be worth a teacher's time and effort. New words are learned through use and discussion in a purposeful context. For example, introducing the terms *igneous, metamorphic,* and *sedimentary* while studying geology may help readers understand what they are reading and studying. These words represent important geological concepts, and students will learn to use these words in the purposeful context of the unit of study on geology, not as isolated vocabulary words. Any words that I plan on introducing and teaching explicitly had better be important words for understanding concepts in a specific unit of study.

We learn to talk like the people we spend the most time with. Teachers learn to talk like other teachers, and geologists learn to talk like other geologists, appropriating the vocabularies of their discipline. In this way, specific vocabularies are rarely learned separately from the developing understandings of what readers are studying.

Featured Comprehension Strategy Lesson for December: Asking Quality Questions

We can learn a great deal about a reader's comprehension abilities by listening to the questions she asks before, during, and after reading a text. The epigraph in this chapter suggests that one's ability to ask quality questions depends on one's interests in, and knowledge of, a particular subject. The more we know about a topic, the better the questions we ask.

Asking questions is an important comprehension strategy for paying attention to what one is reading, anticipating where a story is going, and noticing what is included in the text or left for the reader to fill in. Most quality questions asked during the act of reading focus on information that is not directly included in the written text or images. In other words, inferential questions are more effective in promoting comprehension than literal recall questions. Literal recall questions measure a reader's memory, not necessarily his ability to comprehend. I want readers to pose and answer questions that force them to integrate information from the text, their lives, and the world.

In order to demonstrate to students what constitutes a quality question, I return to some of the Impressions-Connections-Wonderings charts that I have previously created with students. We begin this lesson by looking at the types of questions we asked in response to an expository text, included in the "Wonderings" column of an ICW. Much the same as in the lesson focusing on drawing inferences, I use three symbols, a book, a brain, and a globe, to indicate whether the question can be answered by referring to the text, a reader's experience, or knowledge of the world. We rearrange the questions into three groups and talk about how the questions in these three categories differ.

Certainly, I want readers asking literal, text-based questions; however, this type of question doesn't necessarily lead to critical thinking or comprehension, it just tests one's ability to recall words and information from the text. Literal recall questions privilege the text as the arbiter of meaning, requiring the reader to defer to what is contained directly in the text rather than consider her own knowledge and experience to construct meaning with the text. It is the difference between getting meaning *from* text and constructing meaning *with* text. I believe this difference is significant and not simply philosophical hairsplitting. Inferential, critical questions require the reader to assimilate information from a variety of sources, including the text, the reader's experiences, and his knowledge of the world. These are the kinds of quality questions I want readers, and teachers, to ask.

Using the three perspectives on reading I described in Chapter 1—modernist, transactional, and sociocultural—I provide readers with examples of the types of questions each perspective may support (see Figure 5.1).

The types of questions we pose as teachers have a profound effect on the types of questions students ask. If we ask text-based, literal recall questions, with answers that we already know or that can be found directly in the text, then the readers in our charge

FIG. 5.1 *Three Categories of Questions*

Three Categories of Questions

Questions from a Modernist Perspective

What is the main idea of the story?

What is the author trying to tell you?

How did the author describe the character?

What is the setting of the story?

What are the primary personality traits of the main character?

Why do you think the author wrote the story?

Questions from a Transactional Perspective

What do you think this story is about?

How did you feel as you read the story?

What personal connections did you make as you were reading?

Does this story remind you of any other stories?

Do the characters remind you of anyone?

Can you relate to the challenges the characters faced? How so?

How would you have acted if you were the main character?

How does the book relate to your life experiences?

Questions from a Sociocultural Perspective

Are any of the characters privileged or marginalized?

What attitudes or worldviews are endorsed or diminished?

What assumptions are taken for granted?

How are critical issues (race, gender, class, ethnicity) dealt with?

What alternative interpretations are possible?

What readers would best identify with this story?

Did you feel like an insider or outsider as you read this story?

will do the same. Here are some recommendations for the types of questions teachers should ask and the role these questions play in the reading workshop:

❖ Ask only questions with integrity—honest questions to which you don't know the answers before asking them. Students can tell when they are being set up by a question. Asking questions to which you know the answers leads to playing the "guess what's in my head" game that we have all experienced in school. When we ask honest questions, we get honest answers.

❖ Asking questions in response to students' ideas is better than always asking questions in front of their ideas. If we can get students talking about a book, the questions we ask in response to their ideas tend to help clarify or expand ideas and focus on what interests students, not what interests the teacher.

❖ The questions we ask, and demonstrate for our students to ask, should lead to further inquiry and thoughtfulness. Literal recall questions are dead-end questions, quickly resolved by reference to the exact words in the text. Open-ended questions lead to better discussions and more complex, interesting interpretations.

❖ We should encourage students to ask more questions than we do during literature discussions. The questions that students ask provide insights into their thinking and comprehension and are usually honest questions that indicate what they are thinking about.

❖ We have to demonstrate and discuss the differences between robust questions, those that lead to further inquiry and thinking, and superficial questions that lead nowhere. If we don't call students' attention to the differences among various types of questions, they will assume that all questions have the same value and should be asked in equal frequency.

❖ Teachers should offer statements in response to a text they are reading as frequently as they pose questions to students. We naturally offer comments about a text after reading it when we are talking with a friend or colleague. Why don't we do the same with our students? Offering a statement can elicit as much response from students as asking a quality question. When we want to get an idea into the discussion, we can simply offer a statement and let students build on it.

❖ Asking too many questions, even quality ones, can destroy a good literature discussion. Playing twenty questions may be a good strategy for a first date, but not for a literature discussion.

I extend this comprehension lesson by calling students' attention to the language used to ask questions. We begin with the five traditional question words: *who, what, when, where,* and *why.* These question words usually don't pose much of a challenge for readers, even on standardized tests. The words or phrases that pose the most problems are phrases like *greater than, differentiate, compare, contrast, evaluate, synthesize, according to, which is most likely to,* and others. There are many words and phrases we use in the English language to ask questions, and in order to help students comprehend what they are reading or know what is being asked, especially on standardized tests, we need to help them understand the way questions are constructed.

Literacy Assessments

As we expand the types of responses we require from our students in their reading response notebooks, we need to assess their progress in this endeavor. To do so, I collect students' response notebooks every week and write observational notes about what I am seeing. In addition, I created a response notebook checklist to collect and organize my observations (see Figure 5.2). This checklist represents my preferred vision for students' entries in these notebooks and evolves as the school year progresses.

The response notebook checklist helps give me an overview of students' progress in responding to what they read. I don't use this checklist to give grades for students' response notebooks; rather, I use it as a window into students' developing interpretive abilities.

Connections to the Writing Workshop

Focusing on expository texts for the month of December and beyond provides a perfect opportunity for students to learn about writing in this genre. Writing research reports, taking notes, conducting inquiry projects, learning to paraphrase, and using reference materials for support are primary components of most language arts standards. Some units of study on expository texts focus on a single content area subject, for example, geology, transportation, westward expansion, or architecture. In these units, the texts are used to understand the content area material. In other units of study, the focus is on the format and structures of expository texts, regardless of content. Either way, calling students' attention to the ways that these texts are constructed and organized helps them comprehend this genre and learn to write in it.

Things I Hope to See, Hear, and Have Established by Month's End

1. Students are reading expository texts and checking them out of the library more frequently.

2. I want to have several subscriptions for student magazines circulating by the end of the month, if not sooner. Educational magazines are an undervalued resource in the intermediate grades.

3. Students are slowing down when approaching an expository text, attending to the various extratextual components to guide their reading and comprehension.

4. Our library collection contains an adequate amount of quality expository texts on a variety of subjects. I check out the maximum amount of books I am allowed from the nearby public library and work with my school's librarian to support my personal collection of expository texts.

FIG. 5.2 *Response Notebook Checklist*

Response Notebook Checklist

Response Format

- ❖ includes title, author, date, genre
- ❖ includes complete thoughts and sentences
- ❖ is legible
- ❖ answers response notebook partner's questions
- ❖ answers teacher's questions

Interpretive Repertoire

- ❖ connects story to own life and experiences
- ❖ connects story to other texts and authors
- ❖ anticipates what is coming in the story
- ❖ describes images and ideas
- ❖ asks questions during reading

Uses Elements of Literature in Responses

- ❖ setting
- ❖ character
- ❖ symbols
- ❖ tension
- ❖ moral
- ❖ author's purpose
- ❖ point of view
- ❖ illustrations
- ❖ irony
- ❖ theme
- ❖ mood

5. Students are beginning to evaluate the quality of the sources of information they use for their reports. They are looking for disconfirming information and are researching more than one source of information.

6. I have been able to use think-alouds more effectively, demonstrating my reading strategies and practices when approaching an expository text. We are developing a common language to use when describing what we do when we read.

7. I have been able to weave literature, expository texts, poetry, magazines, and websites into every part of the curriculum.

8. I have gathered an adequate amount of information on each reader to understand his or her strengths and weaknesses as a reader and have used this information to create effective small-group comprehension and literature study groups.

Ideas for Further Reflection

❖ Take inventory of the amount of expository texts that are available in your classroom library. Is there an adequate amount of quality expository texts to support students' investigations of particular research and reading projects?

❖ Linda Hoyt, a fellow Heinemann author and friend, and other educators have published exemplary professional books about expository texts and the elementary reading curriculum. I highly recommend acquiring some of these professional materials and reading through them.

Closing Thoughts

At least 50 percent of the books checked out of school libraries by intermediate-grade children are expository, yet about 95 percent of the books being read aloud to students in these grades are fictional narratives. Therein lies a problem. How will students get exposed to expository writing, authors of expository texts, and expository text structures and components if we don't share more of these texts with them? We must make a concerted effort to read aloud more expository texts in our reading workshops.

As humans, we naturally ask questions when we are confused or are in need of information. However, the questions that get asked in school seem to have lost some of this natural integrity. Teachers ask questions they already know the answers to, something they would probably never do with their friends outside the school setting. As Richard Russo suggests in the epigraph, we need to help students become interested enough in a subject to pose questions for themselves and develop a sense of what's important.

I have used the phrase *calling students' attention to* a great deal throughout this book. I use this term to describe an important aspect of teaching reading. As a literary docent, my role as a teacher is to call students' attention to those things they didn't notice, to see things from alternative perspectives, and to experience texts in new ways. Teaching means to show, and to show means to call attention to what we see.

Exploring Expository Texts

Introduction

Intermediate-grade students need to understand how to navigate the components and structures of expository texts and think critically about the information that is presented. For this unit of study, we spend three to four weeks focusing on the elements of expository texts. We look at a variety of expository texts, magazines, Internet resources, brochures, and instructional manuals to explore how information is presented and made available.

Focus

The focus of this unit is obviously expository texts. However, I am not as concerned about the particular subject matter of the texts as I am about helping students recognize, navigate, and comprehend the features and components of these texts. This unit focuses on expository texts as a genre. In a later chapter, I focus on expository texts and their role in a particular subject area.

Goals and Objectives

❖ introduce various reading and comprehension strategies specific to expository texts

❖ help students understand that reading is a meaning-making process

❖ support readers in understanding the purposes for reading expository texts

❖ analyze and compare information from a variety of resources

Opening Ceremonies

During our opening ceremonies we discussed expository texts and their importance in students' lives. Students were required during this unit to read expository texts for their nightly homework reading. Each morning, students shared reading response notebook entries, noting the kinds of structures found within the texts they chose to read. By reading expository texts each night, students became immersed in the language, style, structure, and components of expository texts.

Cornerstone Texts

To launch this unit, I selected *Volcano*, by Lisa Magloff (2003), as our cornerstone text. I chose this book because of the variety of expository structures and elements used within this single text. *Volcano* includes diagrams, photographs, captions, a table of contents, an index, a glossary, charts, graphs, informational sidebars, headings, subheadings, and a reference list of related websites.

For our afternoon read-aloud, instead of reading a single chapter book, we conducted an author study and read a series of books by Seymour Simon. We read and discussed his expository picture books and investigated the way he presented information in his extensive collection of texts.

Launching the Unit of Study	My primary goal in launching this unit of study was to immerse students in all kinds of expository texts and to help them attend to expository text structures during a literature discussion. I read *Volcano*, thinking aloud as I worked my way through the book, calling students' attention to the various components and structures of the text. I asked students to note in their reading response notebooks what they observed about the text itself, they way I read it, and the reading strategies I employed to navigate through the text. We discussed what they observed and what they heard me demonstrate through the think-alouds. This gave them a better understanding of how to approach an expository text.

To demonstrate the comprehension strategy *previewing a text*, I scanned and skimmed the text, reading the front and back covers and the table of contents. I chose one section of the book to read aloud and invited students to share their observations of what I had read. We talked about volcanoes and what we had learned by reading the text. From our discussions, we created two charts, one displaying information about volcanoes and a second describing components of this expository text. I wanted students to learn about volcanoes, because that was what we were reading about, but I also wanted them to attend to the structures and elements of expository texts in general.

After discussing *Volcano* for a couple of days, I conducted an expository cloze procedure using a page from the book. I made an overhead copy of the page and blacked out key words in the passage. I put the passage on the overhead and read the passage aloud to my students. Students discussed the various strategies they used to figure out what the covered words were. From this procedure, we created a chart of expository reading strategies. We compared this strategies chart with one we had created with a fictional text earlier in the year. Students realized there were many strategies that were similar for each type of text and some that were specific to expository texts. Subsequently, we created a chart that compared and contrasted narrative and expository reading strategies.

During this first week of the unit, I wanted students to be exposed to a wide variety of expository texts. During the second week of the unit, I wanted students to investigate the texts in more depth and learn various strategies for navigating through these texts. Over the course of this unit of study, I taught several reading strategies, for example, summarizing, predicting, and organizing information, in a variety of whole- and small-group structures.

Connecting Reading Expository Texts to Writing Expository Texts	During the third week we launched our inquiry projects. Students researched and created an informational book on a content topic of their choice. They were learning about the structures inherent within their own resources for the inquiry project to support their own writing and creation of an expository text. As students investigated the structures and components of expository texts to create their own books, their ability to make sense of expository texts was greatly enhanced.

To begin, students created a proposal for their inquiry project. The proposal included the topic, the expository genre, the purpose, an explanation for the choice of text, and a detailed description of the intended audience. The proposal was a piece of expository writing in and of itself, but it was also very helpful for students to outline their purposes for writing. Once students proposed their inquiry topics, they began doing research on their topics, locating expository texts and other resources. I also helped them by locating texts pertaining to their inquiry projects.

I then began with a series of whole-group reading lessons on using multiple sources, generating questions, activating prior knowledge, taking notes, and organizing notes. I demonstrated how the expository text could come together by creating a shared text.

Shared Writing   In order to support students' efforts in creating expository texts, we created an example of an expository text together using a shared writing approach. I wanted the whole class to have prior knowledge of a single topic for this shared writing experience, so we revisited the concepts and information from a previous unit of study in science on plants. We brainstormed a list of possible subtopics and headings and then proceeded to create an example of an expository text page.

This page included words in bold print, a diagram with labels, headings, and subheadings, and a photo with a caption. We discussed why we used these components and the reasons behind our choices. We analyzed the purposes for using informational boxes, diagrams, headings, and subheadings. These discussions were very important to develop students' understandings of the structure and purpose of expository texts. We made a table of contents as we thought about the information that could be included if we were to continue writing this book.

Comprehension Strategy Groups   I met with students in comprehension strategy groups and discussed the books they were reading for their inquiry projects. The strategy lessons I taught in these groups began with students identifying the kinds of components and structures found in the books they were using for their inquiry projects. I created reading lessons in response to the needs of each group and individual reader. These lessons helped students comprehend the resources they were using for their projects. Students brought magazines, Internet articles, brochures, texts, and textbooks to these strategy group meetings. I conducted reading lessons on determining a purpose for reading these materials, how to interpret images and diagrams, and ways of using the table of contents and the index.

Writing Think-Aloud   Just as I use think-alouds to demonstrate reading strategies, I also use think-alouds for demonstrating strategies in writing. For these lessons, I thought aloud as I wrote my own expository text in front of my students. I used an overhead for my drafts and a computer with a projector for publishing. Each day I created a part of my text and thought out loud to demonstrate the strategies and techniques I was using. It was important that I explained the choices I was making as I wrote the text. I planned my ideas out beforehand but did the actual writing in front of the students. I kept it to about fifteen minutes of writing each day and then invited students to work on the element that I had just demonstrated in their own books.

After I had demonstrated various components of expository texts, I had students choose mentor texts to use as models for their writing. We worked on these texts for the next few weeks. By the end of this unit of study, we had a long list of reading strategies for expository texts and an array of expository structures and components for students to reference at any time during their writing.

Culminating Experience

As a culminating experience we held a young authors' celebration to share our published books. The published inquiry project included picture books, brochures, PowerPoint presentations, videos, advertisements, newsletters, letters, and websites. We had a classroom publishing party with food and music. Students placed their texts at their seats and rotated around the room, looking at one another's projects. Next to each text was a comment card for students to write ideas, feedback, and positive comments. We invited our primary-grade reading buddies, teachers, other staff members, and the principal in to partake in our celebration.

Closing the Window

This was a complex unit of study because we looked at the content *and* structure of each expository text we read. As a result, students not only researched specific topics but began to consider the quality of the resources they were using with a more critical lens. After this unit, students were not only interested in their inquiry topics but also appreciated the style, structure, and research used to create the resource texts. Students compared and contrasted a variety of resources, choosing to use those with the most reliable information. This in-depth investigation of expository texts helped students prepare for the expository text sections of their standardized tests.

CHAPTER 6

January—Making Our Thinking Visible

We've taught you that the Earth is round,
That red and white makes pink,
And something else that matters more—
We've taught you how to think.

—DR. SEUSS, *HOORAY FOR DIFFENDOOFER DAY*

Introduction

Getting back into the routine of school after the winter break can be challenging for some students and some teachers. Because of our time away from each other, January is a time to regroup, to make sure the procedures we have introduced and worked to establish in the autumn months are revisited and set back in place. It may take a few days to get back on track in January, but this is not a time to lower one's expectations—it's a time to revisit expectations and set new resolutions for the upcoming year.

The month of January involves a variety of learning experiences as we work to reestablish the reading workshop after the winter break. Included in this chapter are descriptions of learning experiences that focus on expanding readers' interpretive repertoires and response strategies and enriching our literature discussions. I also discuss in detail the role of the teacher as facilitator of literature study groups and some new response strate-

JANUARY CHAPTER OUTLINE

January Lessons and Learning Experiences
❖ Investigating Personal Narratives
❖ Understanding Point of View
❖ Investigating Characters
❖ Respond, Categorize, Reflect
❖ Expanding Literature Study Discussions
❖ Facilitating Literature Study Discussions
Featured Lesson in Comprehension for January:
Making Intertextual Connections
Literacy Assessments
❖ Think-Alouds
❖ Literature Study Discussion Recordings
❖ Expanding Reader Response Notebooks . . .
   Again
Connections to the Writing Workshop
❖ Genre Study on Personal Narratives
❖ Writing Letters to Characters

gies to delve deeper into the complexity of the literature we encounter.

Along with the instructional experiences included in this chapter, I describe a unit of study focusing on reading and writing personal narratives. Personal narrative is a genre most students are familiar with, and it provides a strong connection with the writing workshop as students are invited to share their personal experiences through their writing. In addition, Suzette describes a unit of study focusing on the Holocaust during World War II. At first glance, these two units of study may seem unconnected; however, these units provide numerous opportunities to integrate the curriculum as we explore the personal stories written during and about the Holocaust in our social studies workshop and investigate our personal experiences and family stories during the reading and writing workshops. I do not try to force an integrated curriculum when the connections aren't apparent, but when I can connect my science, math, and social science curricula with my literacy instruction, I find it to be a powerful learning experience. This chapter's Window on the Workshop provides examples of how these two units of study evolved and are connected.

> ### RECOMMENDED COMPREHENSION STRATEGIES FROM *LESSONS IN COMPREHENSION*
>
> ❖ 2.5 Point of View
> ❖ 3.5 Attending to Punctuation
> ❖ 4.7 The Literary Talk Show
> ❖ 5.3 Monitoring Understanding
> ❖ 5.7 Making Intertextual Connections
> ❖ 7.2 Letters to Authors and Illustrators

January Lessons and Learning Experiences

Investigating Personal Narratives

Personal narrative is one of the most common forms of story known to humankind. People tell stories of what has happened to them every day, orally and in writing. In fact, literary theorists and cultural psychologists, for example, Jerome Bruner, have posited we live "storied lives," that our identities are developed through the stories we hear and construct. When we get together with old friends or meet new people in social contexts, we often tell stories about ourselves and learn about others from the stories they tell.

To launch the unit of study on personal narratives, I select several of my favorite personal narratives in picture book format and one chapter book that is an extended personal narrative to read aloud and discuss. My selections include several classic examples of personal narrative, stories that contain the basic characteristics of personal narrative, including the first-person point of view, a slice-of-life story line, the past tense, a focus on family events, a focus on a particular event that was important to the author, and the use of descriptive language and setting to get readers to connect to the story. The unit of study also introduces some examples of personal narratives that challenge the traditional characteristics of this genre, pushing our definitions and extending the boundaries of our readings. However, I begin the unit with prototypical examples to establish our working definition of the personal narrative genre.

I always begin a unit of study in the reading workshop by selecting a cornerstone text that will provide the foundation for our discussions. For this unit, I like to use *Owl Moon*, by Jane Yolen (1987) as the cornerstone text. *Owl Moon* contains all of the characteristics of a traditional personal narrative. This picture book tells the story of a young child going owling with her father. It contains wonderfully lyrical and descriptive prose and award-winning illustrations, and it is written in the first-person point of view in the past tense.

We begin by reading and discussing the book for several days, focusing our attention on the language of the story, the setting, the illustrator's techniques, the structure of the story, especially how it begins and ends, and the point of view used to tell the story. Too often, young writers view personal narratives as equivalent with the oral bed-to-bed stories that they share with us on Monday mornings about their weekend escapades. These stories begin when students awake and end when they fall asleep and usually have narrowly conceived titles like "The Day I Went Camping." In order to write better personal narratives, students have to read numerous examples of quality personal narratives and attend to how they are constructed.

In addition to the cornerstone text, I gather a variety of personal narratives to read aloud and provide for independent exploration. After reading and discussing the cornerstone text for several days, we read and discuss a new picture book each day and discuss its characteristics and why it is a form of personal narrative. This portion of the unit of study in the reading workshop helps students make the shift from reading like readers to reading personal narratives like writers.

On a chart or a bulletin board, we construct our definition of personal narrative (see Figure 6.1 for an example). This working definition evolves as our discussions progress and remains open for revision throughout the unit. When I feel that students are recognizing the basic structures and elements of personal narrative, I ask them to begin thinking about some important events in their lives that would be good choices for their own personal narratives. I give them time to share ideas, talk with one another, and jot down some thoughts in their writer's notebooks before launching their writing. The value of the time spent talking and organizing thoughts before writing cannot be underestimated.

After some discussion about possible events for writing topics has occurred, I ask students to try one of the numerous "gathering and organizing for writing" strategies that I have demonstrated in the writing workshop so far this year. For example, I show

FIG. 6.1
Personal Narrative Characteristics

a story about yourself and what you have done

first-person point of view

author tells his or her story of about important event

tell about *one* special event, not your whole life

it is important to describe the setting

use details

use your senses

pay attention to word choice

use poetic language

use metaphors and similes

say things differently

students how to brainstorm, make outlines, create lists, gather ideas in one's writing notebook, construct time lines and story diagrams, organize ideas onto storyboards, and other strategies they might find helpful to get their ideas organized before writing.

After we have organized our topics, I ask students to select one of the personal narratives I have read or provided to use as a mentor piece of writing. Students will closely revisit this piece of writing and use its structures and style to model their own personal narrative after. I assure my students that using a mentor piece is not copying; rather, it is something that most writers do. All good writers read widely in the genre they are writing in and use certain pieces as inspiration for their stories.

The rest of the writing workshop follows the procedures we have established during the year—peer conferences, revising strategies, author's chair, proofreading sessions, and publication. When students have completed their personal narratives, I publish them in a class book to be housed in our classroom library and read by others, and I conduct a young authors' day to celebrate their accomplishments. Parents are invited to listen to stories and share in their children's hard work.

This unit of study provides a rich connection between what we read and what we write. The more we read, analyze, and discuss personal narratives *before* we begin writing them, the better our writing will be. Our writing workshop often piggybacks on the experiences we have in our reading workshop.

Understanding Point of View

When reading literature, in particular personal narrative, it is crucial that readers pay attention to who is telling the story and how a particular point of view affects how the story is told. Determining point of view can be relatively straightforward, simply deciding which character is telling the story or if it's an outside narrator, or it can become quite complex as readers consider how much access to characters' feelings and thoughts the author has made available to the reader.

Point of view is a literary device used to give perspective to the events in the story offered by the narrator, not the author. I begin with an example to introduce point of view to students before moving on to more issues involved with point of view.

One of my favorite picture books is *Gila Monsters Meet You at the Airport*, by Marjorie Weinman Sharmat (1980). In this humorous story, a young boy from New York City is told his family is moving "out west," to Phoenix, Arizona. Although his fears will prove unfounded, he worries he will have to ride a horse to school, his new friends won't know anything about baseball or salami, and gila monsters will meet him at the airport when he arrives. As he is walking through the airport on his way out west, he meets a boy from Phoenix who is moving to New York City. This second boy is worried about moving "back east," where airplanes fly through bedrooms in high-rise buildings, alligators live in the sewers, gangsters drive around in big, black cars, and summer lasts only five minutes.

The contrasting points of view in this story are hard to miss, making this book a thoroughly enjoyable read-aloud and an excellent resource for introducing point of view. This book provides numerous opportunities to discuss our own points of view, misunderstandings, and possible stereotypical attitudes about faraway places.

Three points of view that we should introduce to students are *first person*, where the author reveals events through the main character's perspective, allowing the story to be told through his or her eyes; *third-person full omniscience*, where the narrator can shift focus from character to character with knowledge of every character's thoughts and story events of which no single character would be aware; and *third-person limited omniscience,* where the narrator picks one character and follows him or her around for the duration of the book, telling that character's version of the story.

Readers need to be made aware of the various points of view used by authors to comprehend the literature they are reading. Stories, in particular historical texts, are all presented from a particular point of view or perspective. There is no neutral, objective perspective from which to tell a story. Because of this, readers need to consider not only what is being told but who is doing the telling. Authors use a variety of literary devices to construct a story and provide perspectives from which the story is told. Different points of view change what the reader has access to in a work of literature.

In addition, multiple-perspective texts, for example, *Voices in the Park,* by Anthony Browne (2001), *Black and White,* by David Macaulay (1990), *The View from Saturday,* by E. L. Konigsburg (1996), *Seedfolks,* by Paul Fleischman (1997), and *Making Up Megaboy,* by Virginia Walter (1998), offer readers multiple points of view rather than a single perspective. In these texts, a single event is told through the perspectives of several different characters. By not privileging any one particular point of view, these texts challenge the reader to consider alternative perspectives and interpretations.

Investigating Characters

As mentioned in Chapter 3, character is a primary element in fictional narrative. One of the most enjoyable aspects of reading a good book is becoming involved with a story until you feel like you are walking along with the main character as he faces challenges, conquers his fears, and returns to the safety of his home so much the wiser from his adventures. One of the greatest pleasures in reading literature is the bond that develops between a reader and the characters in the story. I want readers to understand characters' reasons for acting the way they do and to notice the changes they go through as the story evolves in order to develop this bond.

However, there is a difference between bringing characters *to* life, meaning that readers evoke the character and escape into the story world, and bringing characters *into* life, meaning they relate the story world to their own life experiences, critiquing characters' motives, actions, and decisions. Bringing characters into life during the act of reading provides a space to illuminate our experiences and the issues that we deal with outside of literature. I want readers to read both ways, bringing characters to life so they can walk in their shoes and aesthetically experience literature and bringing characters into readers' lives so that literature can impact their ways of being in the world. Memorable characters provide us a window onto the world and a mirror into ourselves.

Two strategies for helping readers attend to the personalities and characteristics of important characters are the use of semantic webs or graphic organizers and interviewing a character. Using a semantic web requires readers to identify attributes of a character and connect them together into an organizational pattern. The purpose of these semantic webs is to remove the character from the story, closely examine her characteristics, faults, and strengths, and put her back into the context of the story to understand the role she played and the changes she experienced.

In a second strategy, which I have called *the literary talk show,* the class creates questions and a selected talk show host interviews a student role-playing a particular character. I assign three or four students to do research on a character we have been reading and select one of these students to role-play that character for our talk show.

The rest of the students prepare questions they want to ask that particular character. We discuss possible questions as a group and select several quality questions for our interview. A student is then selected to be the moderator or talk show host, and he or she prepares the questions for the show.

On the day of the talk show, the student playing the character dresses like the character would dress, with some help from parents and the art teacher, and answers questions posed by the talk show host. In general, students do a wonderful job role-playing various characters, answering questions that delve into the psyche of a character. After the talk show is over, we discuss whether we would have answered the questions the same way that the student playing the character did. This leads to even more wonderful discussions about our own images of the character and how we felt the character acted in the story.

Respond, Categorize, Reflect

I have my students respond on sticky notes to a series of four questions about a book I am reading aloud. I give the students four large sticky notes and ask them to write down their responses to four questions, for example; (1) What did you wonder about? (2) What surprised you? (3) What did you connect to? and (4) What did you notice? The questions may change every time I conduct this invested discussion strategy, but these four questions have worked well for me.

After students have written down their answers, we arrange the notes on the chalkboard in four separate categories, one for each question. We discuss each set of notes individually before moving on to another set. This procedure ensures that students respond individually before seeing other students' thoughts and interpretations. Looking across the whole range of responses, we are also able to notice patterns of response that arise during our discussions.

Expanding Literature Study Discussions

Selecting quality literature to support readers' interpretive abilities and demonstrating how to approach various elements and structures of literature are important considerations in creating effective literature study discussion groups. No matter the quality of the work of literature, the relevance to readers' experiences, or the abilities of the group members to discuss literature, the focus remains a single piece of literature. Sometimes the conversations turn grand, and sometimes they don't.

Another approach for enriching literature discussions is by injecting some picture books into the study. For example, when reading and discussing the novel *Sadako and the Thousand Paper Cranes*, by Eleanor Coerr (1977), we might read *The Paper Crane*, by Molly Bang (1990), *Hiroshima No Pika*, by Toshi Maruki (1980), *My Hiroshima*, by Junko Morimoto (1990), or *Faithful Elephants*, by Yukio Tsuchiya (1988). These additional texts add complexity to the novel we are reading and work in concert with the novel to extend students' understandings, offer alternative information and perspectives, and provide new avenues for discussions. These *text sets*, sets of books, poems, news reports, magazine articles, and other texts with a common focus or theme, provide richer experiences than a novel alone can offer.

Facilitating Literature Study Discussions

In Chapter 4, I suggested that we can better facilitate literature study discussions by becoming better listeners, taking notes for facilitating subsequent group sessions, asking open-ended questions, inviting all members to participate, and waiting to offer our interpretations in the discussions. However, I feel I need to go into more depth here about *how* teachers might facilitate literature study discussions, how they can better respond to readers without dominating the conversation.

Aidan Chambers, in his book *Tell Me* (1996), explains it is important that teachers encourage group members to begin their discussions by stating the obvious. Chambers suggests that by stating the obvious up front, readers can begin to think about things that aren't being mentioned or discussed. Readers need to get past what was obvious to them to attend to the unnoticed when digging deeper into a work of literature. This stating of the obvious helps initiate discussions and serves as an invitation to go beyond the obvious to the unique and idiosyncratic interpretations students have generated.

Many students will wait until the teacher or other students have offered ideas before entering the conversation. That's fine, as long as they are thinking about the book and not waiting for others to interpret the book for them. If students ask me what I think, I often dodge the question by telling them I am waiting to hear what they think or by saying that I need to listen to what they are saying first. Other techniques I use are (1) paraphrasing—restating what students have said to get them to clarify or extend their ideas; (2) piggybacking—encouraging students to add to previously stated ideas; (3) contradicting obvious interpretations—by playing devil's advocate, I encourage students to consider drastically different interpretations; and (4) asking students to justify their interpretations—by asking readers to provide evidence of their interpretations, I try to get them to reconsider, but not necessarily change, what they are thinking. What is important is that teachers attend to what is being discussed, remain open to initial interpretations, and respond in ways that encourage participation. Tentative sharing allows other readers to offer their interpretations without fear of being wrong. The more alternatives we can get on the table in our literature discussions, the more interpretations are made available for negotiation.

Summary of Lessons and Learning Experiences

January is a time for reestablishing workshop expectations and moving deeper into literature discussions. Adding complexity to our novel studies by injecting some picture books and other texts into the discussion and focusing on the role we as teachers play in literature discussions supports the negotiation and revision of interpretations. We must remain vigilant in our expectations, nudging students into more complex thinking about what they read, questioning the sources of their interpretations, and helping them bring new perspectives to the literature they encounter, while at the same time enjoying and respecting the interpretations they construct.

Featured Lesson in Comprehension for January: Making Intertextual Connections

It would probably be better to refer to this comprehension strategy as attending to or noticing intertextual connections because intertextual connections are already made, consciously or unconsciously, by the author when creating the text. *Intertexual connections* refers to the dialogue that new texts have with older texts. These connections can be constructed on a variety of levels of meaning, from simple references to a character's name, to deeper structural and archetypal similarities. Being able to make intertextual connections enriches the reading experience by enabling readers to see common patterns and understanding across classic and contemporary works of literature.

In *How to Read Literature Like a Professor*, Thomas C. Foster (2003) suggests the more we become aware that the texts we are reading are speaking to other texts, and the more similarities and correspondences we notice, the more enriching our reading experiences and the deeper our understandings will be. A reader does not have to notice every intertextual connection infused in the text by the author, nor should a reader worry about the connections she misses because she has not experienced an ample amount of literature. The important point is that every text somehow connects or is based on every text that came before it. Noticing intertextual relationships can add to our reading experiences and help us when we begin to write stories and poems for ourselves.

An obvious but sometimes overlooked consideration when trying to support students in making intertextual connections is reading texts that are apparently connected. All too often, teachers expect students to make text-to-text connections but don't read books that are connected to each other.

Another challenge is the difference between *robust* and *superficial* connections. Students sometimes offer superficial connections, loose connections to the texts that do not provide support for constructing more complex interpretations and intertextual connections. In contrast, robust connections are deeply connected to the themes and important concepts presented in the two texts, help students better comprehend both texts, and allow readers to construct alternative interpretations. We cannot simply accept every personal or literary connection offered by students without pointing out that some connections are more robust, offering more support for our interpretive processes, than others.

Traditional comparison charts have played a prominent role in helping students see connections across various texts. Teachers write the names of books being read down the left-hand column of a chart and various elements of literature and other categories across the top. I have found that by predetermining categories for students to address in a traditional comparison chart, we may reduce this instructional strategy to a literary scavenger hunt, where students simply read enough of the book to fill in the blanks.

Because of this drawback, I have adapted the traditional comparison chart for use in my literature discussions by taking away the categories across the top of the chart. After we read a variety of texts connected by genre, author, illustrator, topic, or theme, I ask students to generate connections across the various texts we have read. When we notice a connection or pattern in the books we have read, we add that as a category across the top of our chart and explore the ways each book approaches that issue.

Another important way to connect texts is to look for the archetypes, or narrative patterns, in the texts we share with students. Northrop Frye (1957) has described four primary narrative patterns in literature: (1) romance—adventure stories containing a quest, a struggle, and a fulfillment of the quest; (2) tragedy—stories that depict humans as vulnerable to nature and evil, loss of innocence, and sacrifice for humanity's benefit; (3) satire or irony—stories of injustice where many characters get what they deserve; and (4) comedy—stories that celebrate the power of the imagination, triumph over obstacles, a rebirth or renewal of the spirit, and magical interventions. Although

I have reduced a very complex literary theory into a single paragraph, I hope you will see how these narrative patterns can be used to help readers make connections across works of literature.

In order for teachers to help readers attend to intertextual connections, they must first notice these connections themselves. The patterns and intertextual connections are there; we just have to help readers notice them and watch for them as they approach new pieces of literature.

Literacy Assessments

Think-Alouds

In addition to the ways that I have used think-alouds to demonstrate comprehension strategies in my reading lessons, I use think-alouds as an assessment device for understanding how readers construct meaning during the act of reading, the comprehension strategies they use, and how they navigate through texts. Think-alouds are a window for gathering reactions and responses to texts during the act of reading. They provide information about what readers are attending to and not attending to. Sometimes referred to as verbal protocol analysis by reading researchers, a think-aloud can provide access to a reader's thinking processes that can't be made visible by assessments that are conducted after the reading is completed.

To conduct a think-aloud, I select a text, indicate when the reader should stop and share his thoughts into a tape recorder, and have the student read the book aloud into the tape. Think-alouds can be done with any text, but I recommend short, complete texts that students can read in a single session.

There are several ways to provide prompts for readers to use to report what they are thinking. Teachers can place sticky labels or dots in the text to signal to readers when to report thoughts, provide some specific questions about what to report on, have the reader simply stop at end of each page, or let the reader report whenever she chooses. There is no one right way to conduct think-aloud assessments. Each variation simply provides different levels of support.

In order for think-alouds to be successful, teachers need to provide numerous demonstrations and detailed, consistent instructions. Teachers need to consider the prompts they offer students for reporting what they are thinking, how to record the think-alouds, and the time it will take to listen to the tapes and analyze the data once collected.

When conducting think-alouds, provide a quiet space for tape recording, let students practice, not play, with the tape recorder, use a quality microphone and recorder, and explain to parents and administrators why you are tape-recording readers. The better the microphone and recorder, the better your chances of picking up what readers report.

Most importantly, don't collect more data than you are willing to analyze. These tapes can build up quickly. You don't have to transcribe them like reading researchers do when they are conducting research for them to be effective classroom-based literacy assessments. I take them along with me on my drive home and start by simply listening to what students have reported. Later on, I listen to the tape while looking at the book and take more extensive notes on what the reader noticed and reported. I listen to the tape initially to get a holistic sense of the reported data. I consider what the reader attended to and what the reader used to make sense of the text as he read. I evaluate the think-aloud based on our criteria for successful readers and then construct some instructional strategies to work on with that particular reader.

Literature Study Discussion Recordings

As students get more comfortable with the tape recorder, why not turn it on during some of your literature study discussions and record what is happening? I remember Ralph Peterson telling me in one of my first literacy education classes that in order to be an effective facilitator of literature discussions, we need to listen attentively to our students as much as we tell them what we think. I wrote this advice down in my notebook, but it wasn't until I had recorded one of my literature study group discussions that his advice made sense. I was listening to a tape of a literature discussion when I discovered the only voice I could hear was my own. Those of you who know me may not be surprised by this, but I actually was. It wasn't until I had recorded the discussion and listened to it that I realized the error of my ways. Recording our teaching on audiocassettes or videos is a powerful professional development experience that is underutilized in schools and colleges of education.

Expanding Reading Response Notebooks . . . Again

In an earlier chapter, I mentioned how I liked to up the ante, trying to make students dig deeper into what they were reading during our discussions of literature. I try to do the same thing with reading response notebooks. As students begin to feel comfortable discussing the basic elements and structures of literature in their reading response notebooks, I revise the book logs for literature study discussions to reflect our developing language of literary criticism.

Certain expectations are established for every reader: writing in the reading response notebook every night, addressing the primary elements of setting, character, and plot, responding to one's response partner or the teacher's questions, and writing legibly. Some expectations are constructed on an individual basis, pushing some students further than others. I expect each student to respond to his or her reading to the best of his or her interpretive abilities. My role is to challenge students to think deeper while at the same time acknowledging and supporting the responses they are making.

In January I revise the book logs we use in literature study discussions to reflect the different structures and elements I have introduced and we have begun attending to in our discussions. Theme, mood, symbolism, point of view, archetypes, and intertextual connections are examples of what may be added. The headings we use in our literature study book logs are derived from the ideas presented during our read-alouds and discussions.

Connections to the Writing Workshop

In the descriptions of the unit of study on reading and writing personal narratives, the connections to the writing workshop are described in detail. One further writing experience that I often include in the reading workshop is writing letters to favorite characters, pretending they are alive so that we can talk with them and ask them questions. In the past, I have asked some of my college students, when I was teaching in both elementary and college classrooms, to respond to my young students' letters. Each of my college students would take on the persona of a character and answer as he or she saw fit. This was a wonderful experience for both sets of students and was more effective than the dialogue journals I had tried between these sets of students.

Things I Hope to See, Hear, and Have Established by Month's End

1. Students are making recommendations to other readers based on more complex criteria than simply liking the book.

2. Students are talking and listening more attentively, not just talking *at* each other in literature study groups.

3. Students are using their reading response notebooks to take notes during comprehension lessons and literature discussions.

4. Students are disagreeing with me about a book or an interpretation. I want my students to realize that I am only one voice in the discussion, not *the* voice.

5. More readers are willing to acknowledge confusion during reading. If I am challenging students to read more difficult material, they will become confused at times. I want them to be able to share their confusion without fear of being ridiculed.

6. Fewer and fewer students are selecting inappropriate materials for independent reading.

Ideas for Further Reflection

❖ As the literature we read gets more complex, our interpretive repertoires must expand to attend to this complexity. Reading books about contemporary literary theories and literary criticism should be an integral part of teachers' professional development.

❖ The reading strategies that we demonstrate are meant to address reading literature in total, not just the actual text we are reading. The strategies we teach must be useful as readers encounter new texts.

❖ Think about where the content for your comprehension lessons has been coming from. Has it come solely from a professional book? Or has it been based on your observations of students? Reflective teachers observe and think about what's happening in their workshops in order to design effective lessons for their readers.

Closing Thoughts

I have read numerous books and educational articles about literature studies describing conversations that were so wonderfully sophisticated that I wondered where the students in that class came from and why my literature discussions didn't sound like that. I sometimes feel incompetent when I read these classroom stories. I wonder what those teachers' secret is to getting these grand conversations going. What do they do that I am not doing?

As a veteran teacher, I have realized that selecting quality literature that relates to the lives of our students, taking numerous classes in children's literature and literary theory, selecting the most proficient readers, and dutifully preparing for a discussion do not guarantee that a grand conversation will occur. I have also realized, through the experiences of writing four books and numerous articles on literacy education, that we rarely speak, let alone write, about the days when everything went wrong. Maybe we should write about our worst days to show teachers that we have had literature study discussions go flat as well.

The truth is that sometimes, even with experienced teachers and intelligent, experienced students, there is little to say about a work of literature. It does not mean that the next day's discussion won't be better. It does not mean that the book was a bad choice. It just means that on that day, with those students and that piece of literature, not much was going to happen. Don't beat yourself up about it; go play kickball and come back and try it again. Sometimes we need to wade through a lot of mediocre discussions before our conversations turn grand.

Internment and the Holocaust

Introduction

After a class trip to Washington, D.C., where my students, some parents, and I visited many museums and American landmarks, including the United States Holocaust Memorial Museum, I launched a unit of study focusing on the Holocaust in response to my students' interest in this topic. During this unit, we read a series of books about internment and investigated numerous resources focusing on the Holocaust and World War II. Although the impetus for this unit was a trip to the Holocaust museum, this Window on the Workshop serves as an example of how to create a unit of study based on students' interests after an important learning experience has occurred.

During the field trip to Washington, D.C., students wrote in reflective journals about their wonderings, experiences, and observations. Students had many questions about how the Holocaust began and wondered what the rest of the world was doing during this time. These entries and student questions were the basis of our unit of study on internment and the Holocaust.

Focus

This unit included a series of readings, lessons, and learning experiences that were constructed to help students begin to understand what events led up to the Holocaust. The books were chosen to help illuminate many perspectives on the war and help students understand how children during the Holocaust dealt with fear, death, and survival.

Goals and Objectives

❖ understand the living conditions for those in concentration camps in Germany and and Poland and the internment camps in the United States

❖ learn about the major events surrounding World War II

❖ compare and contrast information found in textbooks, biographies, poetry, and fictional literature

❖ link themes of internment and persecution during the Holocaust to current events

Opening Ceremonies

Newspapers   Each morning we shared newspaper articles that students and parents brought in written about current acts of internment and persecution around the world or in our local communities. We also searched for articles that focused on individuals or groups that were taking a stand against these acts and moving toward social justice. We created a current events bulletin board to highlight these articles.

Walking Journal   We used the walking journal to express our ideas and thoughts about the Holocaust and World War II in general. Students wrote entries responding to articles, picture books, chapter books, and learning experiences encountered in the reading workshop, and responded to other students' entries. The journal was a way to connect the learning that was taking place in the reading workshop to other parts of the curriculum.

Cornerstone Texts

For this unit, I chose three cornerstone texts. The first was a chapter book titled *Parallel Journeys,* by Eleanor Ayer with Helen Waterford and Alfons Heck (1995). This biography of Helen, who was a German Jew, and Alfons, who was a member of the Hitler Youth, tells their stories in a parallel structure, contrasting the two opposing perspectives. These two people grew up a few miles apart, and this story tells of the drastically different lives that unfolded for each of them. Helen tells the story of her life in the extermination camp at Auschwitz, and Alfons describes his promotions in the Hitler Youth.

The second cornerstone text was *Rose Blanche,* by Roberto Innocenti (1985). In this story, a German girl follows a boy one day and discovers he has been taken to a concentration camp. She does not understand what the place is or why he is being kept there. She brings food to him and others in the camp. In the end of the story, the girl returns to discover everyone has left after the camp has been liberated.

The third cornerstone text was *Home of the Brave,* by Allen Say (2002). This book, containing surrealistic images, tells the story of one man's journey back in time to discover the internment camp of his ancestors in the United States during World War II. The illustrations are dark and ominous as he encounters children wearing name tags and living in the camps. In the end of the story, the tags are set free in the wind.

Launching the Unit of Study

The unit was actually launched as we stepped into the Holocaust museum in Washington, D.C. Going to this museum was a life-altering event that took us through the experiences of and acts of persecution against the Jewish people. There is a children's exhibit called Daniel's story that is less intense and graphic, and many of my students chose to enter into this exhibit. Each child had one or both of his or her parents escorting him or her through the museum. Upon completion of the tour, I asked children to reflect upon their experiences in their notebooks and in small-group discussions.

When we returned to the classroom a few days later, we shared our journal entries. We'd been on a five-day trip around Washington, but the majority of entries and questions centered on the Holocaust museum and the events of World War II. I immediately sought out literature and used the information and resources the museum provided to put this unit together.

We began by listing all of our questions about the Holocaust and the war on a large sheet of paper. The following is a list of questions we generated:

❖ How could the Holocaust happen?

❖ Why didn't the Jews fight back?

❖ What happened to Adolf Hitler and why was he like that?

❖ What happened to the children in the concentration camps?

❖ What were people in the United States doing?

❖ What were the leaders of the other countries like?

❖ Has the United States ever done anything like that?

❖ What were the conditions like for people in concentration camps?

Before our trip, my lessons focused on the three branches of government and the White House. Students had very little knowledge of the Holocaust except what they had learned at the museum. In order to help students understand this historical event, I needed to build a foundation for us to connect our experiences, so I began reading *Parallel Journeys.* We read in the morning, after lunch and before we went home. The book was compelling and students did not want to stop reading it. I interjected the reading of this chapter book with numerous picture books, including *Looking Like the Enemy: My Story of Imprisonment in Japanese American Internment Camps*, by Mary Matsuda Gruenewald (2005), *The Butterfly*, by Patricia Polacco (2000), *Let the Celebrations Begin*, by Margaret Wild and Julie Vivas (1991), and *Hiroshima No Pika*, by Toshi Maruki (1980). We discussed how children around the world survived, coped with, and endured the tragedies of war.

Explicit Instruction

Reading lessons were designed to build upon the expository text reading strategies I had taught during the month of December. Students were using expository texts and media resources to research questions on the Holocaust, so I tried to expand students' repertoire of expository reading strategies even further. In an effort to support students' inquiry into this historical event, I designed explicit lessons on point of view and symbolism.

Point of View   Because the author of each of the books on the Holocaust offered a variety of perspectives on this historical event, it was important for students to understand the historical context in which the authors told their stories. Many authors' stories were told years later through an ancestor's voice. Each perspective was told from a specific historical context and based on the characters' experiences during World War II. It was important to help students understand that no single story was wrong because the information did not match another source. Many of the discussions on point of view also led to lessons on synthesizing information, comparing resources, and differentiating between primary and secondary sources.

Symbols and Symbolism   As we began to research Adolf Hitler and the Holocaust, children became interested in the meanings associated with the swastika. As we read *Rose Blanche*, students noticed how the swastika was set apart from other images. We investigated the history of the swastika and the emotions that were evoked as we looked at a variety of symbols from around the world. We compared the swastika to Pepsi and Nike symbols and to the American and Confederate flags. We also looked at other symbols of the Jewish faith. Students began to realize that symbols carry more meaning when they are considered in historical context. This investigation also led to a side exploration of slang terms used during World War II and the symbol of the American soldier in propaganda posters.

Workshop Experiences	*Propaganda Posters* Our investigation of symbols led to an exploration of propaganda posters used in many countries, especially the United States. There is a subtle difference between advertising and propaganda, and we discussed this difference. A parent volunteer researched and printed out numerous posters found in historical archives. We posted them up around the room and analyzed the symbols in the posters, the possible messages represented in the posters, and how we felt about the various images.

Students wanted to create their own posters for the war. In partners or independently, students constructed wartime propaganda posters and posters for current issues in our community. They used the images they felt were inherent in our community to persuade community members to think and act in a certain way.

Investigation Groups   I invited students to join book clubs for books they were interested in reading. The books students and I chose to focus on were *Terrible Things*, by Eve Bunting (1980), "Letter from a Concentration Camp," by Yoshiko Uchida (1990), *Baseball Saved Us*, by Ken Mochizuki (1993), *Faithful Elephants*, by Yukio Tsuchiya (1988), and *The Story of Ferdinand*, by Munro Leaf (1964), a book that was actually burned and banned by Adolf Hitler. We spent three days reading and responding to these books. Each club then created a presentation to the class to explain the relevance and connection of the book to the focus unit and how it compared with other resources in the unit.

Culminating Experiences

The culminating experiences were a Holocaust and World War II classroom museum designed and created by the students and a presentation to the school board about their experiences in Washington. Students wanted the rest of the school to experience in some way what they had experienced in Washington, D.C. The Holocaust museum had changed them drastically and they hoped to share some of that experience and information with the rest of the school.

In order to approve our field trip, the school board had requested that the students create a presentation when we returned and share information with the rest of the school. Students formed small groups and created a preliminary plan for the museum and created an outline for the presentation. Each group made a presentation of their ideas and we finalized our plans.

Based on the literature, questions, reflective journals, and discussions we'd had about these historical events, at the end of the first week, students formed five inquiry groups. These groups focused on concentration camps, weapons and warfare, life on the home front, the American soldier, and World War II leaders.

After conducting research, each group made a proposal for their part of the museum. They shared the resources they had discovered and were currently reading, the resources and materials they would need, their exhibit design, and how much time would be needed for students to go through their part of the museum. We discussed the components of a quality museum and traveled to a local museum to get ideas. Students designed the layout of the museum and one group volunteered to create a brochure for each student visitor to use.

As a class entered our room, they were greeted by museum docents, ready to guide them through the museum. They began the tour by watching a student skit that we had video-taped titled "What You Didn't Know About Benito Mussolini." Next, visitors went to a multimedia table where they could experience an interactive multimedia presentation on the leaders of World War II and the weaponry and warfare used during the war. Other activities included two plays, one a skit of Japanese Americans being removed from their homes, the other a scene depicting life on the home front; a radio show; and an air raid. My students gave their visitors actual rationing sheets and an air raid schedule.

Then visitors entered into a depiction of a concentration camp. Visitors walked through a re-creation of a women's barrack in Auschwitz, listened to a readers' theatre of *Terrible Things*, and viewed a reenactment of a scene from *One Candle*, by Eve Bunting (2002). They also listened to a role play of Adolf Hitler demonstrating on a map his war strategies to take over Europe.

As the students exited the museum, they were able to meet a real World War II veteran. Students in one group wrote a letter to the editor asking if anyone had information pertaining to World War II soldiers. A veteran who lived in our community responded to the letter, and the students met with him. He came in and helped the group and then volunteered to tell stories and share his experiences with the visitors.

In addition to the classroom museum, students created a PowerPoint presentation for the monthly school board meeting. A small group of students were chosen by the class to present pictures of the classroom museum and the trip to Washington, D.C.

Closing the Window

This was the most amazing unit I conducted with my students during this school year. The trip was something none of us will ever forget and our experiences in Washington influenced our curriculum for the rest of the school year. It was important to meet the district's learning standards and still address the needs and interests of students. Our experiences reached far outside the classroom walls and changed our perspectives on the world.

CHAPTER 7

February—Learning the Rhythms of Poetry and Literature

But all they want to do
is tie the poem to a chair with rope
and torture a confession out of it.
They begin beating it with a hose
to find out what it really means.

—BILLY COLLINS, *THE APPLE THAT ASTONISHED PARIS*

Introduction

Poetry is the most undervalued resource in literacy education. It is also the one genre that engenders fear and loathing in many teachers. Too many teachers in my educational ca-

reer have tied poems to chairs and beat them with a hose until they gave up their meaning as Billy Collins suggests. Unfortunately, it was I and my fellow students who felt like we were being tied to a chair until we were able to find the meaning of a poem and probably a symbol or two in the process. When done right, reading and discussing poetry develops the imagination, exposes students to poetic language, helps readers go beyond literal meanings to consider figurative language and symbolism, and provides opportunities for students to enjoy the rhythms and rhymes of language. When done wrong, it is an educational bludgeoning device that makes novice readers feel inadequate.

In some aspects, reading poetry is different than reading literature, and in other ways it is the same. Louise Rosenblatt (1978) warns us

FEBRUARY CHAPTER OUTLINE

February Lessons and Learning Experiences
- ❖ Reading Poetry
- ❖ Poetic Language Searches
- ❖ Understanding Symbols
- ❖ Understanding Mood
- ❖ Word Storms
- ❖ Poetry-to-Music Connections
- ❖ Readers' Theatre

Featured Lesson in Comprehension for February: Suspending Closure

Literacy Assessments
- ❖ Writing Sample Analysis

Connections to the Writing Workshop
- ❖ Publishing CD Covers
- ❖ Class Poetry Book

not to read a poem to simply find information, as we do with expository texts. Poetry should be read aesthetically, enjoyed for its lived-through experience, its wordplay, and its rhythms, not the historical or scientific content that can be taken away as a result of one's reading. Poetry should be approached like quality literature, that is, one should be aware that a poet uses figurative language and symbolism to construct meanings that go beyond the literal text, there are multiple interpretations associated with any poem, and mood and voice are more important than finding facts.

The featured lesson this month focuses on a literary comprehension strategy I have called *suspending closure*. This term represents a stance to reading that I feel is not being demonstrated in traditional intermediate- and middle-grade classrooms. By suspending closure, we invite readers to entertain the ambiguity inherent in quality literature and poetry. That is, there are numerous meanings available during the act of reading these texts, and readers must remain open to these possibilities, or suspend closure, during the interpretive process.

The process of searching for a single main idea in a poem or a piece of literature is diametrically opposed to the concept of suspending closure. When searching for the main idea, readers are taught to overcome ambiguity and work to reach consensus on the true meaning, or main idea, of a text or a poem. This assumption of a single main idea diminishes the power of readers' interpretive processes and forces them toward premature closure during the act of reading.

In this chapter, I hope to alleviate some of teachers' fears of teaching poetry by demonstrating some simple, yet effective ways to help students discuss, comprehend, and write poetry. In addition, I provide some examples of how I incorporated music, art, and drama into the reading workshop. My goal is to find ways to immerse children in the sights and sounds of poetry, encourage them to read it independently, and identify and analyze the many literary devices without tying students or poems to chairs and beating confessions out of them.

February Lessons and Learning Experiences

Reading Poetry

Poetry is as much a way of reading as it is a particular type of text. We could approach any text and read it as if it were a poem. We could read obituaries looking for figurative language and metaphors, but that may be a bit gruesome. Louise Rosenblatt described two stances readers assume when reading: aesthetic and efferent. I have gone into more detail about these two stances in Chapter 5, but it is important to establish that the aesthetic stance is the one we predominantly assume when reading both poetry and literature.

When reading poetry, our community of readers must allow for multiple, diverse, and even contradictory interpretations to coexist. There is no direct correspondence between the language of poetry and the single, correct meaning one should arrive at after reading a poem. There has been a disruption in the signifying chain that allows ideology, politics, culture, and personal experiences to affect the meanings we construct in transaction with texts. This means our interpretive processes must consider alternative interpretations as viable, assessing the warranted assertions different readers propose rather than simply rejecting unique interpretations outright on the road to finding the main idea of a poem.

To support readers in reading poetry, teachers must read and discuss poems every day, provide opportunities for readers to read poetry independently, and allow small groups to focus on poetry as a text for literature studies. I read and discuss a particular poem, selected for a particular purpose, every day. In the beginning of the year, my selections are intended to get students simply interested in hearing poems and to not be afraid of the word *poetry*. I read humorous poems by Shel Silverstein and Jack Prelutsky, poems about colors from *Hailstones and Halibut Bones*, by Mary O'Neill (1961), limericks, unique poems from collections featuring Ogden Nash and William Blake, and shape poems from *A Poke in the I*, by Chris Raschka (2001). These poems offer readers invitations to explore poetry without intimidating them with unfamiliar language and obscure literary references.

But these are not the poems I finish the year with! As students become more comfortable listening to and discussing poetry, I gently challenge them by reading more complex poems by Langston Hughes, Eve Merriam, Valerie Worth, Nikki Giovanni, and others. We spend time sharing our ideas and focusing on the language poets use to create their works of art. I select poems for our discussions that provide an entry point into their meanings and some challenge when we get inside. It is this blend of points of entry and challenges that makes for the best poems to share and discuss. Here are a few steps readers can take when approaching a poem:

1. Begin by reading the poem completely through to get an overall sense of the poem.

2. Read the poem again, aloud, and highlight interesting words or phrases that you think are important.

3. Write some initial reactions to the poem in your notebook or along the margins of your copy of the poem.

4. Consider the poet, the setting of the poem's creation, and any contextual information you have on the poem and the poet.

5. Read what others have said about the poem, either other students or literary critics.

6. Share the interpretations you have generated with other students and listen to their ideas.

7. Read the poem again, and reconsider all you have thought about it.

Although these steps may be very general in nature, if we approach the reading of a poem with this sense of openness and willingness to listen to alternative ideas, we may create a space in our classrooms where poetry is read, and enjoyed, by all of our students.

The Search for Poetic Language

One of the most obvious differences between poetry and other writing is the language and rhythm of poetry.

Although we may begin focusing on poetry as a genre, our unit of study on poetry quickly expands into a unit on *poetic language* in its many forms. We find poetic language in advertisements, obituaries, picture books, newspapers, magazines, and memos. One of the primary objectives of this unit is getting students to notice and attend to poetic language when they encounter it. This language signals to readers that a text is to be read aesthetically, in the same way the structures and the language of an expository text signal how it should be read. Readers don't have to necessarily assume the stance a text may signal, but they have to be aware of the signals.

One way to help students attend to poetic language is to conduct poetic language searches in our library, our writer's notebooks, environmental print in the classroom, and texts in the world outside the classroom. One of my favorite authors to introduce our search for poetic language in pictures books is Byrd Baylor. Her wonderful picture books, many illustrated by Peter Parnall, include written text shaped like a poem, tall and thin with interesting line breaks. Although poetic language can be found in numerous picture books, I begin with a few that contain obvious examples.

The goal of these searches is to help readers attend to poetic language in all its diversity and to be aware that authors use various literary devices when crafting their stories. We copy snippets from picture books, poems from dinner place mats, phrases from advertisements, and words from the newspaper that have a poetic quality to them, display them on our "Poetic Language" bulletin board, and share and discuss our examples. Hopefully, these searches will carry over into students' writing as they begin to craft poems and other texts that draw upon poetic language.

Understanding Symbols

Thomas C. Foster wrote, "The problem with symbols is that people expect them to mean something. Not just any something, but one something in particular" (2003). And we have learned in school that the best readers will know what that one something is. Fortunately, or unfortunately, that is not the way symbols work.

Symbols are constructed by readers, based on their experiences with texts and life. Figurative language, including symbols, metaphors, clichés, similes, and hyperbole, forces the reader to consider not only the written text but the possible meanings and references to the world outside of the text. In order to interpret figurative language, readers must reject literal meanings and go beyond what is simply written in the text. Like irony in literature, there is a conflict between appearances and reality that must be addressed by the reader in order to go beneath the surface of a poem to uncover its possible meanings.

Donna Santman, in her book *Shades of Meaning* (2005), introduces students to two kinds of inferences: *figuring it out* inferences, and *making more* inferences. Figuring it out inferences are those inferences readers use to make sense of a story, and making more inferences are those readers use to go deeper into a text. Considering the meaning of symbols would be a type of making more inference. Readers interpret symbols by inferring meaning based on their experiences with text and how it relates to the world, looking for clues in the text about what an image or word may be referring to.

Some symbols are obvious; others we would never understand if we didn't read an interview with the author or a critique written by a literary scholar. Too often in schools, we are worried about the symbols that students *miss* rather than the ones they *construct*. For example, in the book *Where the Wild Things Are*, the moon shines through Max's bedroom window in several opening illustrations of the book. Maurice Sendak stated in an interview that the moon symbolizes his mother watching over him when he was a child. No reader, no matter how crafty, would make this connection without reading that interview. As this example shows, understanding symbols sometimes requires readers to read outside the text to make connections to the author's references.

Symbols allow writers to refer to an idea or concept without actually stating their meanings or intentions directly. Things stand for other things in literature. Novice readers often miss these symbols because they don't know that they should be looking for them and because they don't understand the references made to something outside of the text. As teachers, we call students' attention to the symbols we notice, how we came to make those connections, and how to spot clues for when symbols are being used.

Understanding Mood

Authors, illustrators, and poets, like filmmakers, use devices to establish the mood of a piece of literature or a poem. When a movie begins in an old castle, on a dark and stormy night, we know to look for vampires or a monster. Although the signals may be more subtle in writing, there are signs we need to pay attention to in order to understand the mood of a poem or a piece of literature.

One of the best ways to introduce the concept of mood to students is to demonstrate the contrasts between two poems or works of literature with drastically different moods. For example, I like to share with students the two books *Night of the Gargoyles*, by Eve Bunting (1994a), illustrated by David Wiesner in dark pencil or charcoal sketches, and *The Relatives Came*, by Cynthia Rylant (1985), illustrated with brightly colored pencils by Stephen Gammell. The difference between the illustrations and language used in these two books is immediately apparent. We discuss why Wiesner and Gammell chose to use the media they selected, why Bunting and Rylant chose the language they selected, and how their choices affected the mood of each story.

We can help readers understand mood by calling their attention to the setting of a story or a poem, by demonstrating how we would read the piece aloud, and by talking about why we chose to read it that way. We want to explain what clues we use to make our decisions about how to read a piece so readers will know what to attend to as they approach a poem or a piece of literature.

Helping readers understand the abstract concept of mood requires exposing them to many texts and demonstrations by capable readers in order to recognize the techniques authors and illustrators use to create this literary element. I want to see students using literary terms in our discussions, paying attention to the more complex elements of literature, and describing how they came to make their connections. We can read a piece of literature or a poem and miss these elements, but our reading experience will not be as rewarding as if we had attended to the nuances and elements of quality literature and illustrations.

Word Storms

An interesting invested discussion strategy that I created in response to our attention to poetic language is an instructional approach I call *word storms*. Word storms are a process by which readers generate lists of words in response to a poem or a piece of literature. The words they generate can come from the text itself or from their minds. Each student is responsible for generating a list of eight to ten words as I read a poem or a short text through a couple of times.

After students generate their lists, we share the words we wrote and discuss similarities and anomalies on our lists. Our discussions help readers develop a more extensive vocabulary and come to understand the variety of responses their classmates have to a text. Different readers attend to and connect with different aspects of a text or a poem. The words they generate are directly related to what they attended to. In our effort to suspend premature closure in the interpretive process, understanding what other readers attend to and the meanings they construct helps us remain open to new possibilities.

Poetry-to-Music Connections

Most people have developed strong relationships to particular songs during the course of their lives. Songs remind us of past events, emotional experiences, people we have met, and places we have visited. In past years, my students defined poetry as lyrics without the musical accompaniment. There is an obvious connection between the music in our lives and poetry, so why not take advantage of it!

One of the lessons I use to connect music and poetry is sharing with students songs and lyrics that I feel make a connection to the text of a poem and inviting students to bring in examples of music or lyrics that connected for them. For example, when reading *Pink and Say*, by Patricia Polacco (1994), a story of two boys during the Civil War, I brought in the song "The Night They Drove Old Dixie Down," by The Band. Other connections are not so obvious. I remember a student saying that *Nightjohn*, by Gary Paulsen (1993) reminded him of a rap song by 2Pac in which the rap artist struggled with his literate abilities in the same way the main character Sarny did in Paulsen's story.

Intertextual connections do not have to be only among pieces of poetry and literature. We need to encourage students to make connections across music, art, plays, movies, advertisements, calendars, museum exhibits, and other systems and representations of meaning. The more we can help students connect the books and poems they read to other texts and experiences, the richer their reading experiences will become.

Readers' Theatre

One of my favorite things to incorporate into the reading workshop is the dramatic arts. Although I have not mentioned it so far, drama and acting has been ongoing since the beginning of the year. Every year, I begin in the fall with simple charades and ad-libbing experiences. For example, I give students an index card with a particular scenario, for instance, a man who has lost his dog, and ask them to act out this scene so other students can guess what they are doing. The purpose of these drama exercises is to get students used to acting and being in front of others and to prepare them for the full-blown drama production we will do in the spring.

Every year I have created and produced a play to present to the school. Several years, I took a Disney story and adapted it for the stage; for example, we've presented *Alice in Wonderland* in a three-act play, complete with costumes and sets. I still have videos from some of these productions and enjoy revisiting the experience. Another drama activity I have done frequently with students is adapting fairy tales into dramatic productions. For example, we put Goldilocks on trial once for breaking and entering and the wolf on trial for "pigslaughter." Students were given various roles, including judge, prosecutors, police investigators, and bailiffs, and allowed to use any version of the fairy tale as evidence in the trial. Goldilocks got off with paying restitution, but the poor old wolf was sentenced to ten years in prison.

There are many ways to use children's literature in the drama workshop. Students can be taught to quickly adapt a picture book into an impromptu skit, and poems can be used for dramatic readings, especially the many wonderful poems written for two voices. Dramatic arts can bring out the talents and passion of many students who don't make their literate abilities visible in other areas. Not a year has gone by when a student or two haven't surprised me by demonstrating hidden acting abilities and benefited from the dramatic activities we have conducted.

Summary of Lessons and Learning Experiences

Approaching a poem can be a daunting task for many readers. Too often, prior experiences and expectations have squashed students' enthusiasm for this genre, but it doesn't have to be that way. Begin by finding some poems that you enjoy and share them with your students. Invite them to find poems that they enjoy and share them with the class. The more poetry we read and discuss, the more comfortable we will be when approaching the next poem.

Featured Lesson in Comprehension for February: Suspending Closure

I have briefly alluded to the concept of suspending closure earlier in this chapter. Similarly, Margaret Meek (1988) has suggested that readers need to learn how to "tolerate uncertainty." She describes this tolerance for uncertainty as the ability to suspend closure in order to see what occurs as the story unfolds. She suggests that those readers who are aware that authors help them make sense of the stories they are reading are more patient with the beginnings of books than those who expect to recognize straightaway what they have to understand. Readers with a higher level of tolerance for ambiguity and uncertainty are more capable of making sense of complex texts that require revisiting and do not reveal themselves completely during an initial encounter. As readers become more tolerant of the ambiguities presented in contemporary and postmodern literature, and learn to suspend closure in order to consider multiple perspectives and meanings, their interpretive skills and abilities to construct meaning in transaction with texts expand and develop.

Teaching readers to suspend closure is directly opposed to the way readers are prepared to read for standardized tests, which often ask them to find a single main idea (more will be discussed about standardized tests in the following chapter). Suspending closure means remaining open to exploring new interpretive possibilities as they arise. Fortunately, we are able to go back and discuss texts that have been discussed for centuries because there is no final, correct interpretation, only new interpretations to explore.

To demonstrate how to suspend closure, I use many of the multiple-perspective and postmodern texts Suzette referred to in her Window on the Workshop for November (Chapter 4). These texts would challenge the most capable of readers. So why use them with novice readers, you may ask? To demonstrate that reading and comprehending is a process that takes time and focused attention, that interpretations can be revised, and that no one has privileged access to the "real" meaning of a text.

A lesson on suspending closure may go like this. I begin by reading *The Three Pigs*, by David Wiesner (2001), aloud to my students. After only a few pages, students realize that this isn't a simple rendition of the classic fairy tale. The author is playing with the story, as well as reality, in both the written text and the illustrations. We read the book through and write down all of the impressions, connections, and wonderings we have about the book. I explain to my students that many of the questions we have posed will not be answered by the time we finish our discussions; in fact, many of them may never be answered. This may be disturbing to some readers, but we discuss why this happens and what we can do in the meantime.

Our discussions result in offering, agreeing upon, and disagreeing with interpretations in every class period. Just because there is no final interpretation doesn't mean we don't construct new ones every day. Suspending closure is about a process, not about being incompetent. Meanings are offered, beliefs are temporarily fixed, and on we go to other reading experiences. It is the readers' ability to go back and question what we have done and revise their ideas that makes for crafty readers.

Literacy Assessments

Writing Sample Analysis

Up to this point, all of the assessments I have demonstrated and shared with you have focused on the act of reading or readers' attitudes and behaviors. In this month's literacy assessments section, I discuss the importance of looking at students' writing samples for clues about their reading abilities and understandings as well as their ability to write. Especially with emergent readers, looking at writers' spelling and syntactical patterns can reveal a great deal about their reading processes.

There are observation guides, continuums, and scoring rubrics available for analyzing and scoring writing samples. However, what I am suggesting here is looking at a piece of writing and describing what the student tried to do, did successfully, and struggled with. What spelling patterns did she use that provide insight into her decoding of texts? What elements of literature does she tend to use frequently and what ones does she omit? By observing what writers do in the act of writing, and analyzing what they have written down, we get a window into how they read and what they are attending to in the texts they read.

Connections to the Writing Workshop

In much the same way as the genre study on personal narratives in the last chapter provided a connection to the writing workshop, a genre study on poetry brings the reading and writing of poetry together. The poems we read aloud and the poems we share with students become models for the types of poems students write. When students have had exposure to numerous poems and types of poetry, their choices for what to write and how to publish their poems expand.

Students need many avenues for publishing their writing. Every year, I purchase a cloth notebook to use for publishing students' poetry. It is the best seven dollars I spend each year. This blank notebook provides a place for students to publish and display their writing. All poems are edited before being included, and this poetry book becomes a favorite text in the reading workshop.

A student in one of my graduate classes explained to me how she was using CD covers as a place for students to publish their poems. Students designed their own cover art and included poems they wrote or copied some of their favorite poems into this four-inch-by-four-inch poetry anthology. Their collections are easy to transport and are kept safe for years to come.

Poetry can be published quickly and easily, providing opportunities for students to go through the complete writing process, from generating ideas to publication, in less time than many other genres. A young poets' day is a wonderful culminating activity for this unit of study, when parents and other students come to our room to hear us read aloud our poems. We don't do enough celebrating of our hard work in schools. When I finish writing this book, I will have a celebration, so why shouldn't my students celebrate their accomplishments?

There are numerous ways in which literature and poetry are incorporated into the writing workshop. Here are a few additional suggestions:

- ❖ getting ideas for our writing
- ❖ introducing and understanding new genres, themes, and authors
- ❖ understanding literary elements and devices
- ❖ launching writer's notebooks
- ❖ investigating art and visual representations
- ❖ using authors as writing mentors
- ❖ anchoring the sounds of language and poetry
- ❖ understanding what it means to be a writer
- ❖ understanding how writing can be published

Things I Hope to See, Hear, and Have Established by Month's End

1. Students are choosing poetry anthologies during independent reading time.
2. Students are reluctant to accept their initial responses to a poem as their final interpretations.
3. Poems are displayed on our walls and are appropriately connected to items in the classroom, for example, there are poems about fish near the aquarium.
4. Students are attending to the elements of literature I have demonstrated and are using the terms *mood* and *symbols* in our discussions.

Ideas for Further Reflection

❖ Katie Wood Ray's wonderful book called *Wondrous Words* (1999) describes the way she weaves literature into reading and writing workshops. I suggest giving this book some attention.

❖ Think about other ways that the things we do in the reading workshop connect to the writing workshop. Even though I designate separate time blocks for each workshop, it does not mean that I don't see the importance of their interrelatedness.

❖ Think about which readers in your classroom are able to suspend closure and which ones want an immediate answer to their questions about a text. Are these the same students who need to know how to spell every word before they write it down? I often wonder how to approach these students and help them understand that answers are the easy part; questions raise all doubts.

❖ Don't be afraid to go out and find some poems to share with your class. You don't need to have a degree in the fine arts to enjoy poems and share that enjoyment with your students.

❖ Read any of Georgia Heard's books on teaching poetry, or better yet, attend one of her workshops. I guarantee you will find yourself reading and writing poetry for years to come.

Closing Thoughts

Poetry should become an integral part of the reading workshop. The simple nature of the language of poetry demands that readers attend to symbols, metaphors, and figurative language beyond the decoding level in order to comprehend what has been written. Simply decoding a poem by Robert Frost does not indicate that one has made sense of the poem.

Children are exposed to poems, chants, and jump-rope songs from the time they are born. It seems that only in school has poetry become something to be feared. We need to use students' natural sense of rhythm and rhyme, their ability to play with language, and their sense of humor to open up interesting avenues for including poetry in the reading workshop.

Discovering the Rhythms and Language of Poetry

Introduction

Many years ago, I fit the profile Frank described of teachers who feared teaching poetry to children. My fears stemmed from my early experiences with poetry in school and my inability to find the one correct meaning for every poem we read. I figured, if I couldn't find it as a reader, how could I teach my students to find it? During my first year of teaching, I shared my fear of poetry with my principal, and the next thing I knew I was off to a conference to hear Georgia Heard speak about poetry. Hearing her presentation changed my view of poetry forever. I not only learned to love poetry but also developed an overwhelming desire to share poetry with my students and help them learn to love it as well. I found children had amazing insights into poetry when given the freedom to make sense of it on their own terms and a community of readers with which to share their ideas.

Focus

The focus of this unit of study was poetry and poetic writing. In this unit, students were immersed in poetry, learned to comprehend and interpret poetry, and wrote poems of their own. This month's Window on the Workshop outlines how I helped to develop students' appreciation of poetry and combined various lessons to create a three-week unit focusing on the language and structures of poetry.

Goals and Objectives

- ❖ expose students to a wide variety of poetry, poets, and anthologies
- ❖ help many students overcome their fear of poetry
- ❖ teach students strategies for interpreting and enjoying poetry
- ❖ expose students to the rhythms and language of poetry
- ❖ provide opportunities for students to write poetry
- ❖ create opportunities for students to share and discuss favorite poems and poets

Opening Ceremonies

Every day since the beginning of the year, I shared some of my favorite poems with students to expose them to the rhythms and language of poetry and help them feel comfortable with its sounds and meanings. I wanted to expose students to a wide variety of poetry, and simply let them listen to and enjoy it before we began to discuss what poems meant. I read humorous poems, poems about animals, silly poems about school and teachers, and poems about the lives and experiences of children.

In addition, students were invited to read aloud their favorite poems during our opening ceremonies. Students shared poetry and poetic language found in various texts, for example, poetry anthologies, picture books, novels, and magazines, with each other. As the year progressed, students read poems for two voices, student-generated poetry, and poems by their favorite poets.

To initiate our discussions of what poems mean, I pasted the poem "I Too," by Langston Hughes, into our walking journal and wrote some thoughts about the poem. In turn, students pasted favorite poems in the walking journal and invited other students to react to their entries. Students responded to each other and began to paste other poems from anthologies and their own poems in the journal for students to interpret and write about. The walking journal became one place for students to generate and negotiate the meanings of selected poems.

Cornerstone Texts

Cornerstone texts for this unit were *Love That Dog*, by Sharon Creech (2001), and *Polkabats and Octopus Slacks*, by Calef Brown (1998). *Love That Dog* is a book about a boy who hates to write poetry. In fact, the main character thinks poetry is for girls rather than boys. As the school year progresses, he discovers poetry that he enjoys and becomes inspired by the poetry of Walter Dean Meyers, specifically his poem "Love That Boy." Creech writes the entire book in free-verse format, taking us through Jack's transformation as he begins to love poetry and find voice through his writing.

Polkabats and Octopus Slacks is a collection of fourteen off-the-wall poems. Students fell in love with the poems about the Funky Snowman who loves to dance and the Lonely Surfer who surfs in the desert.

Launching the Unit of Study

Since the beginning of the year, we had been reading and discussing a wide variety of poetry. When launching this unit, we revisited many of the poets and poems we had become familiar with and enjoyed. We filled the classroom with poetry anthologies from the school and local libraries and posted our favorites on the walls and a bulletin board. As students found favorite poems and examples of poetic language, they included them in their writer's notebooks.

At the end of each reading workshop, I asked several students to share a poem they selected and enjoyed and explain what they thought it was about. Students would read a poem and offer their initial reactions. After students shared their favorite poems, I shared some of my favorites and invited students to interpret poems contained in various children's poetry anthologies.

To support more in-depth investigations of poetry and poetic language, I invited students to form poetry study groups in much the same way we created our literature study groups. I selected collections of poetry by a single author or an anthology focusing on a particular theme for students to read, share, interpret, and discuss. We read selections from *Something Permanent*, by Cynthia Rylant (1994), *The Dream Keeper and Other Poems*, by Langston Hughes (1996), *Sky Songs*, by Myra Cohn Livingston (1984), *Poetry for Young People*, by Carl Sandberg (Schoonmaker 1995) and *Poetry for Young People*, by Emily Dickinson (Schoonmaker 1994).

Poetry Study Groups   I initiated our poetry study groups by selecting five poems for each group to read and discuss. I spent time observing each group and asked each group to record their ideas on a piece of chart paper. Over the next few days, I rotated the poems among the groups and asked students to continue recording their ideas on chart paper. When all the poems had been read by each group, we gathered as a whole group and posted the charts from each group so we could discuss and compare our interpretations. I asked students to share ideas and explain why they responded they way they did to a particular poem. During these discussions, students made connections to other pieces of literature, their lives, and other poems.

To connect our reading of poetry to the writing of poetry, we discussed where poems hide. This lesson idea came from Georgia Heard and a poem called "A Valentine for Ernest Mann," by Naomi Shihab Nye. Students thought about where in their lives ideas for poetry were hiding, waiting to be discovered. To support this idea, we discussed where we thought famous poets found their ideas. Students read the poems and biographies of selected poets and began to make some connections between poets' lives and the poetry they wrote. This inspired students to create poems focusing on where poems hide, which led to the creation of a class book of these poems.

Guest Poets   Students were so intrigued with the poets we studied that they wrote a letter to the editor of our local newspaper asking if there were any poets in the area who would be willing to come in and share their poetry with the class. In response to the article, two local poets and one parent of a student in the class volunteered to come in. I asked these guest poets to bring in their writer's notebooks. Students were able to see the unique and individual ways each poet constructed his or her poems and how each one organized his or her writing. Students wanted to know why each poet wrote the particular poems he or she shared with students and asked many questions about the language the poet used and how he or she made it sound so good.

Explicit Instruction

Many of the lessons I conducted in the reading workshop focused on the structure and the language of poetry, how poets get ideas for poetry, and specific devices poets use to create poems, such as similes, metaphors, alliteration, and imagery. I introduced these lessons by using poems students were familiar with because students already had a sense of the rhythm and the structure of the poem and had already contemplated the meaning, which allowed them to concentrate on taking a closer look at how the poem was put together.

Shared Reading of Songs   To transition from one subject to another throughout the day, I used songs to signal students to put things away and get ready for a new activity. I selected songs and students brought in songs for these transitions. We created a classroom CD of these songs. During the poetry unit, students asked to create a new CD. Students suggested songs to include and I reviewed the songs for classroom appropriateness. I typed up the words to each song and projected the lyrics on the wall so we could all see them at once. We talked about the song as a piece of poetry and discussed the structure, line breaks, and meanings of the song. We created a songbook and discussed these songs in groups like we did with literature and poetry.

Line Breaks   An important aspect of the structure of poetry is how it is constructed into stanzas and how line breaks are used. To introduce the concept of line breaks, I provided each student with an unfamiliar poem that I had typed in paragraph form without any line breaks. I asked students in pairs to read the poem aloud and mark on their paper where they thought the line breaks should go.

I shared with students how poets used line breaks by connecting this concept to the director of a play. The line breaks are like stage directions that tell the actors where to go and how to move. In much the same way, poets use line breaks to tell the reader where to go and how to read the poem. Students then read their versions of the poem to the whole class. I then shared the original poem and how the poet had broken the lines, and we discussed the differences.

After we did this with several poems, I asked students to take one of their own poems, rewrite it into paragraph form, and share it with another student. The partner then marked the poem where he or she felt the line breaks should go. Then the two students compared and discussed the differences in meaning and rhythm generated by the different line breaks. Students began to pay close attention to the words that sometimes hung at the end of their lines of poetry. They learned to use line breaks to direct the reader to read the poem the way they intended and to find the rhythm they imagined for the poem.

Workshop Experiences

One important component of this unit on poetry is the poetry center. It is a place to experiment with poetry and learn about and enjoy the sounds of poetry. During workshop time students could visit the poetry center at any time. All of the activities that were in the center were introduced and demonstrated to the whole class before becoming independent activities in the poetry center.

Using *Polkabats and Octopus Slacks,* students wrote the words to many of Brown's poems on chart paper, laminated them, and cut the words out and put them into a folder. In the poetry center, students used the words from a poem to create new poems and then posted them on a bulletin board. Each day a small group of students experimented with the words and created a new poem and presented it to the class. Students cut up the words from other poems and put them in folders as well. It was like magnetic poetry, but the words students could draw upon came from existing poems. Other activities involved in the poetry center included a nature box with items students could observe and write about, picture books in which students could search for poetic language, rhyming dictionaries, and activities to help students get ideas for their writing.

A listening center was also available during the reading workshop. Children listened to purchased tapes of poetry or tapes containing favorite poems created by their classmates. They also listened to the songs we had put on CD and read the songbook we had created to accompany the songs. As the year progressed, students published their own poems on tape. Students loved to hear their voices on tape, and it gave them a chance to practice reading poetry aloud.

Using Paul Fleischman's book *Joyful Noise: Poems for Two Voices* (1988) as a mentor text, some of my ELL students used this structure to create poems in two languages for two voices. Students wrote in a language they were comfortable with first and then wrote a parallel poem in English or in Spanish. Students read the poems together, alternating their voices and the languages. Students created these poems in pairs and read them together, carefully choreographing the words in their performances.

There was a wonderful buzz in the room during this unit of study as students shared new poems, laughing out loud at times, and discussed what poems meant to them. At the end of the reading workshop block, students would often perform a readers' theatre or dramatic reading of a particular poem. These experiences helped poetry come alive in our classroom and helped students appreciate this form of writing. Enjoyment came before interpretation, paving the way for students to dig deeper into what they had read.

Culminating Experience

To complete the poetry unit, I combined the reading and writing of poetry by creating a class anthology of our poetry. During the unit, we read many poetry anthologies and studied the different ways they were structured and created. We discussed the various elements of an anthology and discovered that most had an introduction explaining the purpose for the collection.

I asked students to create their own poetry anthologies. Each student was required to select a theme or focus, collect eight poems that fit that theme or focus, and write three to five original poems to include in the anthology. Students then wrote an introduction and a "Meet the Author" page. This was an extensive writing project, but students had been exposed to such a variety of poetry that they had access to plenty of poems for their themes. Before students began to write their anthologies, I shared one of my own that focused on my family. I wrote an introduction to explain the purpose for each poem and introduced myself as the author to model my expectations for students.

We had a poetry celebration at the end of the unit and invited parents, the poets who had visited our classroom, and any interested staff members. Students shared selections from their anthologies and put them on display for the visitors to read and enjoy.

Closing the Window

I have observed over the years that students' writing begins to change after we have discussed poetry. Because of our unit on poetry, students become more interested in how their personal narratives flow and concerned about choosing the right word to begin their persuasive essays. In a community of readers focusing on poetry, children love to hear poetry read aloud, to laugh at its humor, to dwell in its language, to move to its rhythm, and to use various poetic devices to create poems of their own. Poems are not to be tied to chairs and beaten; they are to be savored like a fine wine and shared with the closest of friends.

CHAPTER 8

March—The Role of Literature Across the Curriculum

> There are multiple ways in which the world can be known:
> artists, writers, and dancers, as well as scientists,
> have important things to tell about the world.
> —ELLIOT EISNER, *THE ENLIGHTENED EYE*

Introduction

The month of March is usually associated with blooming wildflowers, warmer weather, and spring break. Unfortunately, March is also associated with the annual onslaught of standardized testing. The strategies and dispositions acquired in the reading workshop may not prepare students for the types of experiences they will encounter on standardized tests. I, along with numerous other educators, advocate teaching students to approach standardized tests as a distinct genre. In much the same way we teach students to approach poetry and expository texts as distinct genres, we need to teach to students how to approach a standardized test passage, with its unique language and structures, in order to demonstrate proficiency on this narrow assessment of literate behaviors.

There is more than one way to read and think about a text, and standardized tests require a very specific way of reading and thinking. As much as I detest the proliferation of testing in the United States, and as much as I write and speak against its narrowing effects on reading curricula and instruction, I realize that it is a fact of life in contemporary American classrooms and must be addressed somewhere in the reading workshop. Teachers who simply assume that readers who are doing well in the reading workshop will do well on standardized tests are making a strategic error.

In addition to addressing standardized tests, this chapter also extends the discussion from Chapter 5 on using literature in the content areas. Although literature is weaved throughout the curriculum over the course of the school year, I describe some particular strategies for helping students use literature to make sense of textbooks and expository texts in the content areas. Rather than looking at expository texts as a genre, in this chapter I discuss using expository texts and textbooks as resources for constructing knowledge in social studies, math, and science.

> **RECOMMENDED COMPREHENSION STRATEGIES FROM *LESSONS IN COMPREHENSION***
>
> ❖ 4.5 Graffiti Boards
> ❖ 5.3 Monitoring Understanding
> ❖ 5.4 Summarizing Texts
> ❖ 5.5 Organizing Thoughts

March Lessons and Learning Experiences

Literature is a way of knowing. As Elliot Eisner mentioned in the epigraph, literature, like other art forms, brings a new perspective to the world, one that provides a different lens on events and phenomena than scientific inquiry and observations do. What one can learn by reading a work of literature about a particular subject, for example the Civil War, is qualitatively different than what a reader constructs while reading a textbook.

Thomas McGowan, one of my professors during graduate school, discussed two different aspects of the social studies curricula: the head and the heart. In his book on American history, *Telling America's Story* (1991), he explained that textbooks give you information for your head, such as dates, facts, and names of important people, while literature provides information that touches the heart and involves the emotional aspects of one's learning. In his opinion, a quality social studies curriculum needs both aspects, head and heart, to be successful. He suggests the best way to get to the heart component is through literature, especially historical fiction.

Content Area Graffiti Boards

In *Lessons in Comprehension*, I discussed the use of graffiti boards, demonstrating how students in small groups represent their ideas about a work of literature on large sheets of butcher paper using symbols, sketches, and short phrases. However, graffiti boards can also be used to construct meaning in transaction with expository texts. After reading aloud an expository text, for example, Seymour Simon's book *Storms* (1989), I had students generate ideas from the book that were important to them on a graffiti board. It was very interesting to see how different students attended to different aspects of what I had read. We shared our graffiti boards with each other and produced an overview of the book from our various representations. This process helped students understand what different readers considered important to know about storms and helped them organize their thoughts.

Summarize 3-2-1

One of the most important processes or strategies for reading the vast amount of text-book pages and expository texts students are required to do as they progress into the middle grades and beyond is to be able to paraphrase and summarize textbook chapters into manageable amounts of information. As students progress into the intermediate and middle grades, they are often required to read a chapter, summarize the important points, and recall that information when necessary for research reports or exams.

The ability to summarize what has been read is not simply the act of reducing information down to smaller amounts of text. In order to summarize what has been read, a reader must be able to comprehend the selection, see the bigger picture, and describe themes, important events, and characters in relatively little space. I developed the summarize 3-2-1 strategy when working with my intermediate-grade students during a unit on astronomy and space exploration. Because of the vast amount of information available on this subject, my students were having trouble managing the large number of ideas they were constructing from what they read.

I began by showing students that many contemporary novels, picture books, and expository texts have a summary written in the Library of Congress section of the peri-text. We looked at what these summaries contained and what was omitted. We discussed how the summaries were not simply shortened versions of the story. Next, I asked students to summarize a book they had read in three sentences. We discussed what they wrote, and then I asked them to write another summary using only two sentences. Finally, I asked them to rewrite their summary using only one sentence. We discovered in this process that one could not simply eliminate one of the sentences to make a better summary. Some students simply wrote longer sentences. We discussed what they wrote and talked about whether they had enlarged their perspectives or simply tried to include everything in the story. Students had to rethink what they knew about the book in order to write about it in fewer words and sentences.

We used the Library of Congress summaries, captions, tables of contents, and book advertisements to investigate how to summarize information. We then used this process on sections of expository texts we had been reading. One thing became clear through these lessons: you cannot adequately summarize something you do not comprehend. Too often, students think a summary is simply a shorter rendition of the same information in the story. In order to summarize, the smaller the amount of text you are allowed to use, the bigger your ideas and perspective must be.

Graphic Organizers

One comprehension strategy that has been taught in many classrooms is the use of graphic organizers or semantic webs to represent what one comprehends or constructs before, during, and after reading. Teachers sometimes use graphic organizers to get a sense of what students know about a particular topic, for example, K-W-L charts, and sometimes use them to assess what students have retained after a particular unit of study. Being able to represent what one has learned in a semantic web is challenging, but it helps readers organize ideas and information and allows them to see connections among the various components of what they have been reading.

As with architecture, form should follow function in graphic organizers. Too often, students are given a Venn diagram or some other predetermined structure for a graphic organizer and are asked to simply fill it in with information. The way students want to organize information or the inherent structures of a work of literature should determine which graphic organizer students choose to use, not the other way around. In order to select an appropriate graphic representation, students have to consider what they have read and how they want to organize that information. To make graphic organizers a successful comprehension strategy, we should provide readers with a plethora of graphic design choices, or better yet, allow them to create their own diagrams to represent what they have comprehended. It is not simply the ability to fill in a Venn diagram that is important; rather, it is a reader's ability to know when to choose a Venn diagram.

Jigsaw Reading

Because of the sometimes overwhelming amounts of reading we require students to do in the content areas, we need to consider ways of dividing up the reading so students don't get bogged down in the amount of reading we require them to do. One strategy to help with this challenge is called *jigsaw reading*. Jigsaw reading is an instructional approach where we show students how to divide up a particular chapter in a textbook or expository text, assign a section for each student to read and take notes on, then provide opportunities for students to discuss the sections they have read. Like so many of the comprehension strategies I have discussed in this book, the most important feature of the procedure is the sharing of ideas in the discussions that take place. Jigsaw reading is a strategy teachers can utilize to help students attend to smaller sections of text and use discussion to construct an understanding of the complete text with other readers. Jigsaw reading also keeps students from getting overwhelmed with too much to read.

Summary of Lessons and Learning Experiences

Constructing meaning with expository texts is different from understanding a work of literature. Each text requires a different approach and different comprehension strategies. The strategies described in this chapter focus on reading for information, a type of reading that readers are required to do more of as they progress through school.

Featured Lesson in Comprehension for March: Official Meanings

In the opening chapter, I discussed at length that there was no such thing as a single, main idea hiding somewhere in a work of literature to be passively discovered by readers. However, when students are confronted by standardized tests, they are probably going to be asked to find a main idea and bubble in the correct choice on the answer key. How do we resolve this conundrum? I explain to students that reading to do well on a standardized test is different from reading to discuss literature in the reading workshop. In the reading workshop, we work to generate, articulate, negotiate, and revise meanings in a community of readers, and these are what I still believe to be the most important aspects of reading. However, standardized test makers operate within a different theoretical framework and are going to ask students to identify and select a predetermined main idea. Although I still don't believe there is a main idea hidden in the text, test makers seem to have no qualms about asking students to identify an answer to match the main idea they have predetermined.

My role is not to help students change their understandings of reading to identify main ideas; it is to help them identify the answer or main idea the test makers want them to identify. This is an important distinction! Although theoretically there may not be a main idea that resides hidden in a text, there is one predetermined by the test makers for the passages they include.

The last thing I want my students to do is waste time trying to defend multiple possibilities for these standardized test passages, in the same manner they do for the literature we discuss. I want them to understand how to identify the official meaning in the context of a standardized test and move on to the next passage. Let me share some ideas about standardized tests before discussing how I address them as a distinct genre.

Some Preliminary Thoughts About Standardized Tests

❖ Standardized tests require students to recognize correct answers from among a group of answers. That means they are dealing only with recall abilities.

❖ There are certain literacy skills that students need to be able to perform well on standardized tests, and these may differ from the skills supported in the reading and writing workshops.

❖ Students must be made to feel comfortable around the test or anxiety will cause them to score worse than they could under better circumstances.

❖ We as teachers must place value upon the test or students will see our disdain and reluctance and possibly perform below expectations.

❖ Preparation builds confidence, and confidence leads to better performance.

❖ Many of our students have the required reading skills yet have trouble demonstrating these skills in the context of a standardized test.

Research on standardized test preparation suggests preparation should be (1) intensive—conducted in the weeks directly before the test; (2) cooperative—teachers and students should work together to discuss and negotiate meaning; (3) nonthreatening—the mention of rewards or punishment for test performance should never occur; and (4) of short duration—if students dwell too long on tests and preparation, their performance tends to deteriorate. Because of this research, I believe it is best to approach standardized test passages as a distinct genre.

A Unit of Study on the Standardized Test Genre

Before beginning a unit of study on standardized tests, I try to *demystify* the tests with my students. I explain why they are used, how they are constructed, how the results will be used, and who creates them. I discuss specific requirements of the testing situation, for example, no talking is allowed, the exercises are timed, and teachers can't really help them during the test. I allow students to share their concerns about the test and we discuss their concerns to help alleviate anxiety.

In addition, I acquire any legally available test-preparation materials and examples of the passages my students will encounter. Before I can demonstrate the various sections of a standardized test and think about how I am going to prepare students for the tests, I must know the types of questions, passages, and materials my students will encounter. Taking standardized tests also requires survival skills. Testing days can be intense for many students and demand their focused attention for long periods of time. I must find ways to help students develop stamina for reading and focusing their attention before they encounter these tests. Remember, it is not cheating to familiarize students with the types of tasks they will face on standardized tests before they encounter them.

I launch the unit by having students brainstorm what they remember about the tests they have taken in the past and clarify any misconceptions they may have. I make a class chart about what they remember and ask students what strategies they have used in the past. I want to understand what they have done in the past and identify strategies that may or may not be helpful in approaching a standardized test.

Once we have discussed our experiences with these tests, I immerse students in reading examples of the questions and passages they will encounter. We read through these and make class charts containing what we have discovered. We consider the various elements and formats of each section, the structure of the questions being asked, and some of the literary devices used to create these passages. Because many students have trouble understanding what is being asked, we create charts of the various terms used in the questions. We discuss some of the words used in the questions and directions, for example, *define, compare, contrast, explain, describe, evaluate, list, identify, summarize, interpret, review, prove,* and *analyze.* Teaching students to identify the tricks that test makers use to fool students is a large part of this unit of study.

I try to help students develop a scavenger-hunt mentality when reviewing the questions and passages. In general, I want them to look for important information in the passage and read only enough of the passage as necessary to answer the questions correctly. I teach students to read the questions before reading the passages in order to determine what will be asked of them. I also make sure that my students know they need to answer *every* question on the test. Guessing is not only allowed, it is encouraged. If there are four answers, choosing one gives the student a 25 percent chance of being right. Even in Las Vegas we know 25 percent isn't much, but it's better than nothing!

Whether we like it or not, standardized tests are directly connected to our jobs and the resources made available to our students. Funding decisions, administrative longevity, grade-level promotions, graduation, and teachers' salaries and bonuses are all closely tied to standardized test scores. Because of the high stakes associated with test scores, teachers need to find ways to help students make their literate abilities visible on these standardized measures.

Literacy Assessments

I described in Chapter 3 how I launched student treasuries and began to help students collect artifacts of their learning to document and demonstrate their literate abilities. In March, we reflect on the collection of artifacts in our treasuries and prepare to share our learning and development with parents during student-led conferences.

Student-led conferences differ from traditional parent-teacher conferences in one significant way: students take the lead in discussing their learning rather than teachers. Students prepare for student-led conferences by reflecting on and organizing the artifacts in their treasuries, while parents prepare by completing a questionnaire about their concerns and observations of their child's learning (see Figure 8.1). Teachers prepare by

FIG. 8.1 *Parent Conference Preparation Questionnaire*

Parent Conference Preparation Questionnaire

1. What improvements have you noticed in your child's learning and schoolwork?

2. What concerns do you have about your child's schoolwork?

3. What has your child been most successful with this year?

4. What has your child struggled with this year?

5. Any other comments or suggestions?

Treasury Reflection Form

Name of artifact: _____

This artifact shows that I am:

organized   industrious   thoughtful   responsible   persistent   honest

artistic   a leader   curious   observant   cooperative   resourceful

What this artifact shows about me as a learner: _____

_____

_____

Why I chose this artifact: _____

_____

_____

FIG. 8.2
Treasury Reflection Form

May be copied for classroom use.
© 2006 by Frank Serafini and
Suzette Serafini-Youngs from
Around the Reading Workshop in 180 Days
(Heinemann: Portsmouth, NH).

reviewing the assessment data they have gathered throughout the year and connecting a student's progress to the state or district learning standards and other criteria.

I ask students to review their treasuries and organize them into specific categories, for example, math, science, and art. I then ask them to reflect on what each piece they have collected shows about their learning and their developing abilities. I have developed a form for students to attach to each artifact in their treasury on which to record their reflections (see Figure 8.2). Students attach a form to an artifact and circle some of the descriptors on the form that explain what aspects of learning the artifact demonstrates. The descriptors on the form are generated during a discussion about what makes a successful learner, reader, writer, and so on. Each year the descriptors change, and there is always an open space for students to include any new descriptors they have generated.

The students create a table of contents to help organize their artifacts and reflections. Before their student-led conferences take place, students write an introductory letter to their parents explaining what they have learned and what has been important to them as a learner during the year. The students read the introductory letter and share the artifacts with their parents during the conferences.

After students have shared their treasures, I meet with parents and discuss the questionnaire they completed and any additional information I feel is important to mention. My goal is to keep students' presentations as the central focus of the conferences while still making myself readily available to answer questions parents may have. Since my first year of teaching I have used student-led conferences in lieu of the traditional parent-teacher conferences during the spring semester. Student-led conferences allow students to demonstrate what they have learned, involve them in the assessment process, show respect for their observations and insights, and give them opportunities to share their accomplishments with their parents.

Connections to the Writing Workshop

The culminating project for some of the units of study we conduct in the content areas is a picture book students create to present their ideas and information they've learned. Students use their knowledge of expository texts developed earlier in the year in the reading workshop to create these picture books. In the past, we have read these student-generated books with our reading buddies and prominently displayed them in our classroom library.

For many of the units of study that I engage students with in the content areas, we create a classroom museum to house all of the resources that we have gathered about a particular topic or theme. To connect writing to this classroom museum project, I have students create a brochure and guide for visitors to use when they visit our classroom museum. I gather various brochures I have collected from my visits to museums, and we discuss their components and structures before students create their own brochures. To extend this experience, we can do a genre study on brochures in the writing workshop.

Things I Hope to See, Hear, and Have Established by Month's End

1. Quality literature and expository texts are being used throughout the curriculum and content areas.
2. Students are using graphic organizers and graffiti boards to comprehend and represent their understandings of what they have read.
3. I have gathered numerous resources about standardized tests.
4. I am more knowledgeable about the kinds of questions and exercises my students will encounter on standardized tests.
5. I've established and conducted a unit of study focusing on standardized tests.
6. Students are more relaxed and confident about taking standardized tests.
7. Students see themselves as capable of assessing their own literate abilities and development and able to articulate what they have learned and are working on.

Ideas for Further Reflection

❖ Read Paul Fleischman's novel *Bull Run* (1993), a multiple-perspective novel about the battle of Bull Run during the Civil War. This book provides examples of different perspectives on an historical event, helping students understand how historical accounts are always told from a particular perspective.

- David Whitin and Sandra Wilde's book *Read Any Good Math Lately?* (1992) provides wonderful examples of ways to integrate children's literature into the math curriculum.
- Create text sets that connect novels under study with other types of texts and media to provide multiple points of entry for students' learning and exploration of a topic.

Closing Thoughts

Suzette demonstrates how a classroom teacher can respond to the interests of her students and use these interests to generate the curriculum across various subject areas. Response-centered instruction, like the instructional experiences advocated by John Dewey and other progressive educators, does not ignore the mandated curriculum; instead, it uses students' interests as a starting point for their inquiries. The students in Suzette's literature study group are considered important resources for other students to draw upon for their investigations into American history. Because of this, Suzette is not the only expert in the classroom. She is seen as one learner coming to know a subject through literature and expository materials along with, instead of in front of, her students.

Textbooks are not the best resource, especially when they are viewed as the only resource for studying a particular subject or topic. Multiple texts and resources need to be located and provided to allow students a way into the curriculum. As we find new ways to expand the use of literature and other trade resources across the school curriculum, we need to consider the strategies readers will need to comprehend what they will read. Approaching a textbook is very different from approaching a novel and requires readers to draw upon different reading strategies to construct information from the text. Using literature to expand readers' understandings to include as well as people's emotions and experiences, facts and information, provides a larger perspective for understanding the world around us.

Looking Closely at Literature Study Groups

Introduction

This month's Window on the Workshop looks somewhat different from the ones I have written so far, as I focus on one particular component of the reading workshop—the literature study group. The literature study group I discuss focused on the young adult novel *Out of the Dust,* by Karen Hesse (1997). The reading of this book extended into two weeks, as we incorporated other resources to support readers' understandings of the Dust Bowl and the Great Depression. Ultimately, the book inspired a short unit of study on the Depression and the Dust Bowl in which we inquired further into this period of American history.

Cornerstone Text

The cornerstone text was *Out of the Dust,* by Karen Hesse. Hesse tells the emotional story of a family living in the Dust Bowl from the perspective of Billie Jo, a young teen growing up during the Depression. Hesse uses a free-verse poetry format to tell the story of Billie Jo's family as they deal with the hardship involved with running a farm in Oklahoma. Billie Jo's strength and courage are inspirational for young readers as she deals with the loss of her farm, the death of her mother, and getting burned in an accident in her kitchen.

***Out of the Dust* Literature Study Group**

I follow the same procedures for launching literature study groups that Frank has described. I placed *Out of the Dust* on the chalkboard for students to preview. Students signed up for the group and we had our first meeting to set expectations for the discussion. At this initial meeting, we scanned the book, reading the information provided on the front and back covers, and read the first three chapters together.

Because each novel poses new challenges based on its structure, genre, and content, I asked students to read a few chapters to ensure they understood what was happening. I asked students to read for thirty minutes the first night, take notes on their reactions to the text, and record how much they were able to read in that period of time. We read approximately fifteen to twenty pages each night, and met to discuss the book three times a week. I have found discussing this novel while students are reading it, rather than waiting until students have read the entire story, is more effective in helping students deal with the difficult and unfamiliar structure of the text.

At the next meeting, students focused on the poetic structure of the text and wondered why Karen Hesse chose to write the novel this way. I brought in *Locomotion,* by Jacqueline Woodson (2003), and *Love That Dog,* by Sharon Creech (2001), for comparison. We discussed the reasons an author might choose to use a poetic structure. Interestingly, in the other two books, the characters were involved in learning poetry in school and the structure of these novels connected to the characters' experiences. However, in *Out of the Dust* there was no reference to writing poetry in school.

In discussing the setting of the Dust Bowl and the vast expanses of land that were once green and bursting with crops, students had a difficult time visualizing the scenery. In response, I brought in the book *Children of the Dust Bowl: The True Story of the School at Weedpatch Camp*, by Jerry Stanley (1992), and *The Great Depression,* by R. Conrad Stein (1993), to help support their understanding of the setting. We researched the Dust Bowl on the Internet and watched videos of dust storms. Students were able to connect to Billie Jo at a much deeper level once they were able to visualize what she was experiencing.

As students read the story and became comfortable with the structure of the novel, they began to discuss various literary elements and changes in structure within the text. As the literature study continued, students made connections to other historical periods and to their lives. To bring the first reading of the book to a close, we read the last four chapters together in class, savoring every word and experience Karen Hesse offered.

Although we discussed the text as we read it, the bulk of our discussion took place after we finished the story. After completing the book, we discussed the themes and ideas that were threaded through the book and decided which ones were worth revisiting. For *Out of the Dust*, students identified the topics and themes of love, friendship, inner conflict, confidence, dust, setting, changes in character, and metaphors as possible discussion points. We chose one or two themes for each ensuing discussion.

We began with the word *dust* and reread sections of the text to find where and how the word *dust* was used. It appeared throughout the text and seemed to take on new meanings with each new context. Students began to interpret the various ways Karen Hesse used the word. On sticky notes, students recorded their interpretations of *dust* in each particular context. We charted all of our ideas about dust before moving on to other topics. Next we chose the theme of love and discussed what it meant to Billie Jo throughout the text.

At the end of this investigation, students prepared a presentation to introduce *Out of the Dust* to their classmates. It was this literature study presentation that was the impetus for launching a two-week unit of study on the Dust Bowl. The literature study group created a powerful PowerPoint presentation that included text about each character and information on the Great Depression and the Dust Bowl. Students shared with their classmates the importance of the setting and the importance of the accuracy of the historical events in the story. Their classmates asked so many questions about the Great Depression and the Dust Bowl that they requested to study it in more depth. This is an example of how a unit of study grew out of students' interests instead of being preplanned by the teacher or mandated in the school curriculum.

Focus

The focus of the two-week unit was the Great Depression and the Dust Bowl and how children endured the tragedies of that period in American history. We used *Out of the*

Dust as the primary resource, but also incorporated visual resources such as websites and videos on this subject.

Goals and Objectives	❖ introduce students to the Great Depression and the Dust Bowl ❖ use a variety of multimedia resources to support student learning ❖ blend the historical information provided in expository texts with the personal experiences provided in novels and selected picture books.
Launching the Unit of Study	After their presentation, I asked the students in the literature study group to take turns reading the book *Out of the Dust* aloud to the rest of the class. They were seen as the experts on this topic, sharing their insights and knowledge, and they directed the discussions with the rest of the class. We read *Children of the Dust Bowl* to connect the information it contained to the personal experiences and stories represented in *Out of the Dust.*
Workshop Experiences	During our reading workshop, students read a variety of books focusing on the Dust Bowl and the Great Depression. I gathered a variety of resources from the school and public libraries, websites, local families who had parents and grandparents who had experienced the Great Depressions, and television documentaries. As students read and researched these topics, they recorded information in their reading response notebooks. We learned about President Roosevelt and what he did during the Depression to help families. We looked at the migration of people from the Midwest to Bakersfield, California, who hoped for work on large farms. We created class charts to record information on the Great Depression, the Dust Bowl, and the westward migration and used these artifacts to further our discussions.
Culminating Experience	For the culminating experience, my students and I thought it would be appropriate to respond to this period in history through poetry. Mirroring the structure of *Out of the Dust*, students selected particular historical events or people, conducted research on their subjects, and drafted poems to express their understandings of these subjects. In some cases, students took notes and represented their understandings in traditional research reports and then selected words and phrases from their reports to create poetry in the same process as writing found poetry. The poems were published and shared in a class poetry book on the Dust Bowl.
Closing The Window	This unit was spontaneous, emerging out of the work of one particular literature study group. It was highly engaging because the students were intrigued by the subject matter. It was not typical for me to use a literature study group as the inspiration for a unit of study, but in this case, students were engaged with a high-quality piece of literature that focused the direction of our curriculum. As Frank discussed earlier in the chapter, there are texts that provide information for the head and literature that provides a window

into the emotions of the characters and events in history. I believe that both are important components in a study like this.

For this unit, we began with a novel that shared the emotions of Billie Jo's experiences and then drew upon expository texts and textbooks to provide the factual data. The students of the literature study group served as guides for the unit as they became experts and informants for the rest of the class.

CHAPTER 9

April—Literature and Social Issues

It is the mark of an educated mind to be able
to entertain a thought without accepting it.
—ARISTOTLE

Introduction

It is important to note that, although I am writing about literature and social justice in the April chapter, I have not waited all year long for discussions about equity, gender, and social issues to be part of the reading workshop. Incorporated in many lessons and discussions are issues of social justice, equality, and democracy. Becoming aware of these issues is about adopting a stance, not about completing a particular set of activities.

Reading literature that addresses social issues, gender roles, race relations, ecology, war, religion, and politics creates an opportunity for what Jerry Harste has called "critical conversations." Children's literature can create a space for students and teachers to question the way the world is represented in literature, analyze the construction of gender, race, ethnicity, and social class, and investigate the themes and concepts that connect literature to the lives of students. Within this theoretical space, the literature teachers select to read and discuss needs to support students' interrogation of the ways in which people like themselves are represented and bring to conscious attention the stereotypes and misrepresentations of traditionally underrepresented groups.

April Lessons and Learning Experiences

Creating a space for students to become aware of social issues and discuss them requires patience and a delicate hand. I realize that some of the issues that may arise during the reading of this literature may make teachers and students feel uncomfortable. To navi-gate these challenging texts, I often begin with issues that are easier to discuss, for example, gender roles, bullying, gangs, and pollution, rather than more controversial issues like alternative lifestyles, sex, and child abuse. Depending on the group of students I have each year, I may not bring forward some issues. It takes a measure of maturity and understanding of the world to discuss many of these social issues.

Over the course of the year, I want to address social issues that arise as we interact with each other, experience multicultural literature, and read about current events in newspapers and magazines. I'm not trying to advocate that we go out and find every controversial topic available and conduct studies on them. However, there are numerous opportunities to help students become aware of social issues through the day-to-day interactions in our classroom. Let me begin by discussing some general classroom expectations and experiences before describing specific lessons and learning experiences that I have used to help raise students' awareness of social issues.

> ### RECOMMENDED COMPREHENSION STRATEGIES FROM *LESSONS IN COMPREHENSION*
>
> ❖ 7.6 Evaluating Responses
> ❖ 8.1 Uncovering Stereotypes
> ❖ 8.2 Understanding Official Meanings
> ❖ 8.3 Interrogating Advertisements
> ❖ 8.4 Asking New Questions
> ❖ 8.5 What We Used to Know
> ❖ 8.6 Analyzing the Classroom Library
> ❖ 8.7 Examining Magazines for Children
> ❖ 8.8 What Have They Done to This Story?

Social Issues in the Classroom

One does not have to look far to find issues of social justice and equity in one's own classroom. In every school that I have taught at, students came from diverse backgrounds, ethnicities, races, social classes, and experiences. You don't have to look outside the classroom for social issues to discuss; you just have to become aware of the issues that already exist in your community. Issues of tolerance, bullying, gender bias, honesty, personal integrity, and civic responsibility present themselves every day in most classrooms. The choice is whether to address these issues or pretend they don't exist. Just because teachers may feel uncomfortable discussing these issues doesn't mean that they shouldn't be addressed. In the hands of a skillful teacher, literature can be used as a space to begin conversations that students may never get a chance to participate in otherwise.

The Class Meeting

One component of our classroom community that has played an important role in helping students address social issues that arise during the course of the year has been the class meeting. During a class meeting, I or my students bring to the class' attention particular issues or challenges that we feel we need to address. I provide a space on a designated whiteboard for students to list challenges that need to be addressed during the class meeting or suggestions for improving our procedures and community. I separate the challenges into those that include the teacher and those that should be handled by the students themselves.

In the beginning of the year we conduct a class meeting almost every day. By the end of September, we hold class meetings about twice a week, unless an emergency demands our immediate attention. The challenges and suggestions listed by students over the years have included such issues as sharing playground equipment, bullying, organizing spaces in the room, sharing couches and pillows during independent reading, and where people should sit during read-alouds. Students play an active role in establishing the procedures and organization of the classroom through these discussions. I purposely do not create rules to address every single aspect of classroom operations because I expect students to take ownership of our classroom and make suggestions about how to improve what we do.

I assign a student the role of classroom meeting director and he or she leads the class discussions for a month, then I assign another student to this position. We begin class meetings by sharing things we have noticed students doing that have made a positive impact on our community before we address any challenges listed on the board. I spend time discussing and demonstrating how to give a compliment and how to politely accept one during our initial class meetings. I want students to recognize, and be recognized for, things that add to our community in positive ways.

When a student writes a challenge on the board, the director will call on that student during the class meeting to explain the challenge he or she posted. The student explains the challenge and asks for suggestions. Other students offer ideas and the class makes a decision. Many issues raised by students are serious, at least to them, and we need to respect their concerns. The time we spend on these meetings and addressing these issues pays dividends as the year progresses.

During class meetings, I take notes and make suggestions when students ask; otherwise I try to remain an observer. I keep track of all decisions and try to remind the class about what we have decided when particular issues arise again. Although some issues seem to come up continually, and some students could talk about certain issues for days, I try to limit meetings to twenty minutes and may table issues for a later discussion if we need to move on.

In addition to reading literature that addresses social issues, and using class meetings to deal with challenges that arise, I conduct some specific lessons during the reading workshop to bring social issues to students' attention. There are numerous lessons focusing on social issues featured in my book *Lessons in Comprehension*; however, I include two additional ones here. The first lesson, on being an insider or an outsider, calls students' attention, during the reading of a particular work of literature, to moments when they feel like they can relate to the characters as insiders, and times when they cannot relate to the experiences being described and therefore feel like outsiders. The second lesson, on unpacking advertisements, forces students to examine the images of people represented in television commercials and print advertisements.

Being an Insider or an Outsider

As I read aloud a picture book addressing a particular social issue, I have two different-color stacks of sticky notes available, one for identifying an insider's perspective and one for an outsider's perspective. I ask students to tell me when they feel one way or another during the read-aloud. We code the text with the two colors of sticky notes and then use these codes to go back and discuss why students felt that way at those particular moments in the story. After demonstrating this procedure to the whole class, I ask students to take sticky notes and try this with selected picture books in small groups. (There is an extensive list of picture books addressing social issues available on my website.) They mark their texts and discuss their perspectives as insiders and outsiders in these small groups before bringing ideas back to the whole class.

I use this activity to call students' attention to particular experiences they may feel comfortable with and those that seem foreign. For example, in the book *Your Move*, by Eve Bunting (1998), the main character faces the challenge of whether to join a street gang or not. Many of the students in my classes have faced this challenge, or may be facing it as we read this story, while others may have no direct experiences associated with gangs. I use this text, and the coding of insider and outsider perspectives, to create a space for students to discuss ways in which they can or cannot relate to what the characters in the story are going through. The discussions help students understand that every reader brings different experiences to a reading and can relate to different texts in different ways.

Unpacking Advertisements

If we wait until students get to middle school to question the images and rhetoric of commercials and advertisements, we have waited too long. My four-year-old niece tells me the brand names of certain products that she "has to have" after seeing them on television or in newspaper flyers. Television and print advertisements present images that can be very enticing. That is their purpose. However, as Aristotle stated in the epigraph, we don't have to *accept* all ideas that we *entertain*. If we don't help students unpack and question the advertisements they are exposed to every day, they may become ignorant consumers, helpless dupes in a sea of false promises who fall prey to every snake-oil salesman who comes along.

I begin these lessons by investigating the flyers that come in most Sunday newspapers. I share with students numerous examples of the ways men and women are portrayed in these ads. Mothers dust houses in a dress and pearls, men are unable to stay with their kids for a minute without chaos breaking out, certain sneakers make you more popular, and certain jeans can help you land the perfect man in these advertisements. As a class, we discuss the relationship between these images and what we know about and experience in the world. Do the ads represent reality? How is life at home and at school different from the life portrayed in the ads? These questions spark some rather interesting conversations. My goal is not to necessarily change my students' buying habits, but to make them aware of how people and products are portrayed and call their attention to the ways that these images affect our actions, thoughts, and values.

Summary of Lessons and Learning Experiences

Before students can take action on social issues, they must become aware of them and learn to recognize how these issues may affect their lives. To take these experiences further, students have organized social issues groups to address particular issues that arose in our classroom and school community. In past years, students have made posters about bullying, become playground monitors to help primary children get along, taken trips to assisted-living facilities to interact with older citizens, forced the cafeteria to abandon its use of Styrofoam eating trays, produced skits about the dangers of street gangs, and raised money to purchase books for a local homeless shelter. These experiences have helped students understand the concept of civic responsibility and become more involved in the issues confronting contemporary society.

Featured Lesson in Comprehension for April: Disrupting Stereotypes

In order to introduce the concept of stereotypes, I use contemporary picture books to engage my students in a discussion focusing on the portrayal of pigs in literature. Focusing on pigs as characters in picture books is a comfortable topic, one children are familiar with through their previous reading experiences, and one that leads to other social issues.

Although the portrayal of pigs in literature seems innocent enough, there are no neutral characterizations in children's literature. All characters in children's literature, whether real or imaginary, portray particular roles and characteristics that reveal an author's version of reality. By reading picture books that contained pigs as characters, I hoped to disrupt my students' commonplace understandings of the role pigs have assumed in children's literature and thereby lead us into a discussion and interrogation of the way that stereotypes are constructed and portrayed in children's literature.

Before we begin reading the picture books selected for this unit of study, I ask my students to describe the characteristics of pigs and to tell me what comes to their minds when I say the word *pigs*. We make a chart of our ideas during the ensuing discussion. My students describe pigs as sloppy eaters, dirty, not smart, fat, pink, muddy, messy, and slobs. Then we make a list of clichés or metaphors that we think of when we mention the word *pig*. This list includes pigsty, some pig, three little pigs, piggy bank, piggies, pigs in a blanket, cool pig, piggie pie, and when pigs fly. Some of these are common folk terms or metaphors while others are references to the roles portrayed in children's literature and stories they have experienced.

For this unit, I select a series of contemporary picture books that contain pigs as the central characters, including *The Three Little Pigs*, by Steven Kellogg (1997), *Pigs*, by Robert Munsch (1989), *Pigsty*, by Mark Teague (1994), *Hog-Eye*, by Susan Meddaugh (1995), *The Three Little Wolves and the Big Bad Pig*, by Eugene Trivizas (1993), *Fritz and the Mess Fairy*, by Rosemary Wells (1991), and *The True Story of the Three Little Pigs*, by Jon Sciezska (1989). More books about pigs are listed on my website. The books I select contain what may be described as a blend of traditional and nontraditional roles for pigs in children's literature.

After creating the lists of pig characteristics and metaphors, we begin to read each of the picture books I have chosen for the study. I read one or two books each day and put them out for students to revisit after reading them. I begin by reading picture books in which pigs are portrayed in traditional piglike roles and then proceed on to books in which pigs are portrayed in nontraditional roles. In addition, we read some expository books on real pigs and students begin to discover that pigs are actually quite smart, as animals go, and that they simply roll in mud to stay cool. The facts presented in the expository texts seem to go against the roles that pigs often portray in children's literature and help us develop an understanding of how stereotypes may get started.

Among the ideas that arise during our discussion are (1) some pigs learned a lesson during the course of particular stories, (2) society seems to value neatness over sloppiness, (3) you should not judge people by how they look, (4) characters change during the course of a story, (5) different stories portray pigs in different ways, and (6) even if others don't think you are smart, you might actually be smart. We conclude the first section of this unit of study by discussing the following definition of the word *stereotype*: a way of thinking that follows a fixed pattern and does not allow for individual differences. I had hoped to disrupt my students' preconceived notions of pigs as literary characters and eventually use this experience to disrupt their preconceived notions of stereotypical portrayals of people.

In order to move the focus of the discussion from fictional animal characters, like pigs and wolves, to fictional human characters, like Cinderella, and eventually to real people and events, we begin to investigate the character of Cinderella in traditional, multicultural, and fractured versions of the fairy tale. I want our discussions from the pig stories to inform our readings and understandings of the Cinderella tales, especially for addressing the stereotypical portrayal of female characters.

We begin by reading and discussing traditional versions of Cinderella, in particular the Disney version. Students consider how female characters in these stories are (1) concerned with their looks, rather than their personality, (2) preoccupied with finding the right man to marry, (3) portrayed as helpless or passive, (4) dependent on others, usually men, for their livelihood, (5) household servants or relegated to doing domestic chores instead of working outside the home, and (6) often portrayed as the evil character in various stories, for example, a mean stepmother, an evil queen, or a witch. During our discussions, it is interesting that both girls and boys remain indifferent to many of the traditional roles assigned to these female characters, in particular Cinderella. Some of my female students express a connection to Cinderella, in that they too want a nice man to marry, want to be taken care of, don't mind doing housework, and worry about their looks every morning before coming to school. Other girls, however, are bothered by these portrayals and suggest that they want more freedom to make decisions about their future.

After these discussions, I begin to read alternative versions of the Cinderella tale (see my website for a complete list). As we read each alternative version of the Cinderella tale, we discuss how Cinderella is portrayed and how the story differs from the traditional Disney version with which we began. Our discussions of these alternative versions leads to the creation of a second list of characteristics for Cinderella. This list includes made her own decisions, didn't follow the crowd, helped herself, didn't need a man, didn't worry as much about her looks, worked for herself, told the men off, acted independent, and seemed self-sufficient.

After discussing the ways in which Cinderella is portrayed in the alternative versions, I read several books in which males exhibit what the boys in my room consider traditional female characteristics and roles, for example, crying, sensitivity to other's feelings, ability to handle domestic chores, and enjoying dancing and cooking. We read *Tough Boris*, by Mem Fox (1992), in which Boris, the tough pirate, cries when his parrot dies. We read *Max*, by Rachel Isadora (1976), in which Max stops by his sister's ballet class every day and participates in the dancing before going on to baseball practice. We also read *Horace and Morris but Mostly Dolores*, by James Howe (1999), a story about three mice in which Dolores doesn't want to bake cheese and do what are considered traditional girl activities but would rather go on adventures with her male friends. Each of these stories contains an example of gender-role reversal or nontraditional roles for males and females. The purpose is to disrupt the commonplace assumptions students have about gender roles and begin to discuss how these roles affect our own lives and perspectives.

The final component in our unit of study on gender stereotypes is to decide how our discussions and readings will lead to taking action about these issues of gender and social inequalities. My students begin by revisiting our list of classroom expectations, rights, and responsibilities that we created earlier in the year. To the list, they added the following ideas:

- ❖ Don't make fun of the way people dress or wear their hair.
- ❖ Set up opportunities for boys and girls to play games together at lunch and recess.
- ❖ No more girls' and boys' lines for going places around the school; divide class differently.
- ❖ Watch for stereotypes in the books we read, and set up a place for students to display books that contain gender stereotypes.
- ❖ Analyze the classroom library for books with stereotypes about boys and girls.
- ❖ Mr. Serafini has to read chapter books aloud that alternate girls and boys as main characters.

Some of the recommendations that come out of our discussions are somewhat cosmetic, while others have an immediate impact on our classroom discussions and operations. Whether these expectations have drastic effects on my students' behaviors is uncertain, but these discussions lead us in directions that would not have arisen without this deliberate focus on gender stereotypes. Throughout this study, I learn that attending to gender roles and expectations, stereotypes, and critical social issues is not something that young readers do naturally on their own. They need to be introduced to these concepts in ways that do not intimidate them or make them unduly uncomfortable. As their teacher, I need to find points of entry into these topics that help students realize that these issues affect all of us as humans and members of contemporary society.

Literacy Assessments

Evaluating Responses

As we move into the last quarter of the school year, I want students to be able to evaluate the kinds of responses that they have made to the literature we have experienced as a class and the texts students have read independently. Although we have explored our responses to literature in various ways throughout the year, I share with students an evaluation instrument that I use with both intermediate-grade and college students to evaluate readers' responses (see Figure 9.1).

I ask students to analyze entries from their reading response notebooks over the course of the year according to the criteria provided in this form. We discuss how readers respond in different ways when they read, from simply enjoying and engaging with a story to making connections and critiquing the style of writing used. I hope students are able to find examples from all three sections of this assessment instrument in their response notebooks. I believe readers who are able to assume these various perspectives during the act of reading are more capable readers than those who only make connections or engage with a text. This instrument represents an expanded view of what readers do. We have talked about the characteristics of proficient and sophisticated readers all year long. This instrument provides support for readers to examine the characteristics they have developed during the school year.

FIG. 9.1 *Evaluating Responses to Literature*

Evaluating Responses to Literature

Engagement/Involvement

can retell a story

able to enter the secondary world of a story

relives the experience of the story

offers immediate reactions (laughs, worries, etc.)

can describe visual images created during the reading

anticipates events next in the story, predicts

follows along with a character

recalls specific events, language, and details from the story

Associations/Connections

makes connections to other stories and texts

makes connections to personal experiences

relates story to events in the world

understands challenges the characters face

puts self in character's place, offers suggestions

Critique/Evaluation

evaluates characters' motives

sees relationship between parts of a story and story as a whole

evaluates quality of a story

infers author's intentions

develops themes

generalizes from literary experiences to life's experiences

analyzes own responses to texts

adopts critical and pragmatic perspectives

reexamines own worldviews

examines internal coherence of story

evaluates the relevance of story to one's life

Connections to the Writing Workshop

There are numerous connections between reading about social issues and opportunities to use writing to address the issues that emerge. One writing experience that has been very popular with my students is using fractured fairy tales to raise awareness of a particular social issue. In the same way that authors we have read have taken the Cinderella story and challenged the gender stereotypes inherent in the original story, my students have chosen other fairy tales and changed settings, characters, points of view, and themes to make a particular point about a social issue. We have published fairy tales addressing endangered animals, poverty, gangs, pollution, and other social issues using the fairy tales about the Three Little Pigs, Snow White, Rumpelstiltskin, and the Three Bears as a framework.

To take the work of the social issues groups to the public at large, students have created issues posters to address bullying, littering, gangs, and conservation of energy. These posters are displayed around the school to raise other students' awareness of these issues. Students have created information brochures and pamphlets to distribute and organized meetings to address these concerns. Writing is an important way to get one's message about issues out to a wider audience.

Things I Hope to See, Hear, and Have Established by Month's End

1. Students are questioning the images portrayed in the books they are reading.
2. Interactions among my students and other classes both in class and on the school grounds are more tolerant.
3. Class meetings are productive, addressing specific concerns in a sincere and mature way.
4. Students are developing an understanding and appreciation of different cultures.
5. Students are taking action about some of the injustices and challenges they see in their communities.

Ideas for Further Reflection

❖ Investigate the Teaching Tolerance and Rethinking Schools online websites (www.tolerance.org/teach and www.rethinkingschools.org) and numerous other Internet resources for ideas about helping students become tolerant of other people.

❖ Don't be afraid to raise some controversial issues in the classroom. Know your community, know what can be shared, and begin where you feel comfortable.

❖ Read some of the theoretical and pedagogical materials available for addressing critical literacy and social awareness listed on my website.

Closing Thoughts

Taking action on issues of social justice begins by calling students' attention to the issues that surround them. One cannot take action without an understanding of the issues involved. Becoming a critical reader involves disrupting what we consider normal, investigating the relations of power in the books we read and the world we live in, and taking action to make the world we live in a better place.

School alone cannot change all the problems of society, but it's a great place to start! Curriculum is a framework for making the kind of world we want to live in. When students become involved in the issues that confront them, they are playing the role envisioned by our founding fathers to ensure that democracy would thrive.

Harry Potter and Social Justice

Introduction

The Harry Potter and Social Justice unit began with a class read-aloud of *Harry Potter and the Sorcerer's Stone,* by J. K. Rowling (1997). During one of our opening ceremonies, a student shared an article in the newspaper describing how a parent group had challenged the reading of Harry Potter books in a nearby school district, and subsequently the school board had banned it from being read aloud, pending further investigation. My students were outraged at these events and were baffled as to why or how this might occur. The questions raised concerning this reported incident led to an investigation of the school board decision and of the issue of censorship in general.

Focus

We launched an in-depth investigation into censorship and taking action for social justice. In this unit we focused on the differences between censorship and selection, how editorials are written, how decisions are made by school boards, the process for challenging a text that is being read in school, what rights students have in these circumstances, and what students can do to challenge decisions they disagree with.

Goals and Objectives

- ❖ construct a well-informed letter to the editor
- ❖ investigate censorship policies in our district
- ❖ learn about our school board and its responsibilities
- ❖ use multimedia resources to research censorship
- ❖ understand the argument against Harry Potter books
- ❖ compare and contrast many texts with magical elements similar to those in Harry Potter books

Opening Ceremonies

As described previously, each morning we read the local and state newspapers. During this unit, parents and students searched these resources for articles that addressed the issue of censorship or Harry Potter books. We created a large chart to keep track of the arguments for and against the censoring of Harry Potter book, and the tactics various religious and parental groups used to remove it from schools and libraries.

Cornerstone Texts

Harry Potter and the Sorcerer's Stone was used as our cornerstone text. In case anyone is unfamiliar with this book, the Harry Potter books are a series of stories about a boy who has been raised by an abusing aunt and uncle and who then discovers he is a wizard. On his eleventh birthday, Harry is taken to Hogwarts School of Witchcraft and Wizardry. The books chronicle his adventures during each school year as he tries to save the world from his archenemy, the evil Lord Voldemort, and various other villains.

Launching the Unit of Study

This unit emerged in response to our reading of *Harry Potter and the Sorcerer's Stone* and the subsequent discovery of articles describing its censorship in public and private schools. Because of its immense popularity, many of my students had already read the book but wanted to hear it read aloud and discuss it with their classmates. A parent volunteered to read it aloud each day and promised to use English accents to enhance the story line.

One morning, we came across an article about how a school district in Colorado was banning the reading of Harry Potter books. Students could read the stories with a permission slip from their parents, but teachers could not read one aloud if a single parent in the class disagreed with its content. Students were confused, as *we* were reading it aloud at the same time as the publication of the article.

We needed to know more about the situation described in the article so we could understand why one group of parents was able to exert so much pressure on the entire school district. We read various articles in the newspaper each day and learned the school in question banned Harry Potter books from being read aloud until further investigation could take place. Students wanted to know why teachers weren't allowed to read the book until further investigation. We discussed how we felt about censorship and connected these issues to our study of the First Amendment. We discussed the effects of our read-aloud component of the reading workshop and what would happen if we were banned from reading certain books, especially Harry Potter books. We recalled the numerous books that I'd read aloud in class that year and reflected on the learning that had occurred and how read-alouds had helped create our community of readers. Once we realized how fortunate our class was to be left unchallenged about our selection of literature, we thought about ways we could help other students in other schools.

Explicit Instruction

It became apparent that students wanted to take action but were unaware of how to begin. So we began by making a list of actions we could take to help the students in the other district. We decided that an editorial would be a great way to start. Students were upset that the students in the other district were not involved in the decision about the books, and they felt an editorial would provide an avenue for those students' voices to be heard.

Before we began writing, we investigated the genre of editorials, their purpose, and the audience. We investigated many editorials from a variety of sources—newspapers, magazines, websites, and newsletters. Each group of students was given an editorial and asked to attend to the structure, language, audience, information, and author. Upon completion of our investigations, students generated criteria for a persuasive editorial. The criteria included descriptive writing, convincing evidence, a focused topic, an appeal to one's emotions, an understanding of both sides of the issue, and a sound argument based on the available facts.

We decided further investigation was needed in two areas: (1) understanding the challenges against Harry Potter books and (2) understanding texts with plotlines and magical elements similar to those in Harry Potter books and why they were not banned in various school districts.

Workshop Experiences

In an effort to persuade the school board to not ban the books, students located the source of the challenges levied against the Harry Potter books. In the newspaper articles, a religious group founded by parents to preserve traditional values and the institution of the family was cited as the source of the challenges. Students conducted research and were able to construct a sound argument against this group. We quickly realized, by reviewing its website, that this was a highly organized religious-political group that was threatened by the values and ideas presented in the Harry Potter books. Students were beginning to understand the issues but still could not make sense of why this group wanted to keep other children from reading the books. We located an article written by a Catholic priest that supported the reading of Harry Potter books. He stated in the article that the books presented harmless fantasy for children. Students found other articles to support their argument written by Christian leaders to negate the notion that Harry Potter was inherently evil.

Students located numerous articles in support and in opposition to Harry Potter books. Students were a little frustrated with the amount of information that existed on both sides of the issue. We spent time discussing the articles and the persuasive techniques used in each. We then moved on to other pieces of literature to gain an understanding of why Harry Potter books were being singled out when so many other similar pieces of literature remained on the shelves in these classrooms.

Comparing Harry Potter with Other Literature   Students decided to make their arguments stronger by comparing Harry Potter books with other pieces of literature that contained similar plotlines and magical elements. As a class we brainstormed a list of books that seemed to be similar in content to Harry Potter books and would warrant further investigation. The list included *A Wrinkle in Time*, by Madeleine L'Engle (1962), *The Voyage of the Dawn Treader*, by C. S. Lewis (1980), and *The Wizard of Oz*, by L. Frank Baum (1991). Students found many similar plotlines and magical elements in these books and used this as evidence to construct an argument in favor of reading Harry Potter books aloud in classrooms. They concluded, based on the results of their comparison charts, that Harry Potter books were being challenged because of their popularity.

Writing Editorials   Before writing, we gave a great deal of consideration to the audience of the editorial as we discussed possible places for publication. Students felt it was important to send some letters directly to the school board. They also deemed it important to send some letters to the primary newspaper where the school was located in hopes that our letters would reach the students and let them know we were there to support their efforts if they decided to take action. Finally, we wanted to send letters to our local paper to share with our school district and community our feelings on censorship and to inform them of our efforts to support reading communities in other cities.

Students constructed powerful editorials, quoting people who offered opposing viewpoints and those who agreed with their perspective. It was obvious that students had a strong understanding of the genre and the ways editorials we used. The finished editorials were persuasive and compelling, and we mailed them to the papers and the school board.

Discussing Public Response to the Editorials   Students never heard from the school board in the district where the books had been banned. The letters we submitted to the newspaper in that area were never published. However, our local newspaper published five of the twenty-one editorials we submitted. This provoked much public response. Many local readers wrote to share their disgust of the Harry Potter books. In their responses, community members quoted the Bible as providing evidence of the need to ban these books. Parents of my students decided to respond to these editorials, providing a contrasting perspective. As time went on, students felt they did all they could about the situation at the other school. The reading of Harry Potter books continued in our classroom without much controversy. We continued to track articles and editorials on the issue to keep abreast of any changes to the situation, but we never faced the challenges the other students did.

Through these experiences, students began asking new questions about the literature and the newspaper articles they read: Whose interests were served by the banning of the books? Whose voices were silenced? Whose story was privileged in the newspapers? Students built upon the discussions from our Harry Potter experiences and applied to other discussions of social justice.

Closing the Window

In the end, the decision remained unchanged in that particular Colorado school district. If a single parent objected to Harry Potter books, the teacher could not read one aloud to the students. Even though they did not overturn the decision, my students felt a sense of accomplishment for taking action and expressing their ideas to the public. Through this experience, they became critical readers of editorials and assumed more responsibility in civic issues.

As a side note, when the first Harry Potter movie was released, the local movie theatre, the only one in our town, elected not to show the movie. My students were outraged because the next nearest theatre was more than an hour's drive away. Children were upset that they would not be able to see the movie with their friends. In response, my students invited the owner of the theatre to visit our classroom and share the reasons behind his decision. He responded that the movie was inappropriate for young children and he did not want them to experience the witchcraft presented throughout the movie.

In the end the movie was never shown in our small town, so we took a field trip to another theatre, sixty miles away. Dressed in Harry Potter garb, carrying magic wands and brooms, we arrived at the theatre. We invited the local media to document the experience. Students were on the front cover of the local newspaper, providing a poetic ending to our experiences.

CHAPTER 10

May—Celebrating Our Literate Lives

Trusting children with books is a revolutionary act. Books are,
after all, dangerous stuff. Leave a child alone with a book
and you don't know what might happen.
—SUSAN OHANIAN, *WHO'S IN CHARGE*

Introduction

As the school year comes to a close, I consider the procedures, lessons, and expectations enacted during the course of the year. I reflect back on the apparent successes and possible failures of my teaching and instructional decisions, the silence that rang through some literature discussions, and the excitement that was created during the investigations of our favorite authors, illustrators, and stories. I celebrate the growth most of my students made and agonize over the students whom I feel I didn't make much difference with.

May is a time to pull things together, to bring closure to a year together and consider our development as literate human beings. Through various assessment and learning experiences, I guide students as we reflect on their growth as readers and writers and compare their literate abilities with the expectations for readers and writers we established at the beginning of the school year. I also invite students to share with me which of the learning experiences were their favorites during the year. Although their choices and mine may differ as to which experiences were most beneficial, it is important to hear what students consider worthwhile.

In addition, I continue the discussions we have had, focusing now on strategies for navigating and comprehending novels. For many of my comprehension lessons throughout the year, I have used short texts, picture books, poems, fables, and short stories as the primary resources. I believe these short texts work best for introducing reading comprehension

MAY CHAPTER OUTLINE

May Lessons and Learning Experiences
❖ Approaching Novels
❖ Summer Reading
❖ Classroom Literature Awards
Featured Lesson in Comprehension Strategy for May: Tensions and Resolution
Literacy Assessments
❖ Taking Inventory
Connections to the Writing Workshop
❖ Letter to Next Year's Students

strategies, allowing readers to experience a complete text during a single lesson and then to reread and reflect on what the text has presented. However, this does not mean that we have completely disregarded the reading of novels during the school year.

I read aloud on average ten to twelve novels a year with my students. I don't get full-class sets of a novel for all students to follow along with me as I read. If a student wants to check out a copy of the novel to follow along, that's fine, but it is not required. I simply want my students to listen to and enjoy the novel as I read it aloud to them and to partake in our discussions about the story when I finish reading. In addition, novels have been the focus of most of our literature study groups. On average, students have participated in four or five literature studies during the year and have read other novels in book clubs. Also, students have been required to have a novel checked out of the classroom library at all times for home and free voluntary reading.

When I am reading aloud, and a teachable moment presents itself, I call students' attention to a strategy or an element of literature I introduced in a comprehension lesson and how it relates to the reading of that particular novel. I try to make the connection for students between how a strategy works in a picture book and how it might work in a novel. Although the reading of novels has occurred throughout the year, and many strategies for approaching this type of literature have been introduced, I want to bring some of these strategies and ideas for approaching a novel together before I send students packing for their summer vacation.

May Lessons and Learning Experiences

By the time May rolls around, I usually have a stack of unread novels, journals, and magazines sitting on my desk at home that I didn't have time to read during the school year. I look forward to having extended blocks of time over the summer to immerse myself in these novels and other texts. In addition, I have purposefully set aside particular novels for my summer travels. I love reading books that are set in the location I am traveling to or that provide background information about the places I will be experiencing. Reading a John MacDonald novel when traveling through the Caribbean just seems to make perfect sense.

I want my students to have the same access to quality reading materials and opportunities to read that I provide for myself. There are several important considerations for sustaining summer reading: having access to bookstores and the public library, having a list of recommended readings, setting time aside for extended reading, and having some opportunities to talk with other readers about what they are reading. Before saying good-bye to my students for the summer, I ensure that these conditions are in place to the best of my abilities.

Approaching Novels

One of the biggest challenges of making the transition from shorter texts, such as picture books, poems, and short stories, to novels is keeping track of the numerous characters, events, and tensions that occur in novels. Readers can go back and reread a complete picture book in minutes, reconsidering what has transpired, whereas a novel may take a week or more to read. Monitoring comprehension and remembering important details over the length of time it takes to read a novel can be challenging for some readers. Keeping track of the various characters and what they know and have experienced, and following along with the extended plot twists of a story, can be challenging for even mature, proficient readers.

To help students enjoy and comprehend longer texts, I demonstrate how I approach a novel and use my reading response notebook to reflect on the story and keep track of what has happened. When reading aloud a novel in class, I begin each day's reading by asking students to briefly summarize the events from the previous day's reading and any important ideas that arose in our discussion. I do this to remind students what happened in order for them to make sense of what I read each new day and because it is a quality reading strategy for students to use when reading novels by themselves.

With novels that have multiple characters and intricate plots, I sometimes use a diagram, time line, or other representation of the story structure to keep track of the various characters or events that have taken place. For example, to keep track of the characters, flashbacks, and connections among the numerous events in the novel *Holes*, by Louis Sachar (1998), I showed students how to create a time line that followed Stanley's life and how it related to his ancestors and his current predicaments. This helped my students understand the surprising connections that were revealed in the epilogue in this wonderful novel. Other strategies that I demonstrate while reading a novel include plot maps, character webs, maps or sketches of the setting, charts of symbols, themes, and changes in the main character, and research references for important connections to expository materials. These strategies are not designed to evaluate comprehension or to generate grades for report cards. I demonstrate them so students can use them to make sense of the novels they select for themselves. The goal is comprehending and enjoying a work of literature, not getting better at making detailed time lines or plot maps. If the strategy doesn't work *in service of meaning*, it is better to discard it and try something else.

Many chapter books that help students transition from picture books to novels contain simple structures and plots to help students feel comfortable as they move into longer works of literature. I have provided a short booklist of recommended transition chapter books on my website. The predictability of these books, often books in a series with familiar characters, helps readers feel comfortable with longer texts. Although the shift from picture books to full-length novels can be challenging for some readers, providing experience with chapter books during read-alouds, providing an assortment of transitional chapter books, sharing some strategies for approaching novels, and helping students make strong connections to the characters in a novel help in this transition. When students can immerse themselves in the story, traveling along with the main character on his adventures and experiences, they have less trouble following the unfolding events of a novel.

Summer Reading

In addition to the strategies discussed for approaching a novel, I send students off with some specific resources and recommendations to support their reading over the summer. As mentioned, I began the year with a field trip to one of the local public libraries, and it is my hope that my students have been using this resource throughout the school year. Some students have access to extended quality learning experiences over the summer, like summer camps, museum visits, and family vacations. Unfortunately, many children are stuck at home with little or nothing to do but baby-sit or watch television. Regardless of students' financial status, there are opportunities available through public libraries, schools, and community centers we should ensure students are aware of.

Before the end of the school year, I invite the local public librarian to come to our class to share any summer programs at the library so my students can take advantage of these opportunities. I also invite representatives from community centers, bookstores, boys' and girls' clubs, YMCAs, and other service organizations to do short presentations for my students. I want to be sure that students have access to quality reading materials and experiences throughout the summer.

At the end of every year of school, I give every one of my students a paperback novel to take home with him or her as my present to celebrate our year together. I go to great lengths to select a special book for each student based on my knowledge of him or her as an individual and what I have learned about the students' reading tastes and preferences. I write a brief note for the student in the book, explaining why I selected that particular book for him or her. I hope that my choices are good ones, and that students will enjoy reading their books over the summer.

I invite students to write to me over the summer and offer them my postal address as well as my email address. I also invite students to share their email addresses with each other, if they have one, and to write to each other about what they have been reading. I would love to get online discussion groups going over the summer, but most of the students I have had in my classes were unable to sustain email accounts. If I were back in the classroom, I would search for grant money to sustain an online literature discussion project with my students.

Classroom Literature Awards

A closing celebration that I conduct every year at the end of school is the presentation of our *classroom literature awards*. We begin by generating some criteria for selecting quality literature and deciding the various categories that we will use to nominate books. Some of the categories we have generated have included best poetry book, best picture book, favorite class poem, favorite illustrator, favorite author, best personal narrative, favorite chapter book read aloud, and best expository text. I seek and accept nominations for each category, create ballots and have students vote for their favorites. On one of the last days of school, I announce the winners and hand out a list of these award-winning texts for students. I use this list as an introduction to my summer recommended reading lists that I provide students before leaving for the summer. The award-winning books are prominently displayed for students to revisit as we finish the year. Each year the award winners are dramatically different. Through this process I learn a great deal about the kinds of books my students enjoyed and which ones I might read again in upcoming years.

Featured Lesson in Comprehension Strategy for May: Tensions and Resolution

Most literature contains a central tension that drives the story forward, keeping the reader interested in what will happen next. Sometimes, these tensions are resolved by the end of the story, and other times readers are left to decide for themselves what happened. It is this sense of tension that makes readers beg teachers to hear more of the story during a read-aloud session. We are thankful that our students want to hear more, but we also must help novice readers realize what the author has been doing to us to make us want to keep reading.

I have chosen to use the terms *tension* and *resolution*, rather than the more ubiquitous terms *problem* and *solution*, because tension isn't always created by a problem, nor ended by a solution. An author may choose to resolve the tension by having no solution to the problem.

Identifying the central tension is not an exact science. There are often numerous tensions that keep the story moving and readers deeply involved. The focus of this lesson is helping students recognize these tensions and resolutions in their efforts to better understand the stories they read, not to simply help them get better at identifying tensions and resolutions.

When readers are reading a novel in one of our literature study groups or for independent reading, I ask them to use sticky notes to keep track of the challenges that the main characters face throughout the story. We talk about which ones are important to the story and how these tensions are dealt with by the author. Does the author resolve the tensions in the story, providing closure for the reader, or does the author leave the story open to interpretation, inviting readers to decide for themselves how things turn out?

I invite readers to use double-entry journals to list the challenges and tensions of the story in one column and the ways the author resolves the tensions on the other side. There are other diagrams and charts that can be used to indicate these concepts, but for most readers, we want to call their attention to the ways the author builds and resolves tension to help them comprehend and appreciate what they are reading.

Literacy Assessments

At the end of the school year, I ask students to review their treasuries, reading response notebooks, reading logs, and writer's notebooks to reflect on their reading selections and responses. I ask them to look for patterns in their reading during the year, thinking about their choices and their omissions. As students consider what they have read and enjoyed, the ways in which they have responded to various works of literature, and the growth they have experienced in their reading abilities, I provide them with a form to create a reading and writing inventory (see Figure 10.1).

I provide spaces for all of the required forms of writing that students completed over the course of the year and room to describe any additional pieces they created. I provide space for students to list the novels, picture books, poems, and other texts they found especially enjoyable or compelling during the year. This inventory provides students with an opportunity to step back and consider what they accomplished over the year. Never has a year gone by when students weren't surprised at the amount they had accomplished in our workshops. These inventories provide students with a sense of who they are as readers and writers and point out some areas in which they could expand themselves as literate human beings.

FIG. 10.1 *Reading and Writing Inventory*

Name: _____

Writer's Inventory

Letters:

Research Project:

Original Picture Book:

Editorial:

Magazine Article:

Personal Narrative:

Poems:

Other Pieces of Writing:

Reader's Inventory

Favorite Picture Book:

Favorite Novel:

Poetry Anthologies:

Individual Poems:

Expository Texts:

Traditional Tales (Fairy Tales, Folktales):

Mysteries:

Realistic Fiction:

Other Important Works of Literature:

Connections to the Writing Workshop

At the end of every year, I have asked students to write a letter offering thoughts and suggestions to a student in the next year's class. This has been an enjoyable experience for me, reading what this year's students recommend for next year's students to be aware of, to understand, and to look forward to. Students have included suggestions for staying out of trouble, which books to read, how to get a drink of water in the middle of a discussion without attracting attention to oneself, which foods to avoid in the cafeteria, which field trips to lobby for and what to bring on them, and other interesting pieces of advice. We share our suggestions with each other before sealing the letters into envelopes for next year's students. This has been a fun and insightful closing experience for both me and my students.

Things I Hope to See, Hear, and Have Established by Month's End

1. Students are using the strategies we discussed for approaching novels.

2. Students are discussing various reading programs and learning opportunities they will take advantage of over the summer.

3. Students are excited about the reading lists I have shared, making plans for what books they will read over the summer.

4. Student are realizing how much they accomplished over the school year as readers and writers.

5. I have some ideas for the learning experiences and lessons I will and will not provide the following year.

6. Students are sad to leave our community of readers behind.

Ideas for Further Reflection

❖ The end of the year is the best time to record some thoughts about what occurred and what you would change for the following year. I always take some time to write in my notebook about things that have been on my mind before taking some time off.

❖ Just like I have a table full of novels at the ready for my vacation, I gather some recently published and recommended professional development materials to read over the summer. Each school semester, fall and spring, I select *one* aspect of the curriculum to work on and read about. I like to focus on one aspect of my teaching at a time, reading and attending conferences in that area, before working on another area. Trying to change or improve every aspect of your teaching can lead to feelings of frustration and make you unsure of the foundations you have built in your teaching.

Closing Thoughts

It is with a sense of sadness, concern, and renewed optimism that I bid my students adieu each and every year. I am sad to see my friends leave, knowing I may never see many of them again. I am always concerned about those students who distance themselves from learning and school, hoping they will find a way to deal with the challenges they will face in society. Finally, I am optimistic that some of the lessons and experiences I have provided will find a home in my students' repertoire of literate abilities, allowing them to find comfort and enjoyment in reading as well as practical applications for the skills and strategies we have worked hard to construct.

Biographies and Persuasive Writing

Introduction

This final Window describes a culmination of the reading and writing experiences we have engaged in throughout the year. The balloon speeches I discuss in this Window on the Workshop were the final celebration of students' research into the lives of particular people. I believe it is one of the most exciting units of study I conduct each year. One summer, as I stood along the Fourth of July parade route in our town, a young girl and boy approached me on the street and said, "Hi, Mrs. Youngs! We're in your class next year and we already know who we are going to be for our balloon speeches." The balloon speeches had become an integral part of our learning community, something every student looked forward to, even those not yet in my class!

Focus

This unit of study focused on students researching the life or characteristics of a real person or fictional character, through biographies and other multimedia resources. They chose one person to *become*, fictional, famous, or infamous, and gathered enough information to allow them to talk and react as their chosen person would.

I gave students the following scenario to guide them through the unit: They were all trapped on a deserted island with only one way off, a hot-air balloon with a basket, but the balloon could carry only one person. Students were to write and perform a speech trying to convince the audience, which would consist of other students, parents, and community members, that their person or character was so important to society that he or she must be the one that was allowed to return. If the character they portrayed did not get off the island, that person's contributions to society would have never existed. Students used this fact to persuade the audience that their character's contributions were the most important.

To begin, students created a three- to five-minute speech outlining their character's contributions to society. I organized student into groups of four characters to compete in heats in order to get to a final round. In addition to doing research on their own character, they researched information on the other characters on the island to make a case against rescuing them. Each group of four competed against each other and sent one survivor forward to the final round. A single winner was determined from the final grouping.

Goals and Objectives

❖ read and become familiar with biographies and autobiographies

❖ use multimedia to gather information

❖ construct a persuasive speech and demonstrate public-speaking skills

❖ use listening skills to engage in a debate

❖ understand the concept of multigenre writing to express information in a variety of genres

Cornerstone Texts	I used two sets of biographies as my cornerstone texts, one focusing on Amelia Earhart and the other on Duke Ellington. I demonstrated how to elicit information from picture book biographies and traditional biographies. Some examples from the two sets are *Duke Ellington: The Piano Prince and His Orchestra,* by Andrea Davis Pinkney (1999), *Music Is My Mistress,* by Duke Ellington (1973), *A Picture Book of Amelia Earhart,* by David Adler (1999), and *Amelia and Eleanor Go for a Ride,* by Pam Munoz Ryan (1999).

Launching the Unit of Study

We began the unit by looking at many wonderful biographies written about famous people. Students were not required to select their characters yet; rather, I invited them to read and enjoy a variety of biographies and autobiographies. Many students eventually chose the characters for their speeches as they became fascinated by reading about particular people. In addition to reading for information, I wanted students to enjoy the genre of biography and the inherent structures, formats, writing, and illustrations in this genre.

To introduce the balloon speeches, I showed students a video of the previous year's speeches. I asked students to take notes on what they noticed and we discussed the process as well as how different students delivered their speeches. The video was available throughout the project for students to view for information or presentation strategies.

I invited students to choose a person or character they really wanted to know more about and would enjoy researching and reading about for a considerable length of time. Their choice was important, and we spent three to five days engaged in the selection process. I brought in a wide variety of biographies, and the local public and school librarians organized a large selection for children to choose from.

I met individually with each student to help him or her understand the expectations of the assignment and to ensure his or her choice was a good match. Many times students were torn between two people, so I directed them to list each person's contributions to society and make an informed decision as to which one would support their persuasive speech most effectively.

One would think the people students selected would be the primary factor in their success during the speeches; however, that was not always the case. I informed the audience on the night of the balloon speeches to focus on the persuasive nature of each speech rather than solely on who the person was. In past years, the Grim Reaper and Jim Carey have won. The quality of a speech was affected by how the student chose to present the facts, not just by the contributions and life of the selected person or character. Other choices have included Leonardo da Vinci, Harriet Tubman, a pediatrician, the Easter bunny, a mom, Thomas Jefferson, Albert Einstein, Lance Burton, God, Santa Claus, J. R. R. Tolkien, a New York firefighter, Oprah Winfrey, and Tiger Woods.

I created a rubric to evaluate and improve their speeches. The categories on the rubric were speech and posture, listening, research, representation of character, and rebuttal ability. I used the rubric to determine a score based on the final written version of the speech as well as the student's performance the night of the balloon speeches.

Explicit Instruction

I conducted a series of lessons to walk students through each step of the speechwriting and debate process. For example, I provided students with a format for outlining their ideas. Some students used the outline format, while other students altered it to fit their speech and presentation style. The outline of the speech was as follows:

I. Attention-Getting Introduction

II. Pertinent Background Information

    A. Childhood

    B. Family Life

    C. Schooling

III. Contributions to Society (list at least five)

IV. Arguments Against Other Members of Balloon Group

V. Conclusion (Could be circular or reword something from your introduction or close with a brand-new point. However you do it, leave them wanting more.)

I demonstrated how to approach writing a speech using Amelia Earhart as my character and modeling the creation of my outline for my students. I demonstrated how I decided which information from Amelia's childhood was important for the argument I was trying to make. Then we spent about one week conducting research on our selected characters or people.

During the second week we focused on creating arguments against the other members of the balloon group. Students gathered information to refute or contradict the other students' speeches. In most instances, I suggested that students make the case for themselves stronger, instead of trying to argue against the overwhelming contributions a person like Mother Teresa had made to the world. They needed to convince the audience they were more important than the other characters and people.

By the end of the second week, once the research and writing were almost completed, I began a series of impromptu speech lessons. The purpose of these lessons was to give students ample time to practice speaking in front of people and to use their listening skills to debate the characteristics of the other group members. In other words, I wanted students to learn to think on their feet during the balloon speech debates. I highlighted proper speaking posture, how to make eye contact with the audience, and how to control one's body movements. I also demonstrated how to take notes on what other students were saying so students could make their arguments stronger during the rebuttal round.

For these impromptu speeches, I suggested a variety of topics, for example, selling your favorite book to the class, persuading the audience to adopt a new class mascot, convincing your parents to let you go camping alone, and pretending you are an astronaut vying for the only seat on the shuttle. I gave each student one minute to persuade the audience and then thirty seconds for a rebuttal. I encouraged students to take notes during the rebuttal round. Students used their notes to refute the information other members presented and were quick to point out statements that were based upon opinions rather than factual information. Depending on the topics and group members of the practice rounds, the winners were different each time, and students were excited for those students who struggled in other areas of literacy learning but excelled in public speaking.

I conducted lessons on how to create a dramatic, attention-getting opening and how to create a persuasive closing that would make the audience change their way of thinking. Students wrote openings with astonishing facts, famous quotes, and humorous anecdotes and drafted closings that pointed out the need for them to be rescued.

We watched videos of great speeches by Martin Luther King Jr. and of presidential debates to observe various speakers' styles and mannerisms. We also observed how the speakers incorporated facts rather than opinions to support their argument or topic of persuasion. These lessons focused on how to synthesize information from a variety of sources and how to check the validity of information by consulting multiple sources.

Workshop Experiences

Students used the reading workshop time to gather information from a variety of sources and to practice reading their speeches with another student not in their balloon group. Students were very independent during this time as they searched for useful information. I worked with individual students who needed extra help comprehending particular resources and finding information that would be useful in their speeches and rebuttals.

In addition, in an effort to formulate arguments against other members in their group, students formed research groups with other students. The amount of information on some characters and famous people was overwhelming, and for some students researching their own person was enough of a struggle, let alone gathering information to refute other group members' claims. Each research group got together and chose one person each day to gather information about. They took turns gathering information on each other's selected characters or people.

Culminating Experiences

The night of the balloon speeches was exhilarating. Students invited family members and friends, and some grandparents even came into town just for this popular event. I introduced the balloon speeches by sharing our rules and expectations with the audience. I explained to the audience how much work went into the speeches and asked them to show respect for each student. I also informed the audience that their vote should be based on the persuasive nature of the speech rather than their personal knowledge or feelings they might have toward a particular famous person.

After the directions, we began the five rounds of speeches. Students chose a number out of a hat to determine the order. Just before the dinner break (parents had volunteered to bring in potluck dishes for the event), I announced the winners of the first rounds of speeches so students could prepare for the final round. Those classmates not selected helped the final-round speakers with information to construct arguments against the other balloon members in the final group. Students had three minutes for their last speech and one minute for rebuttal. The speeches were given, the audience voted, and a final winner was declared. Every year, parents are amazed at their children's public-speaking ability. Even though a winner is declared, all students' efforts are respected, and students feel a great sense of accomplishment no matter the outcome.

When we returned to school the following Monday, we launched a multi-genre writing project focusing on the person they selected. I asked students to propose four pieces their person could have written or pieces that someone else could have written about them. Students had gathered so much information about their person it seemed natural to extend this project into genres other than a speech. Students generated ideas for possible genres, discussed which ones would work best for their character or person, and selected four genres they would attempt to translate their speech into. Students experimented with various genres, audiences, and perspectives. They felt the freedom to be creative and express themselves through new and interesting genres.

Closing the Window

This unit was the ultimate culminating experience for the school year. Students began the year buzzing about who they were going to be for the balloon speeches at the end of the year. Throughout the unit, students were deeply engaged in the speech project, and they had authentic purposes and audiences to guide their writing and research. Each part of the process of creating the balloon speeches and multigenre writing projects helped students develop the necessary reading, writing, and listening skills that would help them be successful not only in their speeches but in all their future endeavors.

Afterword: The Journey Ends . . . for Now

Good teachers continuously reflect on "where we are now" in order to understand "where we can go next."
—MARTIN NYSTRAND, *OPENING DIALOGUE*

Although I have no immediate plans to return to elementary school teaching, enjoying my tenure as a professor of literacy education and children's literature, I know the challenges of starting over each fall from having done so for many years. Summer provided opportunities for relaxation and a rebirth of energy necessary to start anew each September. As our journey around the reading workshop in 180 days comes to a temporary close, I would like to share a few final thoughts with you.

Teaching and Politics

First, teaching children to read begins with faith. Not religious faith, but faith in children that they will work to make sense of the experiences we provide them. In addition, it requires faith in teachers that, if allowed to make instructional decisions, they will do whatever is necessary to help students be successful. Although there are a few teachers who would be better served by leaving the profession, there are many more who do an outstanding job in the face of overwhelming challenges. Unfortunately, it seems that education today is not based on faith; rather, it is based on accountability, mandated curricula, standardized testing, and scripted instruction programs.

Plato defined *slavery* as people living to execute the purposes of others. By definition, it would seem that teachers today are becoming slaves, delivering the curriculum designed by others, giving tests created by testing companies and mandated by legislation, and being forced to follow narrowly conceived instructional scripts intended to have no child left behind. With this shift from professional development to training in commercial programs, what we really end up with is no teacher left reflective.

Bruce Pirie (1997) states, "There is nothing apolitical about silence." That is, by remaining silent about particular assessment and instructional mandates, teachers end up supporting the status quo. Hiding our proverbial heads in the sand has never worked, but it is especially contentious in today's political climate. Teachers must work through their fears of political involvement and learn to articulate their reasons for teaching as they do, and provide parents and stakeholders with information about children's progress and development to offset the stranglehold standardized testing has on assessment and instruction.

Rethinking Comprehension

Linda Fielding and P. David Pearson (1994) describe four practical guidelines, created from a review of the educational research on reading comprehension instruction, for teachers to consider when establishing a quality reading instructional program. Their review of the research suggests providing (1) large amounts of time for actual reading of authentic texts, (2) explicit instruction in comprehension strategies, (3) opportunities for collaborative learning, and (4) time for students to talk with one another, and their teacher, about their responses to what they have read. These four guidelines have been addressed in each section of this book, establishing a connection to the research base associated with reading workshop approaches.

In addition to Fielding and Pearson's four suggestions, I have described throughout this book the four processes of generating, articulating, negotiating, and revising meaning. These processes are enacted in the context of a community of readers, where meanings are constructed, not discovered, by readers actively transacting with particular texts in particular contexts. I leave readers with the following definition of reading comprehension to consider, possibly as an impetus for discussion: reading comprehension is the process of generating viable interpretations and meanings in transaction with text and one's ability to construct understandings from multiple perspectives.

Picture Books as a Resource

If you haven't already noticed, the majority of lessons I have described in this book utilize picture books as the primary resource for the instructional experiences provided in the reading workshop and across the curriculum. Teachers in the intermediate and middle grades need to move past the whole-class chapter book read-along as their primary instructional approach. Picture books aren't just for little kids anymore. They contain complex, quality illustrations and writing and can be used to support sophisticated thinking and discussions. As readers reach the second and third grades, we need to help them resist the chapter book syndrome that seems to occur around that age. The simple chapter books that readers select, for example, Junie B. Jones books or the Magic Tree House series, will not challenge their thinking as much as the picture books created by Chris Van Allsburg or Anthony Browne. Of course I want students to move into chapter books; I just don't want them to leave the world of picture books behind when they do it.

Preferred Vision

In several chapters, I have explained the importance of teachers' developing a preferred vision for their teaching, to be able to articulate the goals and objectives of their teaching and literate environments and to reflect on and evaluate these goals as they establish the various components of the reading workshop. The primary reason I have spent time talking about preferred visions is because it is difficult to know when you are getting closer to your visions if you don't know what they are! By extending the articulation of this preferred vision to parents and administrators, teachers are making a case for the types of instructional experiences they deem most valuable.

In addition to creating a preferred vision of one's teaching, it is also valuable for teachers to articulate their preferred vision for the readers in their charge and to explain this vision to students to help them align with it. While this preferred vision must remain open to revision and provide points of entry for readers of all backgrounds and experiences, allowing one's vision to remain a secret would do a grave injustice to one's students.

The Reading Workshop Revisited

Donna Santman, in her book *Shades of Meaning* (2005), suggests the reading workshop is not a curriculum, but a set of teaching structures and practices that gives students the opportunity to bring their reading lives into the classroom for the purpose of stretching themselves in the company of other readers. In order to stretch readers, we must provide the optimal blend of support and challenge to ensure readers are not frustrated or bored in our classrooms. Wayne Booth (1983) has called this process "co-duction," referring to literature discussion as the cooperative drawing out of ideas and interpretations. This is what the reading workshop is really all about—*changing the nature of the thinking and talking that is associated with the reading of literature and other texts*.

The reading workshop is an organizational framework for enacting the components of quality literacy instruction. It is a theoretical space for changing the way readers think and talk about what they read. In order for these changes to occur, teachers need to provide opportunities for students to read texts that matter to them, establish a community in which readers generate, articulate, and negotiate meanings, understand various literary theories that inform what it means to comprehend, know the elements and structures of children's literature, set appropriate expectations for students to work toward, and provide the necessary support and challenges for students to grow into sophisticated, proficient readers.

Of all the things we can do as human beings, helping children develop to their fullest potential has to be one of the most challenging and most rewarding. I shall end this philosophical journey reminded of the last line from Jules Verne's classic story *Around the World in Eighty Days*, which states, "Truly, would you not for less than that make the tour around the world?" Truly, would you not for less than the future of the children in your classroom travel around the reading workshop in 180 days? I would.

Professional References

Atwell, Nancie. 1998. *In the Middle: New Understandings About Writing, Reading, and Learning.* 2d ed. Portsmouth, NH: Boynton/Cook.

Bear, Donald R., Marcia Invernizzi, Shane Templeton, and Francine Johnston. 2000. *Words Their Way: Word Study for Phonics, Vocabulary, and Spelling Instruction.* Upper Saddle River, NJ: Prentice-Hall.

Booth, Wayne C. 1983. *The Rhetoric of Fiction.* 2d ed. Chicago: University of Chicago Press.

Bruner, Jerome. 1986. *Actual Minds, Possible Worlds.* Cambridge: Harvard University Press.

Burke, Carolyn, and Joby Copenhaver. 2004. "Animals as People in Children's Literature." *Language Arts* 81 (3): 205–13.

Cai, Mingushui, and Rick Traw. 1997. "Literary Literacy." *Journal of Children's Literature* 23 (2): 20–33.

Calkins, Lucy McCormick. 1991. *Living Between the Lines.* Portsmouth, NH: Heinemann.

Cambourne, Brian. 1988. *The Whole Story: Natural Learning and the Acquisition of Literacy in the Classroom.* Aukland, New Zealand; Ashton Scholastic.

Chambers, Aidan. 1996. *Tell Me: Children, Reading, and Talk.* Portland, ME: Stenhouse.

Clay, Marie M. 1993. *An Observation Survey: Of Early Literacy Achievement.* Portsmouth, NH: Heinemann.

Cunningham, Patricia, Dorothy Hall, and Cheryl Sigmon. 2000. *The Teacher's Guide to the Four Blocks: A Multimethod, Multilevel Framework for Grades 1–3.* Greensboro, NC: Carson-Dellosa.

Davenport, M. Ruth. 2002. *Miscues Not Mistakes: Reading Assessment in the Classroom.* Portsmouth, NH: Heinemann.

Eliot, T. S. 1939. *Old Possum's Book of Practical Cats.* San Diego: Harcourt Brace Jovanovich.

Fielding, Linda, and P. David Pearson. 1994. "Reading Comprehension: What Works." *Educational Leadership* 51 (5): 62–67.

Foster, Thomas C. 2003. *How to Read Literature Like a Professor: A Lively and Entertaining Guide to Reading Between the Lines.* New York: Harper Collins.

Frye, Northrop. 1957. *The Anatomy of Criticism.* Princeton, NJ: Princeton University Press.

Goodman, Yetta, Dorothy Watson, and Carolyn Burke. 1987. *Reading Miscue Inventory: Alternative Procedures.* Katonah, NY: Richard C. Owens.

Harste, J. C., A. Breau, C. Leland, M. Lewison, A. Ociepka, and V. Vasquez. 2000. "Supporting Critical Conversations." In *Adventuring with Books*, edited by Kathryn Mitchell Pierce, 506–54. Urbana, IL: National Council of Teachers of English.

Heard, Georgia. 1989. *For the Good of the Earth and Sun: Teaching Poetry.* Portsmouth, NH: Heinemann.

Hoyt, Linda. 2000. *Snapshots: Literacy Minilessons Up Close*. Portsmouth, NH: Heinemann.

Hoyt, Linda, Margaret Mooney, and Brenda Parkes, eds. 2003. *Exploring Informational Texts: From Theory to Practice*. Portsmouth, NH: Heinemann.

Iser, Wolfgang. 1978. *The Act of Reading*. Baltimore, MD: Johns Hopkins University Press.

Johnston, Peter H. 1997. *Knowing Literacy: Constructive Literacy Assessment*. Portland, ME: Stenhouse.

Labov, William, and Joshua Waletzky. 1967. "Narrative Analysis: Oral Versions of Personal Experience." In *Essays on Verbal and Visual Arts*, ed. June Helm. Seattle, WA: University of Washington Press.

Luke, Allen. 1995. "When Basic Skills and Information Processing Just Aren't Enough: Rethinking Reading in New Times." *Teachers College Record* 97 (1): 95–115.

McGowan, Thomas. 1991. *Telling America's Story*. New York: Jenson.

McCormick, Kathleen. 1994. *The Culture of Reading and the Teaching of English*. New York: Manchester University Press.

Meek, Margaret. 1988. *How Texts Teach What Readers Learn*. Stroud, UK: Thimble.

Nikolajeva, Maria, and Carole Scott. 2000. "The Dynamics of Picturebook Communication." *Children's Literature in Education* 31 (4): 225–39.

Nodelman, Perry. 1988. *Words About Pictures: The Narrative Art of Children's Picture Books*. Athens, GA: University of Georgia Press.

———. 1996. *The Pleasures of Children's Literature*. 2d ed. White Plains, NY: Longman.

Peterson, Ralph. 1992. *Life in a Crowded Place: Making a Learning Community*. Portsmouth, NH: Heinemann.

Peterson, Ralph, and Maryann Eeds. 1990. *Grand Conversations: Literature Groups in Action*. New York: Scholastic.

Pirie, Bruce. 1997. *Reshaping High School English*. Urbana, IL: National Council of Teachers of English.

Rabinowitz, Peter J. 1997. *Before Reading: Narrative Conventions and the Politics of Interpretation*. Columbus: Ohio State University Press.

Ray, Katie Wood. 1999. *Wondrous Words: Writers and Writing in the Elementary Classroom*. Urbana, IL: National Council of Teachers of English.

———. 2001. *The Writing Workshop: Working Through the Hard Parts (and They're All Hard Parts)*. Urbana, IL: National Council of Teachers of English.

Rosenblatt, Louise. 1978. *The Reader, the Text, the Poem: The Transactional Theory of the Literary Work*. Carbondale, IL: Southern Illinois University Press.

Russo, Richard. 1997. *Straight Man*. New York: Vintage.

Santman, Donna. 2005. *Shades of Meaning: Comprehension and Interpretation in Middle School*. Portsmouth, NH: Heinemann.

Scholes, R. 1985. *Textual Power: Literary Theory and the Teaching of English*. New Haven: Yale University Press.

Serafini, Frank. 2001. *The Reading Workshop: Creating Space for Readers*. Portsmouth, NH: Heinemann.

———. 2004a. "Images of Reading and the Reader." *The Reading Teacher* 57 (5): 22–33.

———. 2004b. *Lessons in Comprehension: Explicit Instruction in the Reading Workshop*. Portsmouth, NH: Heinemann.

Serafini, Frank, and Cyndi Giorgis. 2003. *Reading Aloud and Beyond: Fostering the Intellectual Life with Older Readers*. Portsmouth, NH: Heinemann.

Smith, Frank. 1988a. *Understanding Reading*. 4th ed. Hillsdale, NJ: Lawrence Erlbaum.

———. 1988b. *Joining the Literary Club: Further Essays into Education*. Portsmouth, NH: Heinemann.

———. 1985. *Reading Without Nonsense*. 2d ed. New York: Teachers College Press.

Stahl, Steven A. 1986. "Three Principles of Effective Vocabulary Instruction." *Journal of Reading* 29: 662–668.

Taylor, B. M., P. D. Pearson, K. Clark, and S. Walpole. 2000. "Effective Schools and Accomplished Teachers: Lessons About Primary Grade Reading Instruction in Low-Income Schools." *Elementary School Journal* 101: 121–65.

Whitin, David, and Sandra Wilde. 1992. *Read Any Good Math Lately? Children's Books for Mathematical Learning, K–6*. Portsmouth, NH: Heinemann.

Wilde, Sandra. 2000. *Miscue Analysis Made Easy: Building on Student Strengths*. Portsmouth, NH: Heinemann.

Children's Literature References

Adler, David. 1999. *A Picture Book of Amelia Earhart*. New York: Holiday House.

Ayer, Eleanor, with Helen Waterford and Alfons Heck. 1995. *Parallel Journeys*. New York: Aladdin Paperbacks.

Bang, Molly. 1995. *The Paper Crane*. New York: Greenwillow.

Base, Graeme. 1996. *The Discovery of Dragons*. New York: Viking.

Baum, L. Frank. 1991. *The Wizard of Oz*. New York: Random House.

Baylor, Byrd. 1994. *The Table Where Rich People Sit*. New York: Macmillan.

Bloom, Becky. 1999. *Wolf!* New York: Orchard.

Brown, Calef. 1998. *Polkabats and Octopus Slacks: 14 Stories*. New York: Houghton Mifflin.

Browne, Anthony. 1986. *Piggybook*. New York: Alfred A. Knopf.

———. 1992. *Zoo*. London: Farrar, Straus and Giroux.

———. 1997. *The Tunnel*. London: Walker.

———. 2001. *Voices in the Park*. New York: DK Publishing.

Bunting, Eve. 1980. *Terrible Things: An Allegory of the Holocaust*. New York: Harper & Row.

———. 1989. *The Wednesday Surprise*. New York: Clarion.

———. 1994a. *Night of the Gargoyles*. New York: Clarion.

———. 1994b. *Smoky Night*. San Diego: Harcourt Brace.

———. 1998. *Your Move*. San Diego: Harcourt Brace.

———. 2002. *One Candle*. New York: Joanna Cotler.

Coerr, Eleanor. 1977. *Sadako and the Thousand Paper Cranes*. New York: Puffin.

Cooney, Barbara. 1982. *Miss Rumphius*. New York: Puffin.

Creech, Sharon. 2001. *Love That Dog*. New York: HarperCollins.

Davis Pinkney, Andrea. 1999. *Duke Ellington: The Piano Prince and His Orchestra*. New York: Scholastic.

Ellington, Duke. 1973. *Music Is My Mistress*. Garden City, NY: Doubleday.

Fleischman, Paul. 1988. *Joyful Noise: Poems for Two Voices*. New York: HarperCollins.

———. 1993. *Bull Run*. New York: HarperCollins.

———. 1997. *Seedfolks*. New York: HarperCollins.

Fox, Mem. 1992. *Tough Boris*. San Diego: Harcourt Brace.

———. 1997. *The Straight Line Wonder*. New York: Mondo.

Gruenewald, Matsuda. 2005. *Looking Like the Enemy*. Troutdale, OR: New Sage Press.

Henkes, Kevin. 1991. *Chrysanthemum*. New York: Greenwillow.

Hesse, Karen. 1997. *Out of the Dust*. New York: Scholastic.

———. 1999. *Just Juice*. New York: Scholastic.

Howe, James. 1999. *Horace and Morris but Mostly Dolores*. New York: Atheneum.

Hughes, Langston. 1996. *The Dream Keeper and Other Poems*. New York: Knopf Books for Young Readers.

Innocenti, Roberto. 1985. *Rose Blanche*. New York: Creative Paperbacks.

Isadora, Rachel. 1976. *Max*. New York: Aladdin.

Janeczko, Paul. 2001. *A Poke in the I*. Cambridge, MA: Candlewick.

Kellogg, Steven. 1997. *The Three Little Pigs*. New York: William Morrow.

Konigsburg, E. L. 1996. *The View from Saturday*. New York: Simon & Schuster.

Leaf, Munro. 1964. *The Story of Ferdinand*. New York: Viking.

L'Engle, Madeleine. 1962. *A Wrinkle in Time*. London: Farrar, Straus and Giroux.

Lester, Helen. 1988. *Tacky the Penguin*. New York: Houghton Mifflin.

Lewis, C. S. 1980. *The Voyage of the Dawn Treader*. New York: HarperCollins.

Livingston, Myra Cohn. 1984. *Sky Songs*. New York: Holiday House.

Lowry, Lois. 1993. *The Giver*. New York: Houghton Mifflin.

Macaulay, David. 1990. *Black and White*. New York: Houghton Mifflin.

MacLachlan, Patricia. 1995. *What You Know First*. New York: Joanna Cotler.

Magloff, Lisa. 2003. *Volcano*. New York: DK Publishing.

Maruki, Toshi. 1980. *Hiroshima No Pika*. New York: Lothrop, Lee and Shepard.

McKissack, Patricia C. 1986. *Flossie and the Fox*. New York: Dial.

Meddaugh, Susan. 1995. *Hog-Eye*. New York: Houghton Mifflin.

Mochizuki, Ken. 1993. *Baseball Saved Us*. New York: Lee and Low.

Morimoto, Junko. 1990. *My Hiroshima*. New York: Viking.

Munoz Ryan, Pam. 1999. *Amelia and Eleanor Go for a Ride*. New York: Scholastic.

Munsch, Robert. 1980. *The Paper Bag Princess*. New York: Annick.

———. 1989. *Pigs*. New York: Annick.

O'Neill, Mary Le Duc. 1961. *Hailstones and Halibut Bones*. New York: Doubleday.

Paulsen, Gary. 1993. *Nightjohn*. New York: Delacorte.

Pawagi, Manjusha. 1998. *The Girl Who Hated Books*. New York: Mantra.

Polacco, Patricia. 1994. *Pink and Say*. New York: Philomel.

———. 2000. *The Butterfly*. New York: Philomel.

Rahaman, Vashanti. 1997. *Read for Me, Mama*. New York: Boyds Mills.

Rowling, J. K. 1997. *Harry Potter and the Sorcerer's Stone*. New York: Thorndike.

Rylant, Cynthia. 1985. *The Relatives Came*. New York: Aladdin.

———. 1992. *An Angel for Solomon Singer*. New York: Orchard.

———. 1994. *Something Permanent*. San Diego: Harcourt Brace.

Sachar, Louis. 1998. *Holes*. New York: Frances Foster.

Say, Allen. 1999. *Tea with Milk*. New York: Houghton Mifflin.

———. 2002. *Home of the Brave*. New York: Houghton Mifflin.

Schoonmaker, Bolin F. 1994. *Poetry for Young People: Emily Dickinson*. New York: Sterling.

———. 1995. *Poetry for Young People: Carl Sandburg*. New York: Sterling.

Scieszka, Jon. 1989. *The True Story of the Three Little Pigs*. New York: Viking.

———. 1992. *The Stinky Cheeseman and Other Fairly Stupid Tales*. New York: Viking.

Sendak, Maurice. 1963. *Where the Wild Things Are*. New York: Harper and Row.

Seuss, Dr. 1960. *Green Eggs and Ham*. New York: Random House.

Sharmat, Marjorie Weinman. 1980. *Gila Monsters Meet You at the Airport*. New York: Macmillan.

Simon, Seymour. 1989. *Storms*. New York: Morrow Junior.

Sis, Peter. 1996. *Starry Messenger*. London: Farrar, Straus and Giroux.

Stanley, Jerry. 1992. *Children of the Dust Bowl: The True Story of the School at Weedpatch Camp*. New York: Crown.

Steig, William. 1969. *Sylvester and the Magic Pebble*. New York: Aladdin.

Stein, R. Conrad. 1993. *The Great Depression*. Cornerstones of Freedom Series. New York: Childrens.

Teague, Mark. 1994. *Pigsty*. New York: Scholastic.

Thompson, Colin. 1988. *The Paradise Garden*. New York: Alfred A. Knopf.

Trivizas, Eugene. 1993. *The Three Little Wolves and the Big Bad Pig*. New York: Macmillan.

Tsuchiya, Yukio. 1988. *Faithful Elephants: A True Story of Animals, People and War*. New York: Houghton Mifflin.

Uchida, Yoshiko. 1990. "Letter from a Concentration Camp." In *The Big Book for Peace*, ed. A. Durell and M. Sachs. New York: Dutton.

Van Allsburg, Chris. 1981. *Jumanji*. Boston: Houghton Mifflin.

———. 1985. *The Polar Express*. Boston: Houghton Mifflin.

Verne, Jules. 1996. *Around the World in Eighty Days*. New York: Viking.

Walter, Virginia. 1998. *Making Up Megaboy*. New York: DK Publishing.

Wells, Rosemary. 1991. *Fritz and the Mess Fairy*. New York: Dial.

White, E. B. 1952. *Charlotte's Web*. New York: HarperCollins.

Wiesner, David. 2001. *The Three Pigs*. New York: Clarion.

Wild, Margaret, and Julie Vivas. 1991. *Let the Celebrations Begin!* New York: Orchard.

Wood, Audrey. 1996. *Bright and Early Thursday Evening: A Tangled Tale*. San Diego: Harcourt Brace.

Woodson, Jacqueline. 2003. *Locomotion*. New York: Putnam.

Yolen, Jane. 1987. *Owl Moon*. New York: Philomel.

Zolotow, Charlotte. 1972. *William's Doll*. New York: Harper and Row.

Index

McGowan, Thomas, 167
McKissak, Patricia, 75
McCormick, Kathleen, 2, 62, 63
meaning. *See also* interpretation;
    negotiating meanings
    breakdown in, 9–10
    comprehension strategies and,
        197
    comprehension strategy groups
        and, 102
    construction of, 16, 20
    finding in texts, 6
    inferences, 102–3
    modernist theory and, 12
    multiple layers of, 71
    negotiating, 6, 13–14, 16, 17
    plurality of, 14
meaning making
    reading as, 7–8
    in reading workshop, 20
    student responsibility for, 8–9
meaning of action, 76
Meddaugh, Susan, 184
Meek, Margaret, 157
mentors, authors as, 108
mentor texts
    for expository writing, 133
    for personal narratives, 137
Merriam, Eve, 153
metacognition, 9
metafictive devices, 94
Meyers, Walter Dean, 162
minor characters, 60
miscue analyses, 44
Miscue Analysis Made Easy (Wilde),
    44
"miscue ear," 44
Miscues, Not Mistakes (Davenport),
    44
Miss Rumphius (Cooney), 75
Mochizuki, Ken, 149
modeling
    goldfish bowl discussion, 95
    reflection logs, 46
    think-alouds, 108
    visualizing, 77–78
modernist (New Criticism) literary
    theory, 11, 12, 14
    comprehension in, 15
    questions from perspective of,
        125
    shifting to transactional or
        sociocultural theory from,
        14–16, 26
mood, 155
Morimoto, Junko, 139
"Mother to Son" (Hughes), 86
Mrs. Wishy-Washy (Cowley), 8
multi-genre writing projects, 207
multiple-perspective texts, 137,
    158
Munsch, Robert, 75, 184
Murphy, Jim, 117
museums
    classroom, 149–50, 174
    docents, 25, 150
    U.S. Holocaust Memorial
        Museum, 146, 147, 149
music
    poetry connections to, 156

sharing songs and lyrics, 41, 52,
    156
Music is My Mistress (Ellington), 204
My Hiroshima (Morimoto), 139

narrative elements, 76
narrative texts. *See also* personal
    narratives
    expository texts *vs.*, 116
    structure of, 94–95
Nash, Ogden, 90, 153
National Council of Teachers of
    English, 19
nature box, writing poetry with, 164
negotiating meanings. *See also*
    interpretation(s); meaning
    in classroom discussion, 13–14
    interpretations, 6, 17, 88–89
    in literature study groups, 88–89
Newbery Award, 68
New Criticism. *See* modernist (New
    Criticism) literary theory
news articles, sharing, 55, 146, 190
Nightjohn (Paulsen), 156
Night of the Gargoyles (Bunting), 155
"Night They Drove Old Dixie
    Down, The," 156
Nikolajeva, Maria, 94
Nodelman, Perry, 2, 18, 94
nonfiction, 116. *See also* expository
    texts
nonlinear texts, 111. *See also*
    postmodern picture books
notebooks. *See also* reading
    response notebooks
    literacy, 36
    for reading inventories, 46
    writer's, 80
notice, rules of, 121–22
novels. *See also* literature
    in classroom library, 38
    reading aloud, 41
    strategies for reading, 196–97
November
    activities during, 87–89
    benchmarks, 108–9
    comprehension lesson: drawing
        inferences, 102–3
    comprehension strategy groups,
        87–88, 101–2
    goldfish bowl, 95
    literacy assessments, 103
    literature study groups, 87–88,
        96–101
    picture book discussion groups,
        91–95
    poetry discussion groups, 89–91
    reading/writing workshop
        connections, 108
Nye, Naomi Shihab, 90, 163
Nystrand, Martin, xii, 208

Obis Pictus award, 68
observation, of readers in reading
    workshop, 52
*Observation Survey of Early Literacy
    Achievement, An* (Clay), 44
October
    activities during, 62–64
    benchmarks for, 80–81

comprehension lesson:
    visualizing, 77–79
literacy assessments, 79–80
reading/writing workshop
    connections, 80
Window on the Workshop:
    becoming a sophisticated
    reader, 83–86
Odyssey, The (Home), 95
official meanings, 169–71
Ohanian, Susan, 195
One Candle (Bunting), 150
O'Neill, Mary, 153
online literature discussion groups,
    198
opening ceremonies
    for community-of-readers unit
        of study, 57
    components of, 55
    for expository texts unit of study,
        130
    for Harry Potter and social
        justice unit of study, 190
    for Holocaust unit of study,
        146–47
    for poetry unit of study, 161–62
    for postmodern picture books
        unit of study, 110
    for sophisticated readers unit of
        study, 83
Opening Dialogue (Nystrand), 208
oral fluency, 8
oral reading analysis, 44, 46
organization
    of classroom, 32–33, 52
    of expository texts, 118, 119–20
organizational structure, of texts,
    119–20
orientation, as narrative element, 76
Out of the Dust (Hesse), 176, 177, 178
outsider's perspective, 182–83
Owl Moon (Yolen), 75, 135

paired investigations, 60–61
paired reading, 89
Paper Bag Princess (Munsch), 75
Paper Crane, The (Bang), 139
Paradise Garden (Thompson), 75
Parallel Journeys (Ayer, Waterford,
    and Heck), 147, 148
paraphrasing, 140, 167–68
Parent Conference Preparation
    Questionnaire form, 172
parents
    information request letters, 46,
        48
    letters to, 46, 48
    questionnaires about student
        learning, 171–73
Parnall, Peter, 154
patterns
    for personal narratives, 141–42
    sharing, 40
Paulsen, Gary, 156
Pawagi, Manjusha, 84
Pearson, P. David, 88, 209
peritext, 42, 112, 168
personal narratives
    archetypes or patterns of,
        141–42

chapter books, 135
characteristics of, 136
investigating, 135–37
literary assessments, 142–43
mentor texts for, 137
picture books, 135, 139
point of view in, 136–37
responding to, 139
sharing, 55, 135–36
text sets for, 139
think-alouds for, 142–43
writing, 136–37
perspective
    comprehension and, 15
    in texts, 6–7
persuasive writing, 203–7. *See also*
    biographies and persuasive
    writing unit of study
Peterson, Ralph, 2, 6, 87, 143
picture book discussion groups,
    91–95
    disrupting a text strategy in,
        93–94
    informal discussion in, 92
    procedures, 91–92
    read-alouds and, 92–93
    self-evaluation of, 92, 93
    student selection of books for,
        92
Picture Book of Amelia Earhart, A
    (Adler), 204
picture books
    in classroom library, 38
    coding passages in, 91, 92
    for community-of-readers unit
        of study, 57–58
    displaying in classroom, 32–33
    disrupting the text strategy for,
        93–94
    with peritext, 42
    personal narratives, 135, 139
    postmodern, 94, 110–14
    for sophisticated reader unit of
        study, 83–84
    student-produced, 174
    value of, 76, 209
    visual images in, 78–79
Piggybook (Browne), 58
Pigs (Munsch), 184
pigs, stereotypes of, 184
Pigsty (Teague), 184
Pink and Say (Polacco), 156
Pinkney, Andrea Davis, 204
Pirie, Bruce, 208
place, 75
Plato, 63, 208
Pleasures of Children's Literature, The
    (Nodelman), 2
plot
    conflict and resolution in, 75–76
    sequencing, 75
poetic language, 153–54
    bulletin board, 154
    searches for, 154
    word storms and, 155–56
poetic structure, 176–77
poetry
    ambiguity in, 152
    approaches to, 152, 153
    benchmarks, 159